T0284947

Praise for *A Gospel f*

This book should be placed on the reading list for all seminarians and set as a devotional text for the two million Korean Christians who have left organized Christianity so that they may follow Christ. It should also be added as the seventeenth chapter of Mark, telling the story of continued witness in the urban industrial mission of Korea and one of the most powerful moments for the Minjung since the days of Jesus Christ.

—Chang Yoonjae,
Ewha Womans University, South Korea

A man with compassion and preferential options for the workers, the Minjung, Cho Chi Song lived a revolution in the church, in the factories, in the public, and in theology. His story is moving—it captivates and motivates—and obliging. I celebrate his attention to women workers. *A Gospel for Workers* deserves to be on bookshelves and lived out in the streets.

—Monica Jyotsna Melanchthon,
Pilgrim Theological College, Australia

Meeting Jesus in the coal mines, factories, and many other places of work is not just the beginning of an individual awakening but a series of profound awakenings of Christianity. The historical examples presented in this book show the multifaceted implications of such awakenings and provide insights that have the power to transform churches and a world ruled more by corporate interests than by the gospel. Highly recommended.

—Joerg Rieger, Vanderbilt University, USA

A Gospel for Workers: Cho Chi Song, Yeongdeungpo Urban Industrial Mission, and Minjung is the testimony of the life and witness of a creative and courageous prophet who offered, through his public witness, alternative models of being and becoming the church in the public sphere. This is not a hagiographical work to valorize one's mentor. Rather, this is a social biography, narrating how deep solidarity with the Minjung working class could transform the cartography of Christian mission. Inspirational and transformative.

—George Zachariah, Wesley Lecturer in
Theological Studies, Trinity Methodist
Theological College, New Zealand

A Gospel for Workers breaks new ground in the study of world Christianity and mission studies generally, and in urban and industrial mission and the origins and growth of Minjung theology in South Korea specifically. It is an essential reading for anyone who is interested in the emergence, development, and growth of Minjung theology in South Korea under the umbrella of the Yeongdeungpo Urban Industrial Mission, as well as the important role played by Cho Chi Song, who was not only a pastor and urban missioner, but an important pioneer of Minjung theology, a tireless advocate for the workers and the subaltern urban poor in Korea's period of rapid industrialization, and a key leader for the Yeongdeungpo Urban Industrial Mission.

—Jonathan Y. Tan, Archbishop Paul J. Hallinan
Professor of Catholic Studies,
Case Western Reserve University, USA

A Gospel
for Workers

SEO DEOK-SEOK

A Gospel
for Workers

Cho Chi Song, Yeongdeungpo
Urban Industrial Mission,
and Minjung

Volume Editor Jione Havea
Translated by David Song
Foreword by Jooseop Keum
Foreword by Kim Yong-Bock
Preface by Bae Hyunju

Fortress Press
Minneapolis

A GOSPEL FOR WORKERS
Cho Chi Song, Yeongdeungpo Urban Industrial Mission, and Minjung

Translation copyright © 2023 Fortress Press, an imprint of 1517 Media. All
rights reserved. Except for brief quotations in critical articles or reviews, no
part of this book may be reproduced in any manner without prior written
permission from the publisher. Email copyright@1517.media or write to
Permissions, Fortress Press, PO Box 1209, Minneapolis, MN 55440-1209.

Library of Congress Control Number: 2023933045 (print)

Cover image: "Dirt Pounding, Seoul" photo by Herbert G. Ponting, 1903
Cover design: Savanah N. Landerholm

Print ISBN: 978-1-5064-9366-4
eBook ISBN: 978-1-5064-9367-1

This book is dedicated with appreciation
for the wisdom, courage, leadership,
friendship, and scholarship of
Kim Yong-Bock
(1938–2022)

CONTENTS

FOREWORD

Mission is all about the face-to-face encounter of people. It is about the stories of God's people responding to the calling to be common witnesses to the hope in Jesus Christ. Mission has an important role in reclaiming the human face, the powerful stories and testimonies of God's people, an experience that we have all enjoyed throughout our time together toward life. The human stories of all God's people contributing to God's mission in the power of God's Spirit can serve as a much-needed continuous challenge to the church and the ecumenical movement.

When I was a Sunday school boy, a teacher often used to teach us the story of the Good Samaritan. Although it was very boring sometimes, she used to emphasize that the Good Samaritan was neither Jewish nor a person in a higher position in the political and religious hierarchy. "He was a gentile but knew enough about how we should love our neighbours." She requested each of us to be a Good Samaritan in our childhood context.

Later, my Sunday school friends and I became university students and members of the Christian youth movement in Korea. As young people who lived under the military dictatorship, our interest in the story moved from the Good Samaritan to the robbed. We asked, "Who is the robbed neighbour in our society?"

Sometime later, we went to urban factories and rural villages to teach the workers and farmers in the night schools. However, as a matter of fact, we learnt more from them about the reality of Korean society. Furthermore, the people in the margins taught us how they share their resources, how much they enjoy the richness of their own cultures, and how much strength and self-dignity they have, despite their poverty.

When these innocent Christian students came back from the lesson, after seeing for the first time the reality of people's lives, their focus on the Good Samaritan story was altered once again. Who are the robbers in our society? What kind of social system produces the victims and the exploited? How do we transform this robbing system? These questions brought the students to take to the streets struggling with the robbers and the system, which justified their robbing in the name of "development." Many of us were kicked out of the university campus by the dictator and forced to become laborers and farmers, organizing people who have a consciousness of the transformation of history and society. Some of us met each other in jail. These were hard times, but we were happy because we thought we were becoming the Good Samaritans, as our Sunday school teacher had taught us.

Rev. Cho Chi Song (alternative spelling: Ji-Song) is the Sunday school teacher for the mission of the Korean churches and Christians. He is an example of mission from the margins. He was a pioneer who lived out the ecumenical mission thinking of the Urban Industrial Mission (UIM) into life, action, program, and movement. Rev. Cho has developed an incarnational model of mission in the suffering context of the Korean *minjung*. He not only lived and worked at the margins but also struggled together with the marginalised people for the transformation of Korean society. However, he did not remain there. He has proved that the subjects of transformation are neither social elites nor the rich and powerful but the community of marginalized minjung.

The incarnation of God took place among the people at the margins. The birth of Jesus was astonishing news for those decision-makers. They never expected that God would be revealed among the ordinary people. God chose the "margin" to inaugurate the kingdom of God. God is encountered among the powerless and in unexpected locations. Therefore, no one can understand the good news of Jesus Christ without incarnating it in the context of the margins. Discussing mission only in a board room or table ecumenism is never enough.

Discipleship without being among the people at the margins is not a discipleship of Christ. The Christendom model of Christianity and mission has been associated for a long time with power. It is impossible for the model to imagine how we could carry out the Christian mission without institutions and resources. However, whatever the means might be, the way of Jesus is the only way to empower the church, mission, and ecumenical movement.

The Council for World Mission (CWM) is immensely grateful for the life and witness of Rev. Cho Chi Song and the community of Yong Deung Po-UIM. It is our privilege to publish their stories in the series *Prophets from the South*. My particular thanks go to the editorial team and translator for their tireless work. Fortress has been one of CWM's closest partners in developing and publishing prophetic mission thinking, including this volume. As a matter of fact, I was originally planning to publish the minjung theology of the late Prof. Yong-bock Kim as a series. However, he recommended publishing the story of Cho Chi Song instead of his own theology. He said that the stories would be more relevant and inspirational for the CWM churches and beyond to imagine mission activities and programs in their own contexts. Therefore, the CWM would like to dedicate this book to Yong-bock Kim, a humble prophet, a forefather of minjung theology, an eminent Asian theologian, and a renowned ecumenical leader and activist.

Rev. Cho challenges us with the questions, *Are we true disciples of the gospel?* and *What does this mean for being Christians in today's world?* I am sure that we will be inspired to find answers and learn how to imagine participating in God's mission in the context. People will know by the instincts of their hearts who we are and what theology we are talking about. People know, by the instinct of their hearts, whether we really believe in the vision of the new heaven and earth. The Holy Spirit is creating many new hopes with people at the margins. Our mission is to reveal this hope from the margins to the world. Therefore, our mission as disciples is proclaiming the hope that "God's kingdom is coming, and already among us!" In the midst of agonies, despair, and cries of life due to the pandemic, wars, and inequalities, it is our mission as transforming disciples to seek alternative values, ways of life, and communities to reveal the kingdom of God on earth by the power of the Holy Spirit.

Jooseop Keum
General Secretary
Council for World Mission

FOREWORD

Root of Korean Minjung Theology

The social biography of Rev. Cho Chi Song is deeply intertwined with the story of the Korean minjung. His life began as Imperial Japan's colonial rule ended and the Pacific War (World War II) ended, due to the victory of the United States and the USSR. He lived through the tragic division of the Korean people (1945) by those so-called victors, the subsequent brutal three-year war on the Korean peninsula (5 million people dead, 10 million refugees, and nearly total destruction of the peninsula), the military coup, and the succession of dictatorships under the Cold War regime during the next 30 years.

Cho chose to live together with urban industrial workers who had been mobilized from impoverished rural areas to serve the military-driven process of economic "modernization," the crude form of capitalist development that was being pushed throughout the third world. The young Cho Chi Song joined the workers in their historical abyss of suffering, as a follower of Jesus the Friend of the minjung. His faith community was evangelical but at the same time sensitive to the suffering of the Korean people in their resistance against the Japanese colonial regime and its totalistic imposition of the burdens of war, as well as their suffering under the national division, the Korean War, and the military dictatorship driving rapid modernization.

Cho Chi Song's deep immersion in the spirituality of Jesus led him to be trained as a minister and to become an industrial evangelist, sharing his spirituality with the suffering minjung—the most exploited industrial workers at the Yeongdeungpo industrial complex in southern Seoul. There, his ministry was mostly among young women workers who had been forced to escape from rural poverty.

In his story of evangelical ministry among the Korean minjung, we find profound spiritual transformations and the social revolutionary dynamics of justice and change.

Although he inherited the evangelical faith of his Korean Presbyterian Church, he was liberated from its denominational and ecclesial dynamics, and he liberated the workers from the required worship services typically led by Christian laypersons and clergy in factories and industrial zones. Instead, Rev. Cho guided them to directly experience the spirituality of Jesus through the formation of faith and spiritual koinonia (fellowship). This brought about significant spiritual transformations of faith in Jesus and led to widespread networking among spiritual and social fellowship groups at industrial workplaces, labor organizations, and later among student movements and social movements. In introducing Jesus to the young workers, Rev. Cho inspired them to recognize themselves as subjects of their own lives and of Korean history. This process was a pivotal point for Korean minjung theology, as the minjung theologians learned their theological sensitivity from the stories of leaders such as Cho Chi Song. The koinonia network of workers in Jesus's spirituality then developed horizontally, giving rise to a network of junior colleagues ("disciples") trained by Cho Chi Song at Yeongdeungpo UIM and a Korean network of ecumenical industrial ministries such as Inchon Industrial Mission.

Furthermore, the Yeongdeungpo workers' koinonia network embraced students and young intellectual activists, giving them on-the-spot training in social justice through exposure to the realities of Korean industrial society. Then and now, Korea's industrial structure is extremely unjust, dominated by the transnational companies—both Korean and international—that exploit the export-oriented industrial zones.

The voices, actions, and stories of the UIM network spread to Korean democratic ecumenical movements including the National Council of Churches (NCCK), the Korea Student Christian Federation (KSCF), and the Ecumenical Youth Council, and to Korean

Roman Catholic Church groups and other communities, stimulating new relationships and raising awareness of social and political realities. The UIM koinonia network thus became a key reference point for the Korean social justice movement.

Cho Chi Song lived in humble friendship with the workers, sharing the Jesus Spirit with them as they struggled to survive and find meaning amid the brutal industrialization process of late twentieth-century Korea. Reading the Bible through the eyes of Cho Chi Song and his koinonia network of worker friends, Korean intellectuals and theologians learned about their own society. For this reason, I acknowledge the workers as important teachers of my own minjung theological lessons. One Korean minjung theologian even declared that Jesus is the minjung.

The stories of the Yeongdeungo koinonia network permeated and strengthened the Korean democratic movement, enabling it to overthrow Korea's Cold War military dictatorships. And the stories continued to flow, traveling through Asia's regional ecumenical network and the World Council of Churches to influence and inspire the global ecumenical movement. This book is unique in the global ecumenical movement, especially now as it seeks to revitalize industrial evangelism in the twenty-first century.

Kim Yong-Bock
Former President of Hanil University
Former Chair Professor at Hanshin University
Former Chairman of the Asia Pacific Institute for Life Studies

PREFACE

A Pilgrim of Love and Justice

Rev. Cho Chi Song was the first ordained pastor for industrial evangelism in the history of Korean churches. He is a representative Christian figure of his time, having walked the way of Jesus during the tumultuous period of industrialization in the twentieth century. His story beckons us to awaken from our dull, passive, and confused states of mind and to roll up our sleeves.

This biography—interweaving the stories of Cho Chi Song, the Yeongdeungpo Urban Industrial Mission, and the rise of minjung theology—is a timely gift for our time, written with great care and affection by Rev. Seo Deok-Seok, a former student and friend of Cho's, as well as a gifted poet. His writing brings back the departed alive to our generation. It is as if the disciples were visited by Jesus the risen, on the road to Emmaus. Just like many of us, they were disillusioned and disheartened. To them, Jesus silently appeared, asking what exactly was on their mind. "What are you discussing with each other while you walk along?"

Those who remember Cho's humble yet fiercely committed character can tell remarkable stories about his life, just as Jesus's disciples told about their teacher. The New Testament scripture originated from the oral testimonies and traditions about Jesus that were first told 2,000 years ago. In each telling and retelling, so great a cloud of witnesses was sustained by the wonder that touched and transformed their hearts profoundly. It is my hope that remembering and retelling the life of Cho may serve as a robust bridge that connects us to such a cloud of witnesses and help us to reconfirm a simple and profound Christian message: the church, the body of Christ, is a friend of the marginalized and oppressed. This biography was penned by a pastor and poet who laments the idolatrous "red neon sign crosses/idly content to feed on electricity" and thirsts for something deep embodying the authentic Christian witness. I trust that this biography could empower us to retell, relay, and relive that witness.

The life of Cho invites Christian readers to reflect on what it means to be "fishers of people" as well as what it means to be "holy." This is all the more so because the institutions of the world we live in, both secular and ecclesial, seem often preoccupied with things far from the good news that restores and promotes life. Cho once tried to capture the exhaustion felt by a laborer in the lyrics of a song that laments, "the only thing I've got left from my paycheck, after paying rent and buying a few briquettes, is debt." He earned the charge of sedition for writing these words and was subject to a 24-hour investigation. In such times of tyranny and oppression, Cho and the UIM staff dreamed and strove for a world in which the workers, as beings created in God's image, could live lives of human dignity. They also fervently practiced the teachings of Christ to love neighbors, especially those who were half-dead as they fell in the hands of robbers, who stripped them, beat them, and went away (Luke 10:30). The story of their ardent desire for social justice and resistance against unjust powers and principalities will haunt the readers.

Industrial evangelism and industrial missions began in the context of strong solidarity with the ecumenical movement and networks that were dedicated to promoting life and justice for the marginalized and dispossessed both in and beyond Korea. Cho, who tried to incarnate the spirit of ecumenism in his own Galilee town of Yong Dong Po, can serve as a compass for today's ecumenical movement at many levels. He challenges us to find an alternative to the current form of dehumanizing globalization, which could be promoted by the vision of life in fullness for all.

We are currently facing the not-so-brave temptation of *Brave New World* (Aldous Huxley) which can be created by a blind combination of technology, mammonism, and individualism. Its offer is shoddy, nonetheless enticing to the unthinking leaders and the mass. We are also facing many transitional shocks that have implications for the whole human civilization, including climate emergency, the Covid-19 pandemic, and the fourth industrial revolution. At this juncture of kairos, those who are awake must stand hand in hand in solidarity. The biography of Cho will lead us to encounter the transformative tradition of Christianity. The book will be an important source of inspiration for anyone who seeks a creative way to address the needs of our time. I hope that it will especially inspire those in the younger generation to look for the authentic spiritual tradition and legacy of the Korean church and the broader ecumenical movement. There will be readers who feel a strange calling to join the "march of the fools" while reading Cho's biography. I joyfully recommend this volume as an introduction to the life of a modern apostle and wise teacher, who can guide us in our struggles for meaning and life.

Bae Hyunju
*Former Professor of New Testament Studies
at Busan Presbyterian University
Former Member of the Central Committee
of the World Council of Churches
Co-President of Korea Christian Environmental
Movement Solidarity for Integrity of Creation*

ACKNOWLEDGMENT

The work involved in producing this book was supported by
Yeongdeungpo Urban Industrial Mission (YDP-UIM)
and Council for World Mission (CWM)

ABBREVIATIONS

ACBMC	American Christian Business Men's Connection
AFL	American Federation of Labor
ANSP	Agency for National Security Planning
CBS	Christian Broadcasting System
CCA	Christian Conference of Asia
CCUI	Council of Churches for Urban Industrial Issues
CCUP	Council of Churches for UIM Policy
CISJD	Christian Institute for the Study of Justice and Development
CSLS	Christian Students' Labor Study
CWM	Council for World Mission
CWW	Council for Workers' Welfare
DOE	Department of Evangelism
DSC	Defense Security Command
EYC	Ecumenical Youth Council
EZE	Evangelische Zentralstelle für Entwicklungshilfe (Protestant Association for Cooperation in Development)
FKTU	Federation of Korean Trade Unions
ICFTU	International Confederation of Free Trade Unions
IEC	Industrial Evangelism Committee
IED	Industrial Evangelism Division
IIE	Institute for Industrial Evangelism
ILO	International Labor Organization
IVCF	InterVarsity Fellowship
JOC	Catholics Youth Workers Movement
KCAO	Korean Christian Action Organization
KCIA	Korea Central Intelligence Agency

KDF	Korea Democracy Foundation
KFCW	Korean Federation of Christian Workers
KMC	Catholics and Methodists
KSCF	Korea Student Christian Federation
LAIE	Yeongdeungpo Lay Association for Industrial Evangelism
LSA	Labor Standards Act
MBC	Munhwa Broadcasting Corporation
NCCK	National Council of Churches Korea
NCNP	National Congress for New Politics
NDP	New Democratic Party
NOPW	Korean National Organization of Presbyterian Women
NTWF	National Textile Workers Federation
NTWF-SGD	National Textile Workers Federation-Seoul Garments Division
PCA	Presbyterian Church in America
PCK	Presbyterian Church of Korea
PCUSA	Presbyterian Church USA
PROK	Presbyterian Church in the Republic of Korea
PTS	Presbyterian Theological Seminary
SGD	Seoul Garments Division
SKH	Anglican Church of Korea
SNU	Seoul National University
SSDC	Student Social Development Corps
UCA	Uniting Church in Australia
UIM	Urban Industrial Mission
UN	United Nations
UPCUSA	United Presbyterian Church USA
URM	Urban and Rural Mission
WCC	World Council of Churches
YDP-IEC	Yeongdeungpo Industrial Evangelism Committee
YDP-UIM	Yeongdeungpo Urban Industrial Mission
YMCA	Young Men's Christian Association
YWCA	Young Women's Christian Association

❧ 1 ❧

BECOMING A FRIEND
OF THE WORKERS

CHO CHI SONG was born on August 28, 1933. He was the youngest child of Cho Byeong-geol and Lee Geun-sil in their home at 137, Eui-dong, Neungsan-ri, Ingyo-myeon, Hwangju County—somewhere between Pyongyang and Gaeseong. Neungsan-ri was a peaceful rural village hemmed in by hills, with a stream of water cutting across its rice paddies.

Traditionally a paper-making village, it was also called *Jongiwol Dongneh.* Hwangju was also an apple-producing country. Every flat patch of the upland was an orchard. Apples were ripe when the cottons burst forth in autumn, painting a rich landscape of red and white around Chi Song's house. Like in most other areas, the residents of the village were all related. One's neighbor was usually an uncle or cousin. People were generous and rarely got into a fight.

The Little Pastor of Hwangjugol

Cho Byeong-geol (Cho Chi Song's father) owned about 3,000 pyeongs (about 2.45 acres) of farmland. He could not feed his family of 10 with his fields alone. So, like many others, he worked 9,000 more pyeongs (about 7.35 acres) as a tenant farmer. Tall and well-built, he could do two men's jobs on his own. Lee Geun-sil, by contrast, was small and delicate in her constitution. The two had three sons and four daughters. Chi Song was the youngest of them. There were 30 years between him and his oldest brother, who used to scrub the little Chi Song by the well whenever he came back from playing outside. Young and frail,

Chi Song was exempt from the family's work, unlike most of his peers. There were enough working hands between his older siblings. All he had to do was feed the cow.

Chi Song was nevertheless diligent in his duty. After school, he went home and took the cow out to graze by the brook. He tied the cow to a stake then went into the water to play or catch fish. Sometimes, he lay down on the grass to gaze at the clouds and sing hymns. Now and then, he got so preoccupied with the play he failed to notice before coming home that the cow did not yet have a full belly. On such nights, Chi Song went out again (after bringing the cow back to the barn) to cut and bring back a large basket full of grass. As young as he was, Chi Song understood how important the cow was for plowing the fields and was learning to take responsibility. His parents rarely had to discipline him, and as the baby among seven siblings, he spent a happy childhood as the apple of every eye in the family.

Chi Song had to walk 20 lis (approximately 8 km) across the mountains to go to primary school, where he received a colonial education. The cultural assimilation policy at the time required students to only speak Japanese. Each student was given a box of matches for scorekeeping and was told to take a match away from every classmate she or he caught speaking Korean. The student with the fewest matches left was given a penalty at the end of each counting period, an "honor" Chi Song received more than a few times.

Lee Geun-sil took her children to church regularly, and while their father never went with them, he was never opposed to their going. In fact, he was quite accommodating and always gave money for the offering should any of the children asked. This was likely due to Chi Song's oldest brother being enrolled in the Pyongyang Theological Seminary. While he was a farmer like the rest of his family during the week, he was also an itinerant preacher on the weekends.

Ordained ministers were something of a rarity in those days. A rural church often did not have its own dedicated pastor. There was a high demand for anyone with the ability to lead a church service, and those who could often went around to three or four different congregations to provide it. This was especially true in Hwanghae Province, where a church had been planted in almost every village thanks to its proximity to the country's first Presbyterian Theological Seminary (PTS). An undergraduate degree in theology was one of the most prestigious pedigrees in the area at the time. This meant Chi Song's brother was a member of the community's most highly educated and respected elite. Seeing his brother work in the fields with a book by his side also taught Chi Song his voracious love for reading.

One of the key events of Chi Song's childhood was attending his church's revival service. The visiting preacher claimed in his sermon on Revelation that Christ will come again in the year 2000. This left a deep mark on the young Chi Song, which drove him to start a very disciplined devotional regimen. The 10-year-old began praying twice a day, once in the wee hours of the morning then again in the dusky hours of the evening. He also set and followed a demanding schedule of reading the Bible and constantly sang hymns of praise. Before long, the villagers started calling Chi Song the Little Pastor, taking note of the uncanny resemblance between the behaviors of the young boy and his seminarian brother.

Chi Song took his devotional commitments very seriously. He felt as if he had committed a grave sin if he failed to perform one of the routines. Yet the church was too far for a child to travel to and from every day on foot. To work around the problem, Chi Song built a prayer hut in the hill behind his house, cutting down a pine tree for a pole and weaving hay for the covering. This became his sanctuary for prayer and scripture reading. He committed to reading 20 chapters of the Bible every day and read through the New Testament 11 times. He also taught himself how to play the church organ, learning how to play most of the songs in the hymnal.

The Yamaha organ was a gift from Chi Song's wealthy cousin who lived in Pyongyang, but it had been sitting idle in the church for lack of anyone who knew how to play it. The villagers therefore marveled when the instrument finally came to life in the hands of a self-taught child. Having been faithful in his initiatives and commitments in faith since a young age, it was only natural that the Little Pastor of Hwangjugol would grow up to be the Lord's minister.

Liberation, Chaos, and Exodus

Korea was liberated from Japanese occupation in 1945. Chi Song was 13 years old and in his third year of primary school. After the Japanese withdrawal, Kim Il-sung's forces took control of the northern areas including Hwangju with the backing of the Soviet Union. This was followed by significant land reforms that transferred the ownership of land to the people who actually worked it. Chi Song's father thus gained the title to the 9,000 pyeongs where he used to work as a tenant farmer, becoming the owner of a total of 12,000 pyeongs (about 9.80 acres) of land.

A new Communist primary school was also created in the village, to which Chi Song transferred as a third-year student. Before long, he started to experience friction with the authorities. Students had scarcely begun singing the *Aegukga* (national anthem) in their morning assemblies following the liberation when the Communists came in and mandated that they now sing the *People's Liberation Song*. Chi Song decided to boycott the new song and the assembly. He walked out of the school with some 20 schoolmates and took to the mountains. When he came home after dusk, his teacher paid him a rude visit. Slapping Chi Song in the cheek, much to the worry of his mother, the teacher exclaimed: "You rascal, how dare you behave so rebelliously!" Chi Song was later given a three out of five for his grade in "behavior and attitude" and was kept from advancing to middle school with the rest of his peers. The reason cited was his "bad ideology." His oldest brother was still a pillar of the community, but Chi Song was now the boy who failed to enter middle school. This did not deter Chi Song, however, and he continued his studies at home.

Chi Song also remained committed to his devotional life, going to church every day for prayer, Scripture reading, and singing at the organ. His seminarian brother had a much greater influence on him than his father did, as he spent most of his time farming and very little on speaking to the children. As a result, the young Chi Song developed a conservative and anti-Communist disposition in his Christianity. This was the norm for most Christians, of course, as the Communists had killed all but one or two Christian ministers out of every 10 in Hwanghae Province. At the same time, Chi Song's brother also showed what it meant to be a balanced intellectual, carrying books like *The History of the Bolshevik Revolution* and explaining to his younger brother that one ought to understand even ideas one sought to oppose.

The Korean War broke out on June 25, 1950. Even before the start, the army started mobilizing students for the war effort from all over the country. Chi Song had turned 18 earlier in March and was conscripted into the reserves of the Korea People's Army. He planned to escape with his friend who shared his birthday and was conscripted on the same day. Chi Song wore his school clothes under his garment all the way to the makeshift barracks where he was to stay for the training. When soldiers came to collect the students' civilian clothes after they changed into their uniforms, Chi Song hid his school clothes and only returned the outer garments.

The plan was to rendezvous with his friend in an empty warehouse far away from the camp in the dead of night before continuing the escape. Chi Song changed into the school clothes he had hidden and slipped out of his barracks around 3:00 a.m. He waited and called for his friend in the warehouse using a whistle they had previously agreed to use as their signal. The friend never showed up. There was no choice but to continue on his own. Chi Song traveled to Gaeseong on foot and stopped at an inn to stay the night before proceeding to take the train for Pyongyang. He used the money his father had secretly given him on the day he was conscripted to pay for the food and lodging. While Chi Song was wearing his student uniform, he was still wearing boots issued by the army. The innkeeper noticed this and discreetly advised him to keep the shoes inside his room. Chi Song complied and stayed inside the room until evening. When it was dark, he continued to make his way for the train station.

Considerable time had passed after the train left the station when the police and state security officers began inspecting the passengers. Chi Song realized, to his horror, that he was carrying incriminating evidence of desertion. He was still wearing the boots. Furthermore, he had unthinkingly brought the army cap and notebooks that were issued in training camp. Chi Song trembled when it was his turn to show the inspectors his luggage. His shaking hands accidentally dropped the pack and spilled its contents onto the floor. Thanks perhaps to the darkness, the inspector did not seem to notice what they were. "A student," he muttered before passing over.

After a narrow escape from capture, Chi Song got off the train at Hwangju station. He went to the house of his sister who lived not far away. His mother happened to be visiting. "Why did you run away?" she asked with a look of grave concern. "You should have just stayed there!" Her fears were well founded, as she had seen other deserters face a worse fate following their recapture. The war started not long afterward, and Chi Song had to continue to hide from the searching authorities. During this period of continual flight, Chi Song's father passed away.

In the winter of 1950, the United Nations forces advanced north and took control of Hwangju. They named Chi Song's oldest brother the village's chief of security and issued him a handgun. Chi Song's brother tried to use his position to keep the villagers from killing the Communists, for he recognized that one's ideological enemy was in fact one's relative or family. Unfortunately, the Communist forces did not extend the same humanitarianism during their retreat, executing 11 people as they passed through the village.

An angry mob of young men and the victims' families surrounded Chi Song's brother in vehement protest. "Why would you protect

Communists? Do not sympathize with them!" He struggled to placate the vengeful crowd. Despite his best efforts, their anger could not be subdued.

The tides of war changed yet again. This time, the Chinese forces pushed the UN line south. The situation had reversed. Now the anti-Communists had to flee. Everyone was in a frenzy to evacuate, but Chi Song's brother stayed behind to handle outstanding matters. He never escaped. Chi Song had to take flight into the mountains like the rest of the Christians, who were automatically executed by the Communists as reactionaries. The pastor at Chi Song's church and his son, themselves his distant relatives, were also killed. Even in hiding, one always had to be ready to flee. It was impossible to tell whether a stranger coming one's way was one of the hunters or the hunted. The best policy was to immediately flee. Quite literally, one had to *run or die.* Such were the times in which Chi Song came of age amid the chaos and bloodshed of a people divided, amid the butchery of members in the same families and communities in the name of ideology.

The UN forces continued to retreat until artillery fires could be heard in Pyongyang. Young people believed their families had to find refuge further south. Chi Song's family also discussed the matter when his older sister came home to give birth. They decided to find temporary refuge in Sariwon about 50 lis (19.6 km) south, hoping they will be able to return in about three days as the UN forces regained ground.

The family started the journey, but Chi Song's mother and pregnant sister soon had to turn back. The air was too cold and the snow too high on the road for his sister to travel just moments before childbirth. Chi Song had to continue without his mother or oldest sister. The remaining party of eight included Chi Song's second-oldest brother, his second-oldest sister, her eight-year-old son, and a handful of other relatives. They boarded the last train south in Sariwon on the morning of December 5, 1950. What was meant to be a search for temporary refuge became a one-way trip. Chi Song never saw his mother again.

The train was already carrying refugees from as far north as Sinuiju, so the cars were completely packed. Chi Song had to push his way onto the roof for a place on the train. The journey lasted a full day before arriving in Susaek in the dead of night. Chi Song's family spent one night in the train station before they were transferred to the Yonggang Elementary School in Mapo. There, the eight were given a single piece of army blanket to keep them from freezing while sleeping on the classroom floor. There was no way to buy food, as nobody accepted the northern money they had. Fortunately, Chi Song's brother had a wide range of contacts among other Christians. One of them connected the family to Youngnak Church, a congregation set up by refugees. Chi Song finally had his first meal since starting the journey. One could not ask for a greater feast than the bowl of barley and soy-paste soup he received. There was a performance of Handel's "Messiah" in Youngnak that year for its Christmas service. Chi Song could never forget how sweet the music sounded after his narrow escape from the clutches of death and war.[1]

From an Army Base to Seminary

Chi Song's family had to evacuate once again when Seoul was about to be overtaken on January 1, 1951. The forces of the south had blown up the Han River Bridge on their retreat. The family had to walk across the frozen river. By the time they arrived in Siheung, they felt too exhausted to move any farther. Some even said they would rather turn back to go home. Yet the Chinese forces continued to push south undeterred. There was no choice but to be on the move again. As they approached Pyeongtaek, the refugees were greeted by leaflets from the UN forces warning they will shoot anyone approaching their lines without question. Apparently, the troops could not distinguish the refugees from the Communists who had reached the vicinity. The family changed course and went to Baran. They initially survived eating porridge made with the rice that Chi Song's sister got from the soldiers. Then the family acquired a supply of flour they could use to make and sell wheat cakes in the market, the income from which they used to support themselves.

Once the Chinese forces had been pushed back, the lines stabilized. Chi Song and his brother started working as day laborers for the US military. Their job was to carry the artillery rounds, munition crates, fuel drums, sacks of cement, and other military supplies from the trains that arrived in Suwon to the trucks bound for the front lines. The ongoing war required the workers to move with haste. Chi Song struggled to keep up carrying loads that were heavy even for a stronger man. The supervisor sometimes beat him for moving too slowly. Chi Song and his brother made 1 *dwe* (1.8 liters) of barley for every day they worked from the dark of morning to the dark of evening. This was the family's source of food.

When the troops repositioned themselves closer to the 38th parallel, Chi Song's brother followed them. Chi Song initially stayed in Suwon with his sister and nephew, but he later took them and moved next to the Gimpo Airfield after the UN forces had retaken Seoul. He wanted to be as close to his hometown as possible. Chi Song got a job working for the US military again, this time carrying supplies from the US cargo planes landing in Gimpo. Most of the supplies in Suwon were heavy weaponry, but in Gimpo they were crates of poultry, bananas, apples, ice-cream, C-ration cans, and other foodstuffs flown in from Japan. The stalls in the food market were empty, but in the airfield there was plenty. The goal of logistics was to send as many supplies to the front lines as possible and to do so as quickly as possible. There was no time to keep track of inventory. Nobody noticed if a famished worker picked up an item or two to take home or to eat.

Chi Song later got another job in the US Eighth Division's artillery formation in Oswe-ri that was tasked with the defense of Gimpo Airfield. This time, he worked for the chaplain's office, hoping to recover the devotional life he used to enjoy in his home church. Many of his tasks were those of a housekeeper, cleaning the offices and taking out the laundry, but he also carried out the chaplaincy's civil assistance projects by delivering goods like powdered milk, powdered eggs, and clothes to the orphanages, elderly homes, and other organizations. He also parked the truck whenever he ran into people in need to distribute the excess supplies he brought from the base.

On weekends, Chi Song volunteered as a Sunday school teacher in Ojeong Church located near the airfield. He composed the class song, to which Kim Heuibo—a fellow volunteer who later became an ordained minister, chief editor of *Kidok Gongbo* (the PCK newspaper), and literary critic—set the text. Kim later visited Cho in his daughter's home toward the end of Cho's life to tell him that the children of Ojeong-ri still sang the song he composed.

Chi Song wanted to attend every weekday service, which was easy enough during the day as the church was close to where he worked. The problem was the evening service, as there was a considerable distance to walk between the church and his home in Oswe-ri. As if in a call back to his childhood, Chi Song worked out a solution. Enlisting a handful of other members from church, he built a small prayer house in Oswe-ri. They reinforced the earthen walls with tin plates and roofed the top with board boxes, both of which were discarded materials from the army base. Originally, the members of Ojeong Church used the hut as the sanctuary for their weekday evening gatherings. Over time, the influx of new refugees and worshippers in the prayer house led to the formation of an independent congregation with a full time Methodist pastor. It was effectively the second church Chi Song built, after the prayer hut he built behind his house. Chi Song also built another hut next to the Oswe-ri church and lived there with his sister and nephew.

Shortly after settling in Oswe-ri, Chi Song married Park Gil-soon on May 7, 1955. Gil-soon was a Sunday school teacher in Oswe-ri church. She and Chi Song were the same age, her birthday coming just three days after his. Her quiet and gentle demeanor reminded Chi Song of his mother and drew him to her. The two watched the flash of the bombs dropped by MiGs going off in a distant airfield against the night sky as they nurtured their love. They had a daughter in Oswe-ri, then a son after moving to Munsan.[2]

The fighting finally stopped over an unchanging line in the central region's stalemate. The armistice was signed, and the bulk of the US forces withdrew. Chi Song found himself without a job. To support his growing family, he decided to take his chances and travel north. He started by simply heading in the direction of his hometown in Hwangju, taking only four books and two hard-boiled eggs with him. He walked about 30 lis (11.8 km) to Gaehwa-ri where he took the boat to cross the Han River. After landing in Ilsan, he took a train that headed north. He got off at Geumchon, the final stop, and started walking again. After hiking a mountain and spending a night under the eaves of a stranger's dwelling, Chi Song reached a US army base in Munsan. He asked the guard for the chaplain. It helped to have learned English in his previous work. There were very few Koreans who could speak English. Jobs were readily available on a US military base for any local who could communicate.

The chaplain gave Chi Song an interview, in which Chi Song mentioned his previous experience working for the artillery battalion in Gimpo and the fact that he had been admitted to a theological seminary. He was informed a few days later that he was hired by the 6th Tank Battalion, 24th US Infantry. Working initially as a server in the officers' mess, Chi Song learned a skill that would prove useful for hospitality in his future ministry. Indeed, the workers of the YDP-UIM commented that Reverend Cho certainly made the best pancakes. Shortly afterward, Chi Song was transferred to the chaplain's office. It turned out this chaplaincy was also responsible for the battalion's civil assistance projects, for which they needed someone who could speak Korean.

It was common among Chi Song's coworkers to steal and sell goods from the base. The US army always had an abundance of supplies, ordering enough goods for 20 or 30 people when they only needed them for 10. The local employees took advantage of this and stole the excess goods and sold them in the markets. One of them even made a quite lucrative business by sneaking out the smaller items like packets of butter and coffee. As the breadwinner for his wife, newborn daughter, sister, and nephew, Chi Song needed more money. Yet he never partook in the theft, even if it meant watching his family go hungry. His coworkers even offered to give him a part of their profits, feeling sorry they were the only ones to benefit from his silence. Chi Song refused. He had a greater fear of wrongdoing than his desperate need for money.

Chi Song's principled character must have caught the attention of somebody on base. The *Stars and Stripes* published a story about him based on a tip they received. The chaplain called Chi Song to his office and proudly showed him the article:

> *The Korean nationals working on the US bases often engage in theft, promiscuity, immoderate drinking, and debauchery. Cho Chi Song, by contrast, knew of no such thing. It is the locals like him who make us proud to fight for Korea. [. . .] Cho is originally from North Korea, but he escaped to Seoul with sister's family because of his opposition to the Communist party. He was admitted into a theological seminary but stopped school because of his financial difficulties. He now works on a US military base, but his hope one day is to finish his studies and become an ordained minister.*[3]

As indicated by the article, Chi Song was accepted by the Presbyterian General Assembly Theological Seminary in 1954 but could not attend school because of the financial hardship he faced after getting married. Reading about this, one of the US army officers and his parents reached out to Chi Song and offered to provide him with a scholarship so he could resume his studies. Having yearned to do so for quite a while, Chi Song accepted the offer. The patrons then asked how much Chi Song would need to pay for the tuition and support his family of five. Chi Song replied that $25 a month would suffice, which was what he received until he completed his studies. Eager to learn as much as he could while he had the chance, Chi Song enrolled in the literature department of Kyonggi University in addition to resuming his program at the seminary.

*We were allowed to transfer from the Presbyterian Seminary
to the philosophy department in Soongsil University as
juniors. [. . .] So you're probably wondering why I chose to
enroll in Kyonggi University as a first-year student. [. . .]
That was so that I could take the general education courses.
As a junior, I would have had to take the major-specific
courses. I wanted the broad subjects you got to take in your
first and second years of college. I ended up taking some 30
credits per semester to take everything I wanted. [. . .] I left
my home in the morning and returned at 11 at night. I
wouldn't be able to do that sort of a thing nowadays.*[4]

Chi Song packed two meals with him when he left the house every morning. He spent the day at Kyonggi University then the evening at the Presbyterian Seminary. There was not much left of the scholarship after paying for the tuition of two schools, but Chi Song was happy despite the austerity to be immersed in his studies.

Chi Song's sponsors were the family of a Rev. David Ingebretsen, a Northern Baptist Minister. When the Korean UIM became known worldwide as the symbol of the South Korean democracy movement in the late 1970s, Cho Chi Song visited the Ingebretsens in the United States. The family was proud to see that the young man whose education they supported was now leading an impactful movement based in the Christian faith.

It was challenging to take 30 credits at two different academic institutions, but Chi Song never missed a class no matter how exhausted. He felt too indebted to the strangers funding his studies from overseas to slow down. As his strategy preparing for the finals,

Chi Song often borrowed the notes of his most capable classmates. He later recounted with a sense of amazement and relief that he somehow managed to pass every class—even when he was sure he would fail. Chi Song managed to graduate without delay, first from Kyonggi University in February 1961, then from the General Assembly Seminary in March 1961. For the former, Chi Song received the state license to teach the Korean language and literature. For the latter, he wrote a thesis on the book of Romans and Pauline theology, titled "Saved by Faith." Then in December, he enrolled at the PTS (not to be confused with the General Assembly Seminary) as a candidate for ordination.[5]

These formative years provided Chi Song with the groundwork that prepared him to serve in the Yeongdeungpo Urban Industrial Mission (YDP-UIM). He learned how to speak English and cultivated an honest work ethic, the separation of his public and private lives, a love of inquiry and learning, and a bias for action when it came to starting a faith community wherever he stood.

After retirement, an elderly Cho Chi Song often joked that he could have easily asked for a monthly stipend of $100 instead of just $25. "I could have been rich," he said, "but I blew it."

From Rural Ministry to Industrial Evangelism

Major General Park Chung Hee and his followers overthrew the government and took power on May 16, 1961. The junta then launched its five-year plan for economic development to secure its legitimacy. These events took place just as Cho Chi Song was finishing his studies. In 1963, the state launched a series of major industrial investments, shifting the focus of manufacturing from consumer goods to exportable products, marking the beginning of new social and industrial relations. The state also imposed low grain prices to induce rural populations to relocate to the cities to provide a cheap source of labor. Public authority was used to sponsor private capital and support its exploitation of the workers for profit.

From its start, Park's regime was very clear about its anti-labor policy. The fifth presidential decree, for instance, stated that it will "freeze wages effective May 15 and prohibit all labor action." The sixth decree then provided the pretext for dissolving every political party, social organization, and labor union. Union officers were arrested from all over the country. The number of unionized workers fell from 320,000 in 1960 to 100,000 in 1961. Despite the continuous increase in the total number of industrial workers over the next five years, the number of unionized workers merely recovered its previous figure at around 340,000 in 1966.

The regime also overhauled the labor laws so that individual workplace unions could no longer exist except via sector-wide representation. The government took over the training of all union officers and ensured they were management friendly. The unions were dissolved in all but name. The shells that remained were utterly ineffective in advocating for the workers. Within this structure of inequality, the number of workers in manufacturing continued to grow. By 1964, there were about 330,000 workers and 16,151 companies in manufacturing alone and 7.02 million wage workers nationally. It was this growing population of industrial and urban workers that the Christians became very eager to evangelize.[6]

The Presbyterian Church of Korea (PCK) was the first protestant denomination to start an industrial evangelism ministry in Korea. In March 1957, the Presbyterians in the United States sent Rev. Henry Jones to head the industrial ministry division of the Christian Conference of Asia (CCA). Jones made a case for evangelizing the industrial population in his visit to Korea before a gathering of the representatives of every protestant denomination in the country. Only the PCK took up its call and created the Industrial Evangelism Committee (IEC, chaired by Hwang Geum-cheon) on April 12, 1957, as an organ of the Department of Evangelism (DOE) of the General Assembly.[7]

A year prior to the IEC's creation, the seminarian Oh Cheol-ho had already begun an experimental industrial ministry in May 1956. He got a job in the cement factory while planting a church for workers in Mungyeong, North Gyeongsang Province, under the guidance of the missionary Robert C. Urquhart (*Eo Ra-bok* in Korean). The PCK capitalized on the experience of the two and placed them in charge of the newly created Christian Students' Labor Study (CSLS). Its first program took place from July to August 1957, in which 14 university students spent their summer working in a cement factory. They also learned the essentials of evangelizing an industrial audience in the evenings.

The PCK launched a more systematic industrial evangelism program the following year. Three women were appointed as industrial evangelists in March 1958, two of whom were assigned to Yeongdeungpo and one to Anyang. Then on April 19, the Gyeonggi and Hannam Presbyteries together formed the Yeongdeungpo Industrial Evangelism Committee (YDP-IEC). This later became the YDP-UIM in which Cho Chi Song served.

In March 1958, the PCK IEC created several industrial evangelism study groups of ordained ministers throughout the country, with guidance again from Henry Jones. It sent four representatives to the Philippines in June to represent the denomination in the first Asian conference for industrial evangelism.[8] In September, the 43rd General Assembly adopted the Rules for Industrial Evangelism and defined industrial evangelism as an "activity to preach the gospel to the working people who were in the factories, mines, ports, transportation, communication, and other industrial sectors," mandating that "a committee is to be formed for such ministry in every geographic area that had two or more companies that employed such workers." The resolution also appointed Oh Cheol-ho the secretary of the PCK IEC.[9]

In September 1960, the 45th General Assembly passed three important resolutions for the industrial evangelism. First, the IEC was elevated to the more permanent status of the Industrial Evangelism Division (IED). Second, the Sunday before March 10—South Korea's Labor Day at the time—was designated as Labor Sunday. The week that followed was to be devoted to raising awareness about labor and industrial evangelism across the churches. Third, the resolution mandated the creation of courses on industrial evangelism in the PTS to raise student interest in the topic.

In 1961, the PCK created the Institute for Industrial Evangelism (IIE) under the IED to offer a three-month training program for seminary graduates and ordained ministers. Participants were to spend a month each experiencing work in the factories, studying industrial issues, and receive practical training to serve in an industrial ministry. In short, the PCK began training a generation of missioners who specialized in industrial evangelism. Rev. George Ogle, a Methodist missionary, also participated in the PCK study groups and itinerant industrial evangelism programs before launching the Methodist industrial mission in Incheon.

In the last chapel service before the summer of 1961, Oh Cheol-ho and Henry Jones addressed the PTS students to recruit participants in the very first IIE summer program that was to start in July. Cho Chi Song was a senior with just one more semester till graduation. As such, he had been thinking about the future course he should take in ministry. Jones left a deep impression on Chi Song with the message that South Korea would soon become so industrialized that even its agriculture will come to depend on the machines. Cho felt moved by the call that the church would need passionate servants who would be able to address an industrialized audience with an effective presentation of the gospel.

My original intention was to get into rural ministry. I never thought about industrial missions [. . .] until I heard Jones say the entire nation will become industrialized. I was

curious. What did he mean exactly by 'industry'? I thought
I might as well participate in the program so I could see for
myself.[10]

Indeed, Cho's initial vision was to start a movement for rural enlightenment and revival like Grundtvig did in Denmark. He was therefore struck by Jones's message that industrialism will even touch agriculture. He signed up for the IIE program.[11]

Meeting Jesus in the Mines

Chi Song was a youth pastor in Sinchon when he participated in the IIE summer program. Participants were sent out in pairs to get jobs in the factories, mines, or other workplaces. They dispersed throughout Busan, Daegu, Daejeon, Incheon, and Gangwon-do to gain their first experience of what it was like to be a worker in a modern industry.

Chi Song got his job in the Jangseong coal mines in Samcheok with his partner, Choi Seong-bong, who was a Methodist seminarian. The employers knew they were hiring students for a church-related program, which was an important difference between the IIE participants and the student activists of the 1970–80s. The latter got their jobs as part of the worker-student solidarity movement while concealing their identities. Nevertheless, the IIE participants still had to hide who they were from their coworkers, and they still had to work the same jobs. The goal was to give the seminarians and ministers a taste of hard labor before they could grapple with the problems of meaningful work, industrial issues, and evangelizing.

The coal mines in the 1960s were "pits" in more than one sense. Although the miners provided the nation's single greatest source of energy, they had to endure horrid living and working conditions. The work was hard and dangerous, as indicated by the fact that miners wrote their wills before starting their job. Yet, their wages were utterly low. The foreman who greeted Cho and his partner seemed puzzled by their visit. "In my 20 years working as a miner, nobody from the church ever came down to this *pit*." Each miner had to carry a pit prop when entering the mines. It was thicker than a man's palm and longer than his height. After traveling hundreds of meters into the tunnel, the miners had to get onto a shaft and travel several kilometers down vertically. At the bottom, the miners had to crawl through narrower tunnels, dragging the pit props behind them on a rope. Once they reached the end, they set up the pit props on all sides of the chamber and started picking away at the coal. A motor pulled a full cart up the shaft before sending an empty one back down. So, the work continued.

The space in the tunnels was tight with sparse oxygen and high humidity. Miners were always out of breath. The heat from the ground caused them to sweat profusely even while staying still. Many chose to work in underwear as the drenched uniforms stuck to their skin and impeded their movement.

With all the coal dust and sweat caking onto our faces, we looked as if we had applied one of those cosmetic mud packs. [. . .] All you could see was the white of our eyes. [. . .] My spit was also black from the coal dust. [. . .] You couldn't tell where you left your lunch box because every surface was covered. [. . .] You had to sweep the floor with your hands to find where it was.[12]

Chi Song had plain rice balls with salt, sweat, tears, and coal dust for seasoning. He knew in his aching bones that the church would never bring a single miner to salvation until it addressed the present wretchedness they had to endure. The coal blocks glistened under the helmet's flashlight every time a pick struck at it. This reminded Chi Song of the lashes that struck the flesh of Jesus Christ.

*If you're a Christian minister who wants to get into industrial
missions, you have to first experience what it's like to be a
worker. . . . You have to feel it for yourself in your body—
the back pain, the drowsiness, the insult, the humiliation,
everything. Then you have to take a good look at the workers
until you can see the depth of their perseverance, the weight
that they bear, the dignity of their character that borders on
religion, even that of Jesus Christ. You have to toil with your
body till you wake up to the utter vanity of the notion that
you could somehow help the workers, share the good news
with them, or somehow be of service to them [without having
gone through what they have gone through].*[13]

Working in the mines had a sanctifying effect. Cho felt spiritual
unity with Christ in carrying the burdens of labor upon his body.
He increasingly realized the need to identify with the workers before
doing anything else in industrial evangelism. It grieved him to know
that the clergy would never see the miner in his suffering. All they
would see was just another man dressed in his Sunday best sitting in
the pews.

After a month in the mines, Cho returned to finish his last semester
and graduate from seminary. He wanted to continue learning about
industrial evangelism, so he joined the monthlong CSLS program in
January 1962. It was directed by the IED, having between 12 and 15
participants, most of whom were Christian students from a seminary
or regular university. It was less intensive than the IIE's three-month
program, and the students only spent their daylight hours working.
The evenings were spent on scholarly lectures and discussions as well as
reflections on what the students had learned.

In his exiting report for the IIE program, Cho identified a number
of tasks for the church to do in the coming years. These included identifying the structures that prevented workers from participating in
religious life, hearing the grievances of the workers, and addressing
their sense of helplessness and resignation. He also believed the church

should do something about the pressure non-Christian workers faced from their employers to participate in worship against their will. The church had to find more appropriate ways to relate to the workers and assist them in their suffering. The work of ministering to the industrial population also had to be an interdenominational effort.

The IED must have noticed Cho's participation in both the IIE and CSLS programs and thought him a promising talent for industrial evangelism. It hired him as a staff researcher for a monthly salary of 2,000 won in March 1962. Cho was tasked with training the new students who participated in the IIE and CSLS programs. He took them around the cement, textiles, and match factories; the steel mills; and the mines. They were intentionally assigned where they could experience the hardest kinds of work. Cho himself became a seasoned expert in a variety of different industrial contexts. He also carried out the basic research the denomination relied on for a range of its industrial ministries.

> *I did all kinds of research under Oh Cheol-ho (who was leading the IED at the time). I collected and processed data, like how many businesses there were in the country, how many men and women were employed by sector, the amount of capital owned by each company, the kind and quantity of products they produced, and so forth. We also collected data on national demographics, economic statistics, industrial accidents, labor unions, government agencies, churches near industrial centers, opinions of the clergy. . . .Our studies were broad. The charts, graphs, and statistics we produced could capture a variety of different topics.*[14]

One could say without exaggeration that virtually every study produced by the PCK DOE in the 1960s had gone through Cho's hands. These studies served as precious points of reference for a host of different activities, including the industrial evangelism study groups and national seminar of evangelism directors.

The IED had more funding than the other organs of the PCK, thanks to the annual gift of $3,000 from the United States. This allowed the division to not only perform its methodical studies but also purchase more modern office equipment. Using typewriters, cameras, voice recorders, and color printers, the IED could create quality materials for educational, administrative, or publicity purposes. For instance, it created a Labor Sunday poster featuring the color photo of a miner, which was reprinted in an advertisement in the Kidok Gongbo's national newsletter. These resources allowed the IED to extend its reach and raise support for industrial evangelism across both the lay and clergy. A television series by the Christian Broadcasting System (CBS) dramatized the life of a worker. It enjoyed such popular success that the station rebroadcast the series. This, coupled with the fact that the members of the IEC were influential PCK leaders, was a testament of the great level of support that existed in the early days of industrial ministry.[15]

Working in the IED was a fruitful time of preparation for Cho Chi Song's ministry. He gained a broad and deep knowledge of various industrial sectors and their workers from firsthand experience. He sharpened his skills of observation and ability to analyze a given workplace. He also learned the importance of education and communication for raising support from a wider Christian audience. He was ready to put his skills to use.

Industrial Ministry

After two years as a staff researcher of the IED, Cho received his ordination on November 21, 1963. During the ceremony in Dongshin Church, the General Assembly and Gyeonggi Presbytery commissioned him as an industrial evangelist, making him the first such ordained minister to specialize in industrial ministry. Oh Cheol-ho gave the ordained Rev. Cho Chi Song a fine leather-bound Bible as an ordination gift. The DOE and Gyeonggi Presbytery (moderated by Rev. Bang Ji-il) announced their decision to send Cho to Yeongdeungpo.

Youngnack Church (whose session moderator was Rev. Han Kyung-chik) took up the charge to support his livelihood. The Yeongdeungpo Industrial Evangelism Committee (YDP-IEC) held Cho's appointment service on February 14, 1964. Influential leaders for the PCK and Gyeonggi Presbytery's missions were in attendance. These included Lee Gwon-chan, general secretary of the DOE; Rev. Bang Ji-il, moderator of the Gyeonggi Presbytery; Rev. Gye Hyo-eon, chair of the YDP-IEC; Rev. Yoo Byeong-gwan from Dorim Church; Rev. Han Kyung-chik from Youngnak Church; and Rev. Oh Cheol-ho, secretary of the IED. Their presence was a sign of the great support that existed for the nascent ministry.

Yeongdeungpo was the largest light industrial complex in the capital in 1964. It had 552 different businesses that employed 40,051 workers in their factories. Dorim Church, which already had a very active industrial evangelism ministry, indicated in its ministry report that most of the workers suffered very poor working conditions because of the highly regressive and exploitative management practices.

> *The working conditions in these businesses are extremely poor. Most owners demand blind obedience from their workers that one could only expect to find in the Roman Empire. They are unwilling to nurture a more creative workforce. . . . Nor do the workers expect things to get any better. They are resigned to their lot. The most they hope for is to bide the time so they can get their pay at the end of the day. Managers are not interested in exploring ways to use adequate rest and leaves as a way of enhancing productivity. The only business strategy they seem to know is to demand more overtime and rely on a totalitarian kind of authority.*[16]

The YDP-IEC had been active since the Korean National Organization of Presbyterian Women (NOPW) sent Kang Gyung-goo to the area as an industrial evangelist in 1958. Kang had been offering a fairly conventional type of ministry, with the only novel feature being that it took place in the factories. Her primary audience was the female workers, whom she visited in their cafeterias and dormitories to hold worship and lead Bible studies. The NOPW records say, "Kang Gyung-goo went around with a kettle of porridge to feed the women who collapsed from the harsh conditions. She is regarded a truly motherly figure among the youth wandering the streets, to whom she delivers a message of forgiveness, comfort, and courage."

As the name indicates, the industrial ministry at the time was simply a more targeted type of conventional evangelism. The primary goal was to bring workers to the churches from the factories. It did not seek to address the distinctive issues of industrialization and its working people.[17] It also operated on the assumption that the key to the ministry's success was the *employers*. Convert them, and the employees would follow suit. The result was that the early members of industrial evangelism often placed greater priority on maintaining their relationship with the business owners over the workers.[18]

Cho did not break from this style of ministry upon getting to Yeongdeungpo. He first had to get familiar with the state of affairs as a new arrival. In the meantime, he supported Kang's existing ministry.

There wasn't much we were allowed to do when I got there other than what we were already doing in the church. [. . .] Things like holding worship or Bible study, visiting the members of the congregation, doing evangelism, bringing in new members, and so forth. Those were the only kinds of things we were allowed to do.[19]

This was reiterated in a ministry report submitted by the YDP-IEC in 1965 after Cho had been there for about a year. It also said the ministry's primary activities were worship and evangelism in the factories, educational lectures, lay evangelism training, local church evangelism, and handing out evangelism tracts.[20]

Factory worship was the single most important activity. It often took the form of an assembly in the cafeteria or auditorium called by the business owner. Attendance for all the workers was mandatory. The employers took their seats on the stage next to the pulpit. The sermons were often written to please their ears. For instance, a typical sermon would say, "Joseph was an honest and hardworking man, so God blessed him. You, too, will receive your reward if you remain faithful in your duties to the company." Many prayers were offered for the company and the owner's security but very few for the workers. The employers welcomed these worship services. They figured that Christianizing their workforce would help set them right with the Lord Almighty while also being good for business.[21]

The more zealous employers went so far as to start a church inside their factories. Such was the case of Hanyoung Church, born inside the Hanyoung Textiles Company. A regular churchgoer, its owner said, "it would hardly glorify God to gather a thousand employees for worship [. . .] inside a smelly dining area." His solution was to build a church. Nor was he alone. Many such factory churches sprung up throughout the country, in most cases making worker attendance mandatory. In one case in Daegu, some of the workers were even penalized for failing to attend service.

There were three factories in Yeongdeungpo at the time with a monthly factory worship—the Donga Dyeing Company, Daehan Textiles, and Daedong Textiles. Attendance was, of course, mandatory. Teenage girls who had just finished working a 12-hour shift at night were no exception. Naturally, they found it very difficult to stay awake. The dormitory staff patrolled the pews to keep everyone awake. Once, a preacher quoted a verse from Matthew 11 saying, "Come to me, all you who are weary and burdened, and I will give you rest."

"What a fool," one of the male workers immediately retorted. "We have to sit here and listen to him talk after we worked all night while he slept in his bed, and he's telling us to rest?"[22]

The preacher could not hear the comment from his pulpit, but Cho did. He liked sitting among the workers, which gave him a clear view of their reactions. The employers may have meant well, thinking they were letting the workers hear the good news. To the workers, however, the factory worship was anything but good news. To them, it was just one more charade to suffer after finishing a wearying shift.

The three companies later built a collective worship hall to house all of their workers in a single service. They invited a Rev. Jeong to shepherd the combined flock, a task he tried to do quite sincerely until one day a worker approached him quite discreetly.

"Reverend," the concerned worker said. "You should stop coming here. There are plenty of other preachers to do the job. I know that you mean well. Why should you be despised for it? You see, none of the workers mean what we sing, even when we're singing at the top of our lungs. We have no choice but to sit through the services. Otherwise, we'll lose our jobs. That's why all the others end up resenting you and speaking poorly about you behind your back."

Jeong talked to Cho Chi Song about this. "What should I do, Reverend?" Cho did not mince words. "Suppose it was your daughter working in these factories. Would you tell her to go to church after a 12-hour shift at night? Or would you tell her to get some sleep? Which is more consistent with the love of God?" Not long afterward, Rev. Jeong resigned from his position after having a disagreement with one of the factory foremen.

Himself an ordained minister, Cho Chi Song was also often invited to preach in the factories. The more he preached, the more he felt that something was wrong. *Industrial evangelism is supposed to serve the needs of the workers*, he thought. *At this rate, we won't even be welcome guests, let alone evangelize anyone.*

Then Cho also received a discreet tip from a worker he had known for three years. "Reverend, many of us are unhappy with the way you fraternize with the employers. You also preach in a way that sounds pleasing to them." Cho was shocked, but the problem was now clear.

"I had a vague sense that I was doing it wrong. Now that a worker said this, I was sure of it. [. . .] That's when I started talking to the workers instead. My focus had drifted, but I was going to gradually come back and find my way."[23]

Indeed, after that conversation, Cho started to spend more time with the workers directly rather than through the factory worship. He set aside the appearance of a high and lofty preacher who was always escorted to the pulpit by the employers. Instead, he put on the persona of the workers' friend. He started visiting the factories at midnight or very early in the morning so he could speak with the workers who had night shifts. If he could not catch a worker for a conversation, he spoke to the security guards for an hour or two instead.

I remember the reverend making rounds on his bicycle around the factories. He visited us like he visited the members of his own church. He asked things like how the managers were, how we were treated, or how things were overall in the factories. [. . .] I found out later through the news that he had to endure a lot of hardship under the military dictators because of his involvement in the UIM. [. . .] I'll never forget the way he poured out the energy of the best years of his life going around concrete jungle of the factories. [. . .] While I was never a part of the UIM, whenever it's Christmas or the New Year's, or whenever I think about the cross of Christ, I think to myself that perhaps Rev. Cho was what Christ would have looked like should he have walked among us in those days.[24]

Workers were still treated as second-class citizens, called by derogatory terms like *gongsooni* or *gongdori*, which ascribed them a diminutive status simply for working in the *gongjangs* or factories. Visiting each of the factories on his bicycle, Rev. Cho came to share in the workers' pain and sorrow. He was fully convinced that they were the ones Scripture spoke of in Luke 14:21. Thus Cho started his lifelong ministry of becoming a friend and part of the workers' lives.

NOTES

1 Seo Deok-Seok, *Interview for the Biography*, Transcribed by Hong Yoon-gyung (2011), 5th Interview.
2 Seo Deok-Seok, *Interview for the Biography*, 5th Interview.
3 Original English could not be found. Re-translated from the Korean translation.
4 Kim Yong-Bock and Yoo Seung-hee, *Cho Chi Song's Oral History* (Vol. 12, 2011), 32A–36A.
5 Seo Deok-Seok, *Interview for the Biography*, 5th Interview.
6 NCCK, "The May 16 Coup and Labor Movement of the 1960s," *Testimonies from the Ground: Labor in the 1970s* (Pulbit, 1984).
7 Chang Sook-kyeong, *The UIM and Labor Movement in the 1970s* (Seonin, 2013), 32–33.
8 Chang, *The UIM and Labor Movement*, 32–33.
9 Jeong Byeong-joon, "50 Years of UIM," *I Am Working As My Father Is Working* (PCK National Mission Ministry, 2007).
10 Kim and Yoo, *Cho Chi Song's Oral History* (Vol. 12, 2011), 32A–36A.
11 Seo Deok-Seok, *Interview for the Biography*, 5th Interview.
12 Kim and Yoo, *Cho Chi Song's Oral History* (Vol. 1, 1986), 4.
13 Kim and Yoo, *Cho Chi Song's Oral History* (Vol. 1, 1986), 21.
14 Kim and Yoo, *Cho Chi Song's Oral History* (Vol. 1, 1986), 67.
15 Oh Cheol-ho, *Industrial Evangelism Handbook* (PCK Education and Resourcing Ministry, 1965).
16 Yeongdeungpo UIM 40th Anniversary Committee, *Yeongdeungpo UIM: A 40-Year History*, (1998), 53.
17 In Myeong-jin, "History of the Yeongdeungpo UIM," *Yeongdeungpo UIM: A 40-Year History* (YDP-UIM, 1998), 58.
18 Cho Chi Song, "A Brief History of the UIM," *Yeongdeungpo UIM: A 40-Year History*, YDP-UIM (1998), 58.
19 Kim and Yoo, *Cho Chi Song's Oral History* (Vol. 12, 2011), 32A–36A.

20 Kim Myeong-bae, Yeongdeungpo UIM Files Vol. 1, YDP-UIM & Soongsil University Center for Culture and Mission Studies 2020, 21–31.

21 PCK Department of Evangelism UIM Committee, *The Church and UIM* (PCK Education & Resourcing Ministry, 1981), 95–96.

22 Kim and Yoo, *Cho Chi Song's Oral History* (Vol. 12, 2011), 32A–36A, 11.

23 Kim and Yoo, *Cho Chi Song's Oral History* (Vol. 12, 2011), 32A–36A, 11.

24 B. H. Won's story blog, http://moriamount&faith.blogspot.com/ 2007/10/8.

2

INDUSTRIAL MISSIONS

A Gospel for Workers

CHO STARTED TO gradually change the course of his ministry. He tried to be more balanced in his sermons and started to address the workers' needs in addition to that of the employers. He broke from the typical mold for Sunday sermons that had been copied in the factories. At times, he began delivering a preferential message for the workers.

One can turn to his sermon on 2 Thessalonians 3:12 as an example. The verse says, "such persons we command and exhort to do their work quietly and to earn their own living." Sermons on this verse typically pronounced blessings for the diligent workers who were content to receive what they are given, asking for no more nor less. Cho gave it a different spin: "The command to earn your living not only means you ought to work for what you eat, but that you ought not take away from what someone else has earned."[1]

The change started to make employers feel uneasy, as expected. Rev. Yoo Byeong-gwan, chair of the YDP-IEC, tried to intervene. "Mr. so-and-so isn't very happy about your preaching."[2] The intent was not to chastise but to caution. The new sermons might make the employers resistant to industrial evangelism. The assumption, of course, was that ministry would be impossible without the cooperation of the employers.

Cho had sensed that he was in a bind. It was becoming difficult to address the needs of both the workers and the employers. Facing pressures from both, he had to pick a stand. Yoo Byeong-gwan's caution served as the liberation he needed. Cho had felt cynical about preaching in the factories for some time anyway. If the employers did not want him to do it, neither did he. It was the perfect opportunity to quit leading the factory worships and start looking for another way.

Meeting the Workers Outside the Factories

The companies stopped inviting me to preach. [. . .] The rumors were that 'Cho changed, he's different'. [. . .] The word reached the ears of the IEC. [. . .] So I went ahead and told them. I'd really rather not continue to preach in the factories. I thought it actually detracted from the cause of evangelism.[3]

Starting fresh, Cho recognized that he had entered the ministry with more zeal than he had understanding. He decided the first order of business was to clearly define industrial evangelism and communicate it to the others. That led to the printing of *Saneop Jeondoji (The Industrial Evangelism Tract)*, each of which had four pages explaining topics like work ethic, labor laws, work-rest balance, stewardship, and Christian financial ethics. The text was written in plain language and was accompanied by cartoons. Each print had 3,000 copies, and there was a total of 30 prints. That meant there were enough copies of the tract circulated for each of the 40,000 workers in Yeongdeungpo to have received two copies. Cho spent most of his time handing out the tracts to meet the workers directly without having to go through their supervisors.

Around the same time, Yoo Dong-sik began introducing the concept of lay theology for the first time in Korea in the Yonsei University School of Theology. His message that the lay were equally capable and called as the clergy to be Christ's disciples captivated Cho's imagination. He found the concept revolutionary when he realized that he did not have to evangelize the working people himself. The workers themselves could do it![4] He was convinced that the ministry could grow simply by having lay workers become the agents of industrial evangelism. Cho now directed his energy to organizing the lay

Christians in the factories. Previously, Kang Gyung-goo had formed a loose Christian network by the name *Shinbong-hwe*. Cho replaced it on May 13, 1964, with the Yeongdeungpo Lay Association for Industrial Evangelism (LAIE). It had lay representatives from 14 different factories and began to serve as the core for organizing Christians in each workplace.[5]

By the end of 1964, there were 34 businesses that either had a branch of the LAIE or a connection with the YDP-IEC, including Hanyoung Textiles, Chosun Leathers, Daedong Textiles, Donga Dyeing Company, Mipoong, Panbon Textiles, Panbon Spinning, Daehan Wool, Hanguk Textiles, and Donga Sewing Machines. In 1965, a total of 1,000 people attended 21 lay gatherings in the factories.

The LAIE facilitated fellowship, devotional life, and volunteering among its members. Its activities included worship, prayer, dialogues, educational lectures, social events, music hearings, meetings, etc. Vibrant lay evangelism ministries started in the local churches like Dorim Church, Yangpyeong Church, Yeongdeungpo Church, and Youngnam Church.[6]

Cho phased out the reliance on the owners and supervisors. His new model was to organize and train lay believers so they could voluntarily organize their own worship, fellowship, and education. The previous model required the cooperation of the employers to bring the workers together for worship or Bible study. Now, the workers themselves were the agents of evangelism. This shift of agency came to the fore again in the small-group movement of the 1970s.

The ministry needed a place to meet and train the workers outside the factories. Cho leased a two-story red-brick building. It was across from his house in the alley that cut below the Dangsan-dong overpass and opened toward the Han River. It was the first UIM (still the IEC) Center. Cho made two large tables using fiberboard he bought from the Daeseong Timber Company, where Rev. Lee Guk-seon of the PROK[7] happened to run his industrial ministry. The tables were used for classes, meals, and table-tennis. Cho also put up a large map of

Yeongdeungpo on his office wall. He placed a pin to mark the location
of every factory from which he knew at least one worker who was a
Christian. He then marked the distance from the ministry center to
the factory with a red pen. A piece of paper attached next to each pin
summarized the factory's information such as its products, number
of employees, and the names of its LAIE members. The map was the
dashboard for all industrial evangelism activities in Yeongdeungpo.

> *We used to have a map of Yeongdeungpo in our office that
> was half the size of this wall here. [. . .] I marked the location
> of every company, and I put up notes on how many people
> were employed there, who were the people I knew there.
> Toward the end, we discovered we had a connection to nearly
> 250 different companies.*[8]

Workers organized into a local branch of the LAIE borrowed a
local church or cathedral for their meetings. Rev. Cho visited them
in Yangpyeong-dong, Daelim-dong, or Guro-dong to lead their Bible
study. Unlike in the worship services where the employers were present,
workers felt free to have a robust discussion about their real thoughts
and experiences.

A common issue was that the employers often did not keep their
promise to give Sundays off. Christian workers felt torn about working
on a Sunday, concerned they were not keeping the commandment to
rest on the Sabbath and keep it holy.

> *Is it true we can't go to heaven if we work on the Sabbath?*
> *My employer gets to go to church where he is an elder
> every Sunday, dressed in his nice clothes. Yet he makes us work
> all the same except to have a quick worship service during
> lunch break.*
> *Who's supposed to be barred from heaven, then? The
> workers who did what they were told? Or the elder who made
> his employees work on a Sunday?*

Cho chimed in after listening for a while:

> *I heard a story about a man who owned a gas station next to*
> *an expressway in the United States. He was an elder of the*
> *church, but he still kept his store open on Sundays. He was*
> *worried about cars running out of gas when the store was*
> *closed. [. . .] Some of them could be on their way to church.*
> *[. . .] So the elder figured, God would understand if he*
> *stayed open to sell gasoline. Now, let's suppose this wasn't your*
> *reason. Let's suppose you're someone who doesn't have to work*
> *seven days to make a living. Would it please God if you chose*
> *to work yet another day just to make more money?*[9]

The discussions naturally delved into matters of concrete application. While this was never an issue for the workers, other members of the clergy bristled to hear what was being discussed. The churches in Korea predominantly followed the doctrine of verbal dictation, believing that every word in the Bible was the inerrant and directly inspired word of God. This rigid interpretation of the Bible was actually a break from the broader tradition of the reformation, but it was the local order of the day. Cho's colleagues found the very notion strange that one's context should be brought into consideration to determine how to apply the commandment to keep Sabbath. One of the members of the LAIE also found these discussions novel, never having heard any of it in her years as a deacon. She brought the question to her pastor: "Rev. Cho from the IEC says we're allowed to work on the Sabbath." Her pastor responds: "What in the world is he teaching? I'm afraid this might be heresy."

The pastor was further shocked to hear from his deacon that the topics of LAIE discussions were not always religious. How could a Christian fellowship possibly discuss labor, economics, or social ethics? "A minister should only talk about the gospel," he said. "Why would Cho talk about labor? That's what a Communist would do, not a Christian pastor. Deacon, you must stop attending these meetings."

The deacon asked Rev. Cho the tragicomic question if he was sure he had gone to seminary. The factory owners also began talking about how "Rev. Cho changed" or "preaches differently than he used to." They realized that getting Cho Chi Song to preach to their workers was going to impede their business as usual.

The reactions were anticipated. Undeterred, Cho continued to build the curriculum for the LAIE teaching program. The first iteration covered topics like stewardship, economics, and labor unions. The following iterations progressively gained additional topics: industrial issues, economic ethics, labor movements, natural sciences, social sciences, and humanities. The fourth, fifth, and six iterations placed a greater emphasis on labor-specific issues, such as overseas industrial evangelism, theory of labor relations, labor movement history, and the Labor Standards Act (LSA). It was a robust educational program. Lectures were given by top speakers on each topic, including seminary and university professors, missionaries, and labor experts. By the end of 1966, a total of 300 LAIE members had completed at least one full curriculum.[10]

After establishing a relationship with the workers, Cho began meeting them in groups from each factory, production line, or section. Workers trusted Cho's judgment on many of their workplace issues, as he often had better insights about their own factories from the rounds he used to make. While continuing to grow the LAIE quantitatively, Cho also started preparing for its qualitative leap.

He organized around 250 groups of workers and matched them with dedicated lay leaders like Kim Gap-jun (Hanguk Textiles), Kim Dong-hyeok (Daedong Textiles), Kim Ryeo-seong (Goryeo Molding), Kom Yong-baek (Miwang Industries), Na Joo-sik (Namyoung Nylons), Park Young-hye (Hanguk Textiles), Seok Jong-chil (Samgwang Glasses), Lee Man-jin (Je-il Moolsan), Lee Myeong-jip (Daehan Weaving Company), Lee Seung-man (Panbon Textiles), Lee Jeong-gil (Hanil Dorco), Cho Seung-rae (Hankook Tire), Cho Yong-chan (Haitai Confectionery), Cho Hye-ja (Hanguk Textiles), Jeong

Hae-ryong (Daedong Textiles), and Han Sang-chool (Dongyang Sewing Machines). This experience with organizing the LAIE groups later proved invaluable when organizing the women's small groups in the 1970s.[11]

A Congregation of Workers: The Labor Union

Organizing the workers to evangelize other workers soon faced a major limitation. First, not all the workers were equal peers. Many of the starting members of LAIE got themselves promoted to section chiefs of middle managers, thanks to the quality education provided by the LAIE curriculum. Ironically, the privileges they gained through their involvement with the LAIE soon became the fetters that bound them to their senior management. They started to care more about what their employers wanted. Cho believed that LAIE could not fulfill its original purpose through members who joined the rank of supervisors.

The members also had their discontent. The LAIE had invited several speakers who were economists, labor activists, and instructors in government training centers in order to enhance the quality and diversity of its education. One of them was the famed economist Dr. Cho Dong-pil. Some of the association's members, however, were displeased with being lectured by non-Christians: "This is supposed to be a training for Christian evangelism. Why are we bringing nonbelievers as speakers who smoke on our premises?"

Word of this reached Bang Ji-il, who was integral in bringing Cho Chi Song to Yeongdeungpo. He took Cho out for lunch. "There's been a lot of noise," the senior reverend said. "I don't think you should keep going this way. A pastor should focus on pastoring."

Also having come from North Korea, Bang Ji-il cherished Cho like he would his son. He repeatedly told the young minister not to put himself at the center of negative attention. When it became clear Cho would not yield, Bang relented. The only means of evangelism known among the established clergy was to convert individuals and bring them to church. They were unfamiliar with the concept that the gospel ministry could be served by getting the workers to experience the justice of God through the transformation of their society. Bang did not fully understand Cho's method. Nevertheless, he trusted the young missioner, knowing he was motivated by a sincere commitment to the workers and his faith.[12]

Cho found himself facing two fronts again. The employers still despised his pro-worker sermons. Now, Christians were pressuring him to stop providing the secular portions of the LAIE worker education. He realized that the church was just as reluctant as the government or corporations to discuss workers' issues. He believed any step forward in industrial evangelism would require building awareness and support across the church. Cho thus started the Industrial Evangelism Seminar for ordained ministers.[13]

Over the course of four iterations from 1965 to 1966, Cho noticed an interesting pattern in the LAIE education. The first class in spring 1965 was a session titled "What Is Stewardship?" and mostly featured explicitly Christian content. The subsequent classes were also taught by renowned professors of theology. Their theological content was top quality, but most of the workers except for the most pious Christians remained disengaged. When the audience was directed to have a discussion among themselves on the topic of Christian ethics, the longtime churchgoers retorted, "What's there to discuss?" To them, going to church and believing in Jesus was the full extent of Christian ethics. This convinced the non-Christians in the audience to keep their silence. There was no point in arguing about the exploitation and inhumane treatment of the workers by their Christian employers. Religious talk rang hollow for most workers, removed from their daily lives.

The real discussion began when the formal program was over. The air in the room changed as the workers gathered around with cups of barley tea.

Our shift was over, and they still made us work for two more hours to meet the production quota. They don't even pay us overtime!

That's mild. We're not supposed to start our shift until eight, but everyone knows you're late if you're not there by seven. If you get there 10 minutes past seven, they cut a day's pay.

Do you know the head of human resources in our company? Everyone knows he has the wandering hands. Rumor says there isn't a pretty girl he hasn't harassed.[14]

It was only through the informal sessions that Cho learned the full extent of the issues that the workers were dealing with. His formal programs had done very little to address them. The workers did not need more education about the church or theology. They needed to know how to make immediate improvements in their lives. They needed the ability to demand proper wages, take collective action, and exercise their lawful rights. So the LAIE programs gradually shifted focus, dealing more with the issues of labor, society, and economy. By its sixth iteration, the program mostly dealt with the issues of industrial society. Only a minority of the topics were still explicitly religious.

Over the years, Cho fleshed out what the gospel of Jesus Christ should look like in the Yeongdeungpo factories. The good news for the workers was that Christ—and his body—participated in their suffering. Cho felt the followers of Christ ought to step into their issues to help them raise their wages and create the conditions in which they could actually take joy in their creative activities. That was what salvation would look like for the workers.

Cho was concerned that the LAIE was retreating to a narrow focus. Its leading members seemed more interested in bringing workers into the churches rather than going into the factories. They became used to the comfort of staying where they were, sitting in the pews and speaking the established language of Christianity. The call for the believers to go out had turned into a call to the nonbelievers to come in. The ministry had hit another dead end. This exposed the false assumption that all evangelism had to do was to bring the workers to sit inside a church building.

> *The members of LAIE were entry-level workers when I first met them. After a few years, they got promoted to be managers and section chiefs. That changed their thinking. I realized [. . .] that I cannot continue running the ministry this way. I dissolved the LAIE not very long afterwards. [. . .] I told myself it was for the better.*[15]

Thus, the experiment that started in the summer of 1964 ended in 1966.

Meanwhile, the YDP-IEC made its first contact with labor union leaders on April 9, 1965. Nine union leaders came to the mission center to meet with the 16 branch leaders of LAIE. They discussed the state of industrial evangelism and labor unions in Yeongdeungpo. The YDP-IEC was interested to learn what issues were handled by the unions and what message they had for the Christian church.[16]

This led to bimonthly meetings between the YDP-IEC and union officers who were Christians to discuss the issues in each of the factories they represented. They agreed to start a joint study of the Christian basis for labor activism and ways that Christians may engage. It was the ministry's first step toward involvement with concrete labor action.

Cho selected around 10 out of the 300 graduates of LAIE education for a new set of trainings. Each was a member of a labor union, some of them officers. Their new goal for training was to be better equipped for labor union activities. Someone named this new regimen "the Chain," highlighting the fact that the goal was to produce individual organizers who could work together like the interlocking chains of a bicycle.

The Chain covered an extensive range of topics over the course of six months, which included labor laws, collective bargaining rights, labor-management relations, production and wages, and labor movement history. It offered high-quality labor education that included topics even the union officers found difficult to access back in the day. For example, the YDP-IEC was one of the very few places in Korea in the 1960s where someone could attend an academic lecture on industrial and organizational psychology.[17]

Cho also traveled to other countries to learn different ways he could approach the ministry. He visited Japan and Taiwan to learn about their model of industrial evangelism from March 13 to April 4, 1966. Then, he participated in a program for union leaders in the University of Manila from October 7 to December 22 per the referral of the International Labor Organization (ILO) and Federation of Korean Trade Unions (FKTU). He was joined by labor union leaders from 13 different Asian countries and was the first clergyman to complete the training.

Accompanied by three FKTU officers, the trip to Manila allowed Cho to deepen the partnership between the unions and the YDP-IEC. Upon coming back, Cho was invited as the speaker for the FKTU worker trainings. The first of these—which was also the first time a church minister was invited to address a labor union—was the Yeongdeungpo Union Leadership Development Program that took place in the Yeongdeungpo Cultural Center on July 23, 1966. In turn, the YDP-IEC invited FKTU officers as speakers in its programs. These exchanges became frequent.[18]

The ministry staff often got together with the union leaders to pool their best ideas for worker education. They often met simply to have a conversation. Over time, it became evident that the YDP-IEC offered higher quality programs than the FKTU. Explaining that they did not have access to the same resources, the FKTU requested that the YDP-IEC take over its officer training. The YDP-IEC agreed and began training potential officers nominated by the FKTU. Each cohort met once a week for six months. The YDP-IEC trained 16 cohorts total, becoming South Korea's hub of union leadership development.

> *When we first started going into the companies, we used to look for the CEOs and managers. Then we looked for the section chiefs, then we looked for the employees. [. . .] And now when we stepped foot into a company, we went straight for their union office. [. . .] The unions were so grateful that someone from the clergy was taking an interest in them. [. . .] We started training the union officers together. [. . .] I'd say the YPD-IEC organized a good number of the local branches working with the FKTU.*[19]

Cho identified four main issues in his updated report to the YDP-IEC. One, the workers suffered from extremely low wage levels. Two, the ministry was short-staffed. Three, it was very difficult for the workers to make the time to participate in religious life given the way they were employed in the factories. Four, it was incumbent upon the ministry to define its role in addressing such issues in the factories.[20] The report indicated the ministry was gaining a wider scope. Beyond just increasing church membership, it was now interested in getting believers to address the host of problems festering in the factories.

The ministry's encounter with the labor unions gave it the ability to recognize structural problems in addition to issues of individual spirituality. It was the missing piece required to serve the workers in their context. It took some trial and error, but Cho and the YDP-IEC finally had a working solution to the questions that have been posed to the ministry: What does it mean to preach the good news to an industrial audience? How are the workers saved? Who are the agents of this ministry? Cho's answer was, "the labor union."

> *The unions were not the only way to protect a worker's rights and dignity, but they were the best way. In a way, the labor union was a worker's church. [. . .] It was at that*

congregation where workers learned their rights as human beings. It was there they learned the art of democracy, or the love of their neighbors, or the value of sacrifice and service. Being in a union taught the workers what it meant to be persecuted for righteousness, how to fight for justice, how to stand up for the rights of another. And they could learn all that through action. They could learn what it means to make peace. The unions were the context in which the UIM had to do its ministry. They were the instruments of the workers' salvation.[21]

The unions pointed the way to an important breakthrough that the ministry needed after realizing the limitations of both the factory worships and lay evangelism trainings. Workers were now understood to be a suffering people who had been pressed down in the earthly kingdom of industrialized society. The labor union was the congregation of workers who held to the new hope. It was, in other words, a worker's church. Accepting this conceptual framework signaled the next phase in the industrial ministry of Yeongdeungpo. By acknowledging the workers' burden, it had committed to sharing it—as their friend. A thorny path awaited both.

From Industrial "Evangelism" to "Missions"

Having spoken to workers in nearly 250 different factories, Cho knew the workplace environment in Yeongdeungpo like he knew the palm of his hand. The vast majority of workers did not even know their basic rights and did not have access to union representation. This state of affairs made Cho very angry.

A young woman told me about the horrible things she had to endure as if it was all a part of normal life. Well, they were not a part of a normal life. It made me boil with anger. [. . .] She had to show up at seven o'clock in the evening and make

*a few thousand parts before the end of her shift at seven in
the morning. They gave her half an hour to eat at midnight,
after which she had to rush back to work. Sometimes, they
didn't even allow that break. After working again until three
or four in the morning, she got an hour or two to sleep at her
workstation before they woke her up. Even when it became
seven, she wasn't allowed to leave until she filled her quota.
She couldn't leave until she remade the defective parts. [. . .]
How could anyone survive in this kind of environment?
These were young girls. They should have been full of life. Yet
there they were, looking pale and sick, incapable of speaking
coherently. How could anyone see this yet feel nothing? How
could anyone serve in an industrial ministry yet do nothing
about this?*[22]

Most workers thought it was a luxury to ask for their rights or
better working conditions in the 1960s. Having seen the extent of
their exploitation, Cho believed the justice of God will never reign in
the land until the workers were treated with dignity.

Many of the workers in Yeongdeungpo were young women
and girls who had left their rural homes in search of work in the
cities. Most of them only had an elementary school education.
Many were too young to be employed, so they often used their
sisters' names to get their jobs. The employers knew this but turned
a blind eye, since it provided a convenient excuse to lower their
wages or even withhold their severance. Complaints were shut down
by blaming the workers for using fraudulent identity. Workers often
worked 18-hour shifts for less than a living wage and no overtime
compensation. They also often left without being given their legally
mandated severance.

The climate was decidedly against the workers. None of the
3,000 women working in Haitai Confectionery could even think of
asking management for a fan in their workstations to cope with the

summer heat of 40°C. Anyone who did would have been fired without recourse. Cho believed nobody with a religion or conscience could possibly eat the Haitai products if they knew the conditions in which they were made.

The following was another experience that convinced Cho that the ministry needed to take action: He was waiting for a 16-year-old worker by the name Soon-ok when she came rushing into the office. He sat the girl down to catch her breath. She had run all the way from the factory as soon as she finished her night shift to make it in time for her appointment with the reverend. The factory was 4 kilometers away. When asked why she did not take the bus, she replied that it would have taken two bus rides to get to the mission from the factory. Cho told her to wait while he prepared some noodles for her to eat. He felt his anger boil like the water in the pot. Despite being overworked, the girls were being paid so little they could not afford an extra bus fare. Soon-ok was just one of the 300 other young women working in her factory. The cruelty had to stop.[23]

Cho was attracted to the labor unions because of their dynamic ability to unite individually powerless workers into a force that could assert their rights, correct wrongs, and improve their environment. He believed the church could do far more for the workers by letting them experience the love of God rather than preaching about it. This meant helping the workers recover their ability to live in dignity.

Believing that labor unions were an effective instrument to this end, Cho Chi Song began equipping union leaders. He offered his training program 21 times over three years starting in 1969. Around 100 unions were formed with 40,000 members in Seoul and Incheon with the support of UIM organizations. Virtually every labor union in Yeongdeungpo had been organized with the support of the Yeongdeungpo UIM or had officers trained by the mission.[24]

In January 1968, the CCA held a conference in Bangkok for staff missioners to review the progress of industrial evangelism in

Asia. It had been a little over 10 years since the PCK first created the IEC. Missioners from the various represented countries agreed on a number of very important points. One, they agreed to give "industrial evangelism" the new name of "urban industrial missions." The idea was to expand the scope of ministry beyond individual spirituality to address the comprehensive set of human and social problems created by industrial urbanization. The participants also affirmed the need for concrete intervention in the labor issues if the UIM is to be part of bringing deliverance to the oppressed workers. Central to this task was supporting and multiplying the labor unions.

The theme verse of the UIM had also changed. Previously, the verse was "my Father is still working, and I also am working" (John 5:17). The new verse was "the Spirit of the Lord is upon me, because he has anointed me to bring good news to the poor. He has sent me to proclaim release to the captives and recovery of sight to the blind, to let the oppressed go free, to proclaim the year of the Lord's favor" (Luke 4:18–19).

> *The previous verse was more a message to the workers, implying that they ought to work diligently. But Luke chapter 4, verses 18 and 19 were a message for us missioners, telling us to stand with the workers and get engaged in the labor issues so that we can release the captives and set the oppressed free.*[25]

This change in tone was made possible by missioners like Cho who recognized the workers could not be freed from their wretched, dehumanizing conditions through individual spirituality alone. The only way to achieve justice was to challenge the structural contradictions of an industrialized society. Only then would the soil be ready for the gospel to take root.

Part of what went through Cho's mind during this period of transition from evangelism to missions can be found in texts like the following:

*The focus of worker missions should not be on individual
salvation or religious ceremony. The focus should be on
implementing justice in our industrialized society. That
is accomplished through the fair distribution of corporate
profits. We ought to start by investigating the facts. We have
to ask whether the wages are being raised properly, whether
the laws are being followed, whether the Labor Standards
Act is being followed. Then we have to expose who is actually
breaking the law to ensure that the workers are not excluded
by the very laws that are meant to protect them.*[26]

It also helps to know that part of the change was driven by the
adoption of a *missio Dei* theology. The early drivers of industrial evangelism subscribed to the traditional view that the only way to do missions
was to "evangelize" or bring about "individual salvation." Cho and his
peers, however, counted "humanization" and "social salvation" to be
part of the proper domain of God's ministry.

In keeping with the decisions of the CCA, the PCK also
began using the term "urban industrial mission" (UIM) instead of
"industrial evangelism" in the 56th General Assembly in 1971. The
Catholics and Methodists (KMC) also recognized the importance of
labor unions around the mid-1960s, shifting the emphasis of their
worker-related ministries from religious aspects to the protection
of worker rights and promotion of solidarity. The KMC and its
Incheon UIM benefited from the experience of George Ogle, who
had been a part of industrial missions in the United States.[27] The
Catholics Youth Workers Movement (JOC) also had a very active
ministry.

In 1965, these and other various players—the PCK, PROK,
KMC, SKH (Anglicans), and Catholics—joined to create the National
UIM Staff Conference to facilitate mutual exchange and training.[28]
Then, in January 1969, they created the National UIM Alliance representing each of their UIM organizations.

The PCK and KMC also created the YDP-UIM. Cho Chi Song was joined by KMC Rev. Kim Gyeong-nak and Rev. Ahn Gwang-soo starting on May 19, 1969. The YDP-UIM remained a joint PCK-KMC ministry for six years until April 1975.

The YDP-UIM and Yonsei University Institute for Urban Studies founded the Association of Ministers in Urban Industrial Areas. The founding covenant was to have all the denominations work together in areas where they had active UIMs. This interaction across the different ministries, denominations, and geographic areas made it possible to organize a collective response to issues in the future. The YDP-UIM especially prioritized the activities of the National UIM Alliance. Cho served as the PCK's representative, and the ministry was a very active participant in the organization.

The change in the UIM's goals also required a change in methodology. Cho explored his options during a six-month trip to Chicago from September 1970 to April 1971. He went per the invitation of the Presbyterian Church in America (PCA) to learn about Chicago's labor activism and social activism. He spent three months in a training for labor union leaders at Roosevelt University, a month with rural activists, and four months in the Organization for a Better Austin. He also visited various rural, civil rights, and Christian activist organizations around the Chicago area.

On his trip back to Korea, Cho stopped by West Germany to secure financial assistance from the Protestant Association for Cooperation in Development (EZE) for the construction of the new mission center. He took the opportunity to also learn about the social development projects of Friedrich Ebert Stiftung and the community activism in the poor sections of Paris.[29]

The activists Cho met during his time in Chicago were practitioners of Saul D. Alinksy's theory of community organizing. Their example of applying Alinksy's principles inspired Cho with a few ideas.[30] Some of the elements he saw were especially applied in the later women's small-group movement, which became one of the dynamic events in the history of the YDP-UIM. The friendships Cho forged in the United States and Germany also became a source of much-needed strength when the YDP-UIM came under persecution.

That Sinners May Repent

Lee Man-jin was the first fruit of the union officer training by the YDP-UIM. He was once the general secretary of LAIE. Now, he was the founding organizer of the labor union in Je-il Moolsan, a seasoning producer located in Mullae-dong. Its owner, Lee Byeong-cheol, had a zero-tolerance policy for labor unions. His anti-union legacy can still be felt in Samsung, another company he founded. Naturally, Lee Man-jin and his fellow union leaders were immediately fired.

To respond, the YDP-UIM filed a petition to the local labor office. It also distributed copies of the petition to create pressure to reinstate the fired workers. The company eventually restored Lee Man-jin and the rest of the union leadership. It also formally recognized the union and its right to collective bargaining. The workers even got a union office inside the company. This was a significant milestone as the first successful intervention by the YDP-UIM in a real labor dispute. It took a lengthy struggle, but real gains had been made.

The victory strengthened the conviction that helping resolve labor issues was the correct direction for the ministry. There was still much to be done in terms of the support for union activism. There were nearly 330,000 workers in 1,000 different companies in Yeongdeungpo in 1968. Only about 55,000 of them in 76 companies had access to union representation. This meant only a small fraction of the workers were enjoying their basic rights under the LSA.

Workers could not resist the state of modern slavery imposed on them without access to robust union representation, much less ask for rights. This was the case in Hanguk Textiles, where there was a labor union that existed only in name. Its office and roster of officers notwithstanding, the ineffectual union never engaged in collective bargaining, worker education, advocacy, or any other substantive activity.

The spark that led to change was a worker by the name Kim Gap-jun, who was a graduate of the first LAIE worker education program and regular member in Bang Ji-il's Yeongdeungpo Church. When Hanguk Textiles disallowed Cho Chi Song from entering its premises for his "problematic preaching," Kim arranged for the use of a church across the street where Cho could continue to meet the workers through a LAIE Scripture study. She was integral to bringing her coworkers together as the number of weekly participants grew from 20 to 50. She was also far more active than the union steward in her capacity as the female employees' representative. Coworkers turned to her rather than the union to resolve minor issues like job reassignments or coordinating leave.

Park Young-hye was one of the people who came to her first YDP-UIM meeting through Kim Gap-jun. Cho took special note of her and asked if she would like to work in the YDP-UIM credit union created in 1969. When Park quit her job at Hanguk Textiles to take the offer, she made an astounding discovery. Hanguk Textiles had never paid its workers severance compensation. Park asked Cho what she should do about the situation. "Of course you should get them to pay you," Cho said, "severance is part of your rightful wage." Cho also instructed Park to find the others who left the company without their severance.

Park found 40 others. Together, they were owed more than 6 million won. It was a larger sum in those days than an average Korean got to see in a lifetime. The YDP-UIM characterized the money as arrears that had been misappropriated by the company. The YDP-UIM sent a bill of overdue wages to the company while reporting a case of LSA violation to the Seoul Labor Administration in the name of the former Hanguk Textiles workers.

Park Young-hye took about a dozen of them and marched to the company gate. They demanded the severance that they earned with their "sweat and blood!" The company locked the gate, calling Park a "crazy woman." It had never paid severance, and it was not about to start now out of fear for Park and her rabble. The rabble, however, proved to be very persistent. They showed up to the gate at the start and end of every shift every day to demand payment for their severance. Some of them ran for the open gate and almost made it inside, but the guards grabbed and tossed them back out like pieces of luggage. Some others who were especially agitated planted themselves under the company vehicles, refusing to get out until their demands were met.

Over time, all 2,000 workers in Hanguk Textiles learned that their company had been robbing workers of their legally entitled severance. Representatives from the JOC, protestants, academics, labor activists, and social research organizations gathered on May 17, 1971, per the invitation of the YDP-UIM and decided to show collective support for the former Hanguk Textiles workers' struggle for severance. The issue started to attract attention from the rest of society. Feeling the public pressure, the Seoul Labor Administration reported Hanguk Textiles to the prosecutors for wage arrears.

The demonstration had been going on for several consecutive days when the Noryangjin Police suddenly arrived and arrested the demonstrators. Every one of them was taken away, including Park Young-hye and two other demonstration leaders, Park Yong-on and Yoo Myeong-seon. The purported cause of arrest was "unlawful collective action." The demonstrators went on a hunger strike during their detention in police custody. They were emaciated when they got out after a week.

As soon as they were released, the demonstrators regrouped. They chose a new chairperson and secretary to substitute for Park Yong-on and Yoo Myeong-seon before marching straight back to their former employer. Seeing the starved demonstrators marching toward them, the company sensed things could take a bad turn. It had also become the target of a police investigation by the reluctant labor authorities who faced public criticism for their failure to take action.

The company finally came out to negotiate. It promised to pay the severance but said it did not have the money yet. "Give us a date," the demonstrators said. The issue dragged on for a while longer as the company repeated the process of setting a deadline to placate the demonstrators before pushing it back when the date arrived. Time was not on their side, however, as it allowed more of the former employees to hear the news and join the fray. Workers who had quit as many as three years before started showing up on the company doorsteps.

When the demonstrators marched in again, a desperate management swore that it would pay them right away. The incredulous demonstrators proceeded to occupy the CEO's office. They were not going to leave until they had the money. Flustered, the CEO himself called Cho Chi Song for help.

When Cho asked why he wanted to see him, the CEO said "the girls" wouldn't believe him despite him giving them his word. "Why should we believe you?" The women immediately fired back. "You lied to us several times!" The managers in the room were startled at how assertive the previously docile workers had become. The CEO said he could pay the workers as early as the next morning, but he just needed more time to get the calculations sorted out.

Cho figured the workers would not have had to camp in the office if the company was ready with the money. "Show us where it is," he said. The CEO opened a large fridge off to the side in the office. There were two large sacks of cash inside.

"Just take it," the CEO said, "and do whatever you want with it."

It seemed the company was going to keep its word this time. It was clear it had the cash. Cho gave the demonstrators his word that the issue will be sorted out the next morning in the mission office. He told them to go home for the day. The ferocity of the demonstrators from moments earlier was nowhere to be found. After hearing Cho's assurance, they left the office in peace.

"I've never seen workers who had so little faith in their boss," the CEO muttered out of resignation. "You can run my business instead, reverend. I quit."

The next morning, the company sent the two sacks of money to the YDP-UIM along with its head of human resources and four accounting assistants. The five of them stayed there to process every severance claim over the next month with Cho Chi Song in the room as the witness of payment.

The struggle for severance in Hanguk Textiles began as a small organized action among the members of the YDP-UIM. Over time, however, it gained the support of intellectuals, clergy, JOC, and other social organizations. The incident became a powerful warning to all employers who had violated the labor laws with impunity. Hanguk Textiles had accumulated a considerable amount of severance arrears as an employer of 2,000 workers. If nothing else, the event taught other companies that the failure to pay the workers on time could end up being bad for business.

Cho Chi Song was proud of what the movement had achieved. He explained that the UIM ministry was also about "saving the employers," as it allowed them to turn from their ways and be saved. "Thanks to us, they started obeying the laws and treating their workers fairly. [. . .] We started our labor activism so that both the employers and employees could enter the kingdom of heaven, hand in hand together."[31]

He also believed that respecting the rights of the workers was ultimately good for the company. "Ethical management" was still an unfamiliar notion. The YDP-UIM was ahead of its time to argue that lawful management practices were the only way forward for businesses in the future.

Meanwhile, the struggle exposed the utter ineffectiveness of the labor union in Hanguk Textiles. The sitting steward lost the confidence of the workers and was moreover exposed for embezzling union dues. The central union also withdrew its support for him. This was the perfect opportunity to reform and democratize the union.

Cho believed Kim Gap-jun was someone who could lead the change. He tried to convince her to run for union steward, but Kim declined saying she did not want to stand in front of the others. Instead, she nominated Ji Dong-jin for the role.[32]

The company caught whiff of the attempt to breathe new life into the union. In an attempt to prevent it, it tried to isolate Ji Dong-jin from the rest, placing him on weeding and garbage duty out on the lawn. To fight back, Kim Gap-jun and some 60 others organized the action for union normalization. The group passed the inaugural four-point resolution on July 9 in the YDP-UIM. Over 1,000 workers joined the boycott of their shifts for a sitting demonstration out in the lawn. Their demands were the reinstatement of Ji Dong-jin, assurance of non-retaliation against the 1,085 signatories, removal of the curfew that prevented dormitory workers from leaving company premises, and assurance of unobstructed union activities. The union held the delegate assembly the following day on August 10, which proceeded just as Kim Gap-jun had planned. Ji Dong-jin was elected the new union steward and appointed the rest of the leadership along with deputy stewards Bang Yong-seok and Jeong Sang-beom. A genuinely worker-controlled, democratic labor union had been created.

After failing to get their man elected for union stewardship, the company turned to union-busting tactics to regain control. It used every method in the book to target core members—job reassignments, sweet-talking, forced overtime work, and violence. When the workers boycotted their overtime and tried to walk out of the factory on September 3, the company sent security guards and supervisors to assault the workers. It then shut down all operations the following day along with the cafeteria, refusing to provide breakfast and lunch to the dormitory workers. This angered some 600 workers who marched to the Myeongdong Cathedral in protest.

Union officers were suddenly taken into police custody on September 4. Most were released shortly thereafter, but deputy stewards Bang Yong-seok and Jeong Sang-beom were kept in the Yeongdeungpo

Detention Center. To assist with their release, Kim Soo-han, an NDP legislator and counsel for the Hanguk Textiles Labor Union, raised the issue during his parliamentary questions to the prime minister and justice minister. The government replied that it would take appropriate actions to address the issue. On September 15, Bang Yong-seok and Jeong Sang-beom were released.

Struggling against an employer as large as Hanguk Textiles sent a very effective signal to the other companies that they could no longer break the law with impunity. The YDP-UIM's strategy between the late 1960s and the early 1970s was to work within the institutionally recognized framework of the labor unions. The primary objective was to get employers to keep the labor laws and regulations while getting workers to recognize the rights they had according to the same. The mission also preferred resolving disputes through a four-way engagement with the employer, government (i.e., the labor administration or the police), and workers. Civil disobedience had not yet been added to the repertoire. Some criticized that this method involved too much compromise and did not go far enough in advocating for the workers. It was, however, a valid and necessary strategy at a time when there were very few worker organizations mature enough to take forceful action.

The following are more examples of the labor actions that the YDP-UIM was a part of between 1968 and when the Yushin regime took power in October 1972. On October 17, 1969, Sigmatex Korea fired six unionized workers with the support of its pro-management union for demanding a general assembly to address the company's failure to pay holiday compensation to the workers who worked on election day. The YDP-UIM helped the general assembly to take place. In 1970, the YDP-UIM assisted the workers trying to unionize in the Donggwang Trading Company after a number of wrongful terminations and failure to pay severance. In February 1972, the YDP-UIM helped the workers of Crown Electronics counter the company's union suppression and normalize activities. In June 1972, the YDP-UIM brokered a meeting between the police, labor administration, and the Mindo Mannequin Company to negotiate the full payment of all wage arrears. Finally, in September 1972, the YPD-UIM helped the temporary status workers of Pangrim Textiles get equal protection under the LSA.

The Death of Kim Jin-soo

A sewing worker named Jeon Tae-il set himself on fire on November 13, 1970. He tried to expose the murderous working conditions his coworkers had to endure through his self-immolation. His death shocked students and intellectuals throughout the country and started a wave of new interest in the labor movement. Students formed clubs to study labor issues. Some of them got undercover jobs in the factories to support the organizing of workers. The surge of labor organizing resulted in the creation of 2,500 new unions in a single year in 1970.[33]

This was the backdrop against which the YDP-UIM held a seminar on labor and management issues in the textile industry on December 6, 1970. The official purpose was to find ways to promote greater cooperation between workers and managers. The true purpose was to create a subsidiary in the national textile workers' union for the weaving sector specifically. The cover story was required by the fact that the authorities had heightened their surveillance in the wake of Jeon Tae-il's death. Exactly two weeks after the event, the Seoul Garments Division (SGD) of the National Textile Workers Federation (NTWF) was created on December 20. It was headquartered in the YDP-UIM office.[34]

This was followed by the creation of the Hanyoung Textiles Labor Union, a branch of the NTWF-SGD. The lead organizer was Kim Yong-wook, who represented the workers as a panelist in the seminar. Rev. Kim Gyeong-nak of the YDP-UIM supported the process. Kim Jin-soo also participated in the organizing meetings as a representative of the workers living in the Anyang area. Some 400 workers attended the inaugural meeting on December 28 in the company cafeteria.

Management was startled to discover there was a labor union in their company. They immediately fired Kim Yong-wook and three other union officers in an attempt to neutralize the union. Then, they forced some 200 workers to resign on December 31 before declaring a shutdown of all operations.

The company recruited Choi Hong-in, Hong Jin-gi, and Jeong Jin-heon as its anti-union lieutenants. The trio had been fired for violent behavior by the same company—Jeong was especially notorious—but the foreman rehired them and offered to pay handsomely for their services in breaking down the union. He even offered, in a show of unusual generosity, to protect their employment status should they get themselves into trouble again. True to their role, the three never worked. They were usually drunk and asleep during the day inside the guard's shed. When they woke up, they loitered around the workstations and beat the palms of the workers with screwdrivers to intimidate them. Using threats, they pressured the fearful ones into signing a pledge to leave the labor union.

The workers who had been forced to resign were rehired on January 10. The employment of the four union officers, however, still remained terminated. The workers filed for wrongful treatment and requested remediation from the labor authorities. The regional labor commission ruled on February 10 that the four should be reinstated. The company did not comply and filed to appeal, to which the union responded by reporting a labor dispute. Meanwhile, Kim Jin-soo was working with Hahm Seong-gil and Kim Yoon-gi to rebuild the union by recovering the workers who had signed to leave the union under duress.

The Seoul Labor Administration opened the Hanyoung Textiles case on March 18. Yoo Hae-poong, the factory foreman, lambasted the trio for failing to suppress the union sufficiently. The unhappy trio went to a nearby store to get themselves drunk around 5:30 p.m. They came back to the factory intoxicated and picked a fight with Kim Jin-soo when they saw him working at the loom. Jeong Jin-heon hit Kim Jin-soo on the back of his head with the handle of his screwdriver. Kim frowned to express his displeasure. Then suddenly, Jeong stabbed Kim with the screwdriver on the back of his head.

Kim was rushed to the nearby Yeongdeungpo St. Mary's Hospital. Wang Seong-soo, his coworker, lied to the doctor and said that Kim had tripped to injure his head. This prevented the doctor from learning the true extent of the injury. The hospital staff merely applied some styptic and bandages. Only when it was clear that the bleeding was not stopping did they transfer Kim to the larger Yonsei Severance Hospital. The time was already 11:00 p.m. The company continued to hide the true cause of the injury. It ordered Wang to continue the lie that Kim had tripped and hurt himself during an argument. The doctors were kept in the dark about the severity of Kim's injury.

When news of the incident reached them, Kim's mother and sister rushed to him in the hospital. They were also joined by Park Geong-young from the NTWF-SGD (National Textile Workers Federation-Seoul Garments Division). The left side of Kim's face had been swollen beyond recognition. He could not open his left eye. He called out for his frantic mother, saying, "Mama, save me, I think my head is breaking."

Kim Jin-soo soon fell into a coma. After learning what really happened, Park Geon-young called the UIM and SGD (Seoul Garments Division). The next day, Kim Gyeong-nak and Ahn Gwang-soo of the YDP-UIM came to the hospital, together with Park Eun-yang of the SGD. The three told the doctor what really happened and demanded that Kim received appropriate treatment. He was immediately taken to the operating room. The surgeon discovered that the screwdriver had penetrated 2.5 centimeters. It had already caused critical damage to the brain. The inflammation had already spread to every region. It was unlikely Kim was going to survive. Even if he did, he was not likely to recover all of his functions.[35]

Meanwhile, Han Ik-ha, the CEO, was busy deflecting responsibility. "Why should we be responsible," he said, "when the incident was caused by a few workers who got into a fight?" Adding insult to injury, he said, "we are not charity." Jin-soo's mother was livid when she was told what Han Ik-ha said. She marched to Hanyoung Textiles and demanded that he gave her back her son, foaming at the mouth and throwing every object she could grab in the CEO's office. The only reaction this incited was a contemptuous scowl. "Get the hag out of here," Han Ik-ha ordered. "Where does she think she is?"

As she was being dragged out, Jin-soo's mother yelled back, "Heaven will judge you for this!"

The next day, the Hanyoung Textiles Labor Union called for a general assembly to denounce the company's workplace terrorism and demand a full investigation of what really happened. The central union, however, did not reciprocate their resolve. The NTWF (National Textile Workers Federation) turned a cold shoulder. The issue seemed to get buried as one of the many stories of company persecution seen across the branches of the SGD. It was unclear how to find a solution without the ability to mobilize broad collective action.

Kim Jin-soo continued to deteriorate in his coma even after the two surgeries. The YDP-UIM and a number of other religious organizations tried to raise the issue in public discourse by reporting Hanyoung Textiles to the labor administration and writing to the president, cabinet ministers, FKTU, police, newspapers, and television stations in early April.[36] It was hard to gain traction, however, given the upcoming presidential election in April and general elections in May. The government was very careful not to allow another social issue to agitate the public as did the death of Jeon Tae-il. As such, it merely made the gesture of initiating an investigation to buy time. It took 25 days before the incident was covered for the first time in a newspaper (*Hankook Ilbo*) on April 10. The FKTU and the police reluctantly announced their finding that the incident "was a personally motivated crime of passion." The prosecutors supported this, saying

Jeong Jin-heon committed a personal crime of passion, never questioning the possible link between the assault and the union-busting instructions given by the factory foreman.

Kim Jin-soo's family and supporters were visited in the hospital by Lee So-sun, the mother of the late Jeon Tae-il. Accompanying her were Choi Jong-in and Lee Seung-cheol from the Cheonggye Garment Workers' Union. Having similarly experienced the loss of a child and friend in a labor struggle, the visitors suggested going to the FKTU to protest the sham investigation. On April 15, Kim Jin-soo's family, Park Geon-yeong, and around a dozen Hanyoung Union workers marched to the FKTU headquarters. To their astonishment, they discovered that the FKTU staff was completely oblivious to the issue. The chairman, Choi Yong-soo, was not even in his office. Some of the distressed Hanyoung workers damaged the office property. The police came to take them away, and Park Geon-yeong was jailed after his arrest.

Kim Jin-soo never woke up from the coma. He died on May 16, 1971, two months after the attack. His family, labor union, and the YDP-UIM demanded that the company pay 3 million won in damages to the family. They also demanded the company recognize the union's right to collective bargaining and guarantee its unobstructed activities.

The company insisted it will pay no more than 500,000 won, while the government bureaucracy was sluggish about processing the many reports and complaints. If anything, the bureaucrats were busy transferring responsibility. The labor administration, for instance, had completely taken its hands off the issue.

Angered by their lukewarm reaction, Kim Jin-soo's family declared that they would delay the funeral indefinitely until a proper resolution had been reached. The YDP-UIM then revealed two critical documents refuting the company and government's claim that Kim's death had nothing to do with union suppression. One was Choi Hong-in and Hong Jin-gi's written statements about the incident. The other was Yoo Hae-poong's earlier pledge to protect the trio's status.

These were carefully prepared moves informed by the lessons learned from the death of Jeon Tae-il. Back then, activists had lost the initiative to the government, which hurried to get the body buried, before they could organize meaningful pressures for change. The YDP-UIM was determined not to repeat the same mistakes. Cho Chi Song had immediately started planning a response when he heard the news upon returning from Chicago on March 20.

The plan must have worked, for Cho soon received a visit from the company's emissary. Han Chul-ha was Han Ik-ha's younger cousin and a professor at the PTS.[37] While Cho had never been his student, the company must have hoped that a professor from his alma mater could convince Cho to let the issue pass over quietly. Han Chul-ha questioned the YDP-UIM's theological justification for getting involved in a labor dispute. Cho questioned what would remain of God's justice if Christians did nothing to address a wrongful death. "The company and its employers can reach a compromise," the professor said, "that would be God's justice; there is no reason for the UIM to get involved."

Cho believed Han Chul-ha lost his theological balance because of his connection to his cousin and his company. Han Ik-ha also turned out to be an elder at his church. Part of the issue was going to be a theological fight. Students from the Christian Academy had already expressed their interest, some of them seminarians at the PTS. One of them was In Myeong-jin, who was later trained by Cho Chi Song and hired onto the YDP-UIM.

In Myeong-jin took a group of seminarians to Han Chul-ha's house around 11:00 at night. They fiercely debated his defense of the company, but their professor insisted that Christians ought to stay out of a problem created by a few workers who got into a fight. The theologian took it upon himself to be the negotiator for his cousin's company.

After more than a month in their stalemate, the two sides agreed to each take a step back and reached a settlement on June 19. The company agreed to take full responsibility for the incident and pay Kim Jin-soo's family 750,000 won in damages and 1,067,910 won to cover the hospital bills. The company also contributed 150,000 won and Christian organizations 120,000 won to cover the costs of the funeral.[38]

Kim Gyeong-nak officiated the funeral service at 3:00 p.m. on June 25 in front of the Severance Hospital Morgue. A thick perimeter of police officers surrounded the ceremony. University students hung up the banners they made overnight.[39]

"Reveal the cause of death."

"Kim Jin-soo is the second Jeon Tae-il."

"Let me live again."

"The Labor Standards Act. Why won't you repeal it if you won't enforce it?"

The funeral was the collective effort between the Council of Churches for Urban Industrial Issues (CCUI), Christian Academy, and Korean Student Christian Federation (KSCF). Father Han Jong-hoon, president of the CCUI, served as the chair of the funeral committee, and Rev. Cho Seung-hyeok served as its secretary. Cho Chi Song was the funeral director. The rest of the committee was filled by ecumenical representatives from the CCUI. The ceremony was also staffed by student volunteers from eleven universities. In Myeong-jin was the representative of the volunteers.[40]

The eulogy lamented the repetition of a tragedy that should have ended with Jeon Tae-il. Six messages were issued, each directed at a particular audience. The government was denounced for its failure to protect workers from the threat of wrongful deaths. Employers were urged to lay down their selfishness and recognize that they shared a common fate with the workers. Journalists were reminded to fulfill their role as watchdogs of society. Students were invited to become advocates and allies for the workers. Workers were called to stand together in unity. Finally, the eulogy rebuked the church for failing to fulfill its prophetic calling and allowing the world to trample upon the workers. It emphatically called for the church to wake up and hear the cries of those who had been robbed.[41] Then the procession took Kim

Jin-soo's body from Hanyoung Textiles to Moran Park, where he was buried next to Jeon Tae-il.

Properly defined, the incident was a case of murder that took place as a part of union suppression and workplace terrorism. The employer who issued the orders should have ultimately been held responsible. He was a Christian, no less. However, only the hands that pulled the trigger—Jeong Jin-won, Choi Hong-in, and Hong Jin-gi—were found guilty. The company itself was never held accountable. The tragedy was caused by the prevalent mindset that an employer may use any means necessary to suppress and control the workers.

It also exposed the FKTU and other higher union organizations' susceptibility to government persuasion and coercion. In this case, they clearly betrayed the interests of the workers and took its side with the employer. Discontent with the national unions began to grow. In November 1971, the YDP-UIM declared its divorce from the FKTU, citing its anti-worker tendencies.[42] It then held a "truth forum" on the state of labor activism in Yeongdeungpo to effectively expel the FKTU-SGD headquarters from the mission office.

The Kim Jin-soo incident convinced the YDP-UIM that it could no longer place its hope in the established union organizations. What they needed was a new grassroots movement that was of and by the lowest workers. The FKTU confirmed the need for a total break in an unambiguous display of allegiance to power in its December statement of support for Park Chung Hee's national emergency declaration and activation of national security laws. It did the same again when Park announced the "October Restoration (or Yushin)" in 1972. Then, the FKTU denounced religious organizations for their UIM and labor activism in articles it submitted to the *Hankook Ilbo* on January 19, 1974, December 9, 1974, and January 22, 1975. Each of them was written in the strongest terms. In response, 16 Christian activist organizations across the denominational divide publicly issued the "Exhortations to the FKTU." Now that the establishment within the unions had shown its true colors, the UIMs had to start looking for ways the workers could reclaim democratic control from the lieutenants who did the employer's bidding.[43]

Looking back, Cho believed Kim Jin-soo's death could have been far more explosive than the death of Jeon Tae-il. The latter died in an act of self-sacrificial protest, but the former was a victim of workplace terrorism that was ordered by management. He also believed the activists were more successful this time in dealing with the aftermath of the incident. The concerted response of the UIM, students, and Christian activists did get the company to pay damages to the family, recognize the union it tried to destroy, and cover part of the funeral costs. However, Cho also believed an opportunity for much greater momentum was lost after commemorating the incident in a few memorial ceremonies. Part of this was because Kim Gyeong-nak left the YDP-UIM to study in the United States. He was the primary missioner who dealt with the Kim Jin-soo issue. More generally, however, the YDP-UIM just did not have the capacity to create and sustain broader momentum. As the following pages will show, they were about to be spread too thin to even deal with the government's persecution. The Kim Jin-soo incident was just the beginning of the YDP-UIM's involvement in some of the most intense struggles of the 1970s.

NOTES

1 Kim and Yoo, *Cho Chi Song's Oral History* (Vol. 1, 2011), 10.
2 Kim and Yoo, *Cho Chi Song's Oral History* (Vol. 1, 2011), 10.
3 Kim and Yoo, *Cho Chi Song's Oral History* (Vol. 1, 2011), 11.
4 Kim and Yoo, *Cho Chi Song's Oral History* (Vol. 1, 2011), 11.
5 Yang Myeong-deuk, "Ministry Reports from July April–May, 1964," *Freedom for the Oppressed* (YDP-UIM & Dongyeon, 2020), 42.
6 Yeongdeungpo UIM 40th Anniversary Committee, "Two Paths for Industrial Evangelism: Organizing Working Christians," *Yeongdeungpo UIM: A 40-Year History* (YDP-UIM, 1998), 72–80.

7 Presbyterian Church in the Republic of Korea, also known as PROK.

8 Kim and Yoo, "Early History of the Yeongdeungpo UIM," *Cho Chi Song's Oral History* (Vol. 1, 2011), 11.

9 Jeong Yeong-cheol and Sohn Eun-jeong, "Cho Chi Song's Interview," *Documenting the Oral History of the Democracy Movement* (Korea Democracy Foundation, 2002).

10 Kim and Yoo, "Early History of the Yeongdeungpo UIM," 11.

11 Yang Myeong-deuk, "Ministry Reports from January 1965," *Freedom for the Oppressed* (YDP-UIM & Dongyeon, 2020), 57.

12 Yang, "Ministry Reports from January 1965," 57.

13 Kim Myeong-bae, "Ministry Reports from 1965," *Yeongdeungpo UIM Files* Vol. 1 (YDP-UIM & Soongsil University Center for Culture and Mission Studies, 2020).

14 Kim, "Ministry Reports from 1965."

15 Kim, "Ministry Reports from 1965."

16 Yeongdeungpo UIM 40th Anniversary Committee, "A Few Issues of Industrial Evangelism," *Yeongdeungpo UIM: A 40-Year History* (1998).

17 Kim Myeong-bae, *Yeongdeungpo UIM Files* Vol. 1 (YDP-UIM & Soongsil University Center for Culture and Mission Studies, 2020).

18 Kim and Yoo, "Early History of the Yeongdeungpo UIM."

19 Kim and Yoo, "Early History of the Yeongdeungpo UIM."

20 Kim Myeong-bae, "Ministry Reports from 1965," *Yeongdeungpo UIM Files Vol. 1* (YDP-UIM & Soongsil University Center for Culture and Mission Studies, 2020), 49.

21 Yeongdeungpo UIM 40th Anniversary Committee, "UIM: Messengers of the Labor Union Movement," *Yeongdeungpo UIM: A 40-Year History* (1998), 112.

22 Jeong and Sohn, "Cho Chi Song's Interview."

23 Cho Chi Song, "A Half-Piece Story the UIM," unpublished lecture notes.

24 PCK Department of Evangelism UIM Committee, *The Church and UIM* (PCK Education & Resourcing Ministry, 1981), 111.

25 Jeong and Sohn, "Cho Chi Song's Interview."

26 YDP-UIM, "The Past and Present of the Yeongdeungpo UIM," *Yeongdeungpo UIM Files* Vol. 1 (YDP-UIM & Soongsil University Center for Culture and Mission Studies, 2020), 126–127.
27 George E. Ogle (Korean name: Oh Myeong-geol) started the Incheon UIM as a missionary sent by the UMC in 1954. He contributed to the development of an ecumenical UIM policy and leadership training regimen through the UIM Staff Conference in July 1965. He was also involved in the democracy movement of South Korea, such as in criticizing the so-called People's Revolutionary Party Incident. This got him deported from the country on November 14, 1974, by Park Chung Hee's Yushin regime. He was awarded the Civil Merit Medal in June 2020 by the Moon Jae-in administration.
28 Yang Myeong-deuk, "Ministry Reports from July 1965," 73–76.
29 Cho Chi Song, "Memoir," unpublished text; Kim and Yoo, "Early History of the Yeongdeungpo UIM."
30 Cho, "Memoir."
31 Jeong. and Sohn., "Cho Chi Song's Interview."
32 Seo Deok-Seok and Sohn Eun-jeong, "Kim Gap-jun's Interview," Interviews of Related Individuals for the Biography (YDP-UIM, 2011).
33 KBS Newsroom (November 13, 2020).
34 Kim Myeong-bae, *Yeongdeungpo UIM Files* Vol. 3 (YDP-UIM & Soongsil University Center for Culture and Mission Studies, 2020), 273.
35 Korea Democracy Foundation, *The Fire of the Age 3: Kim Jin-soo* (2003).
36 Kim Myeong-bae, *Yeongdeungpo UIM Files* Vol. 4 (YDP-UIM & Soongsil University Center for Culture and Mission Studies, 2020), 62–66.
37 Kim and Yoo, "Early History of the Yeongdeungpo UIM."
38 Kim, *Yeongdeungpo UIM Files* Vol. 3, 275.
39 Kim Gyeong-nak worked with Cho Chi Song when the Yeongdeungpo UIM was joint ministry of the KMC and PCK.
40 Council of Churches for Urban Industrial Issues (CCUI), "Order of Kim Jin-soo's Funeral Service" (unpublished, 1971).

41 Korea Democracy Foundation, *The Fire of the Age 3: Kim Jin-soo* (2003).

42 Chang Sook-kyeong, *The UIM and Labor Movements in the 1970s* (Seonin, 2013), 98–99.

43 PCK Department of Evangelism UIM Committee, *The Church and UIM* (PCK Education & Resourcing Ministry, 1981), 152–153.

❦ 3 ❧

THE MARCH OF THE FOOLS

WHILE THE YDP-UIM was still grappling with the Kim Jin-soo incident, the New Democratic Party (NDP) made massive gains in the general elections on May 25, 1971. It gained 89 more seats, which surpassed the 69 seats required to block a unilateral constitutional amendment by the ruling party. Park Chung Hee managed to hold onto his presidency in the race against Kim Dae-jung a month earlier, but it was only by a lead of 950,000 votes. The difference was smaller than the 3.09 million invalid or abstention votes. It was reasonable to suspect that Park had lost the election.

Sensing a threat to his hold on power, Park Chung Hee declared a state of national emergency on December 6 and had the leaders of student activism rounded up and sent to the military. On December 27, he had his party's lawmakers pass the "Special Act for National Security," which required labor unions to submit a request for a binding government arbitration before they could engage in any collective action or bargaining. Needless to say, this stifled most if not all meaningful union activities. On October 17, 1972, Park issued a "special presidential declaration" dissolving the National Assembly and freezing the activities of all political parties. All of this culminated on December 27 with the declaration of the "Yushin Constitution" that now gave the president even greater emergency powers.[1]

The Small-Group Movement

The comprehensive ban on all social assembly placed severe limitations on the three basic labor rights of association, collective bargaining, and collective action. The surveillance state also started to close in. Agents from the police, Korea Central Intelligence Agency (KCIA), and Defense Security Command (DSC) monitored the YDP-UIM from across the street, photographing and taking note of every visitor. The missioners were followed, and their phones wiretapped. One by one, union leaders started to fall out of contact with the YDP-UIM.

Whatever freedom labor unions used to have was completely taken away in the 1972 Special Act for National Security. This also cost the YDP-UIM its ability to interact with union activists. The ban on social assembly and organizing also caused a dramatic contraction in all union activities. It was common for union leaders whom the YDP-UIM, JOC, or Methodist UIM spent over a decade training turn into pro-management agents overnight after being contacted by the KCIA. Cho recounted:

> *We were about to take off, as we had just organized a handful of new unions including the textile workers' union. We also created a group for union officers called the* Nowoohwe *(or* Workers' Friendship Association*). But then came the national security act. We had hardly caught our breath when the specter of "Yushin" and the beast of "emergency measures" started their rampage. [. . .] All the union leaders went into hiding. Sometimes, it was the Christians who were the first to run away.*
>
> *Yet the YDP-UIM could not give up. We couldn't get into the factories. We couldn't get into the churches. Now, we couldn't get into the labor unions. [. . .] So we had to improvise what we could, and that was the* small-group movement. *[. . .] There were already a number of small groups that had been meeting since the late 1960s. This was where we redirected all our energy. There was no other avenue left. We put everything into organizing new groups and training them.*[2]

Cho applied many of the lessons he learned in Chicago in designing the small groups. The activists there had based their movement on rigorous social theories and proven tactics, making highly calculated moves with predictable results. The US labor activists had especially accumulated a wealth of experience through their activism in the large corporations like the automobile industry. There were also many academics who provided robust theories to support the practitioners. Cho was especially drawn to Paulo Freire's concept of "conscientization" and Saul Alinsky's "community organizing."

There were both similarities and differences between the way those two concepts were applied in Chicago and what Cho had been trying in Yeongdeungpo. One key difference was that the LAIE relied on the religious goodwill of its members to drive the movement forward, while the Chicago activists relied on the unified strength of organized workers who had a critical awareness of their social identity. Cho realized that the only sustainable way to serve the workers was to first bring them to an understanding of who they are and empower them with the strength that comes from organizing. There was little use relying on the goodwill of individualized Christians.

Later on, Cho also abandoned his hope in the integrity of the union leaders. He used to believe that training better leaders would automatically make the unions more democratic, which would make them better advocates of their members' rights. In reality, the leaders were often the first to cave under pressure or sweet-talking. The YDP-UIM now understood that its ministry had to grow from the bottom up, starting with the least of all workers. It had to find a novel way to organize workers without catching notice amid the political climate of the Yushin anyway.

Cho took his inspiration for the small groups from the "section" of the JOC. Trained members (or militants) in the JOC were organized into sections that served as the basic unit of action and ministry. Section members studied and trained with each other to gain critical awareness before initiating organized action. Having seen the effectiveness of this model in Cardinal Joseph Cardjin's ministry in France, Cho decided to adopt it.

There were already several groups that the mission could use to launch a new campaign. Hundreds of groups had been formed in the LAIE in the 1960s. Contact with and among their lay members were still intact. Several hobby groups had also been formed among users of the ministry's credit union cooperative, which met regularly to knit, cook, make toys, arrange flowers, etc. These two served as the basis of the new small-group movement.

After analyzing the impact of the emergency decrees, the missioners created a small-group design that could bypass the ban on public assemblies and organization. The goal was still to organize workers across entire factories, but each group had to be between five and 10 members. Groups with more than 10 were split, while groups with fewer than five were dispersed so that each member could join another group. Every member of a group had to come from the same work section and belong to the same gender. This created a natural affinity between the members. The ultimate goal was to set up a context in which the workers could raise their own consciousness. Groups that started by meeting over a common interest or hobby eventually became the networks that could be mobilized when needed for action.[3]

In Myeong-jin, who worked with Cho for nearly a decade, said "Once the group members gained 'critical consciousness' about where they worked in the factory, they acquired the ability to take action and create change. The fact that you all worked in the same place created a natural affinity."[4]

Once a group had been formed, the workers had complete control over what to do with it. The only directions the missioners gave were the initial principles for getting started and that they were to meet once every week for an hour or two.

Prospective members were given about a week to think through their choice. "You could get fired or seriously upset your family," the missioners explained. "Why don't you take some time before you decide if you still want to be a part of this?" Many of the workers dropped out at this phase. Those who chose to remain started their first meeting by choosing a group name and electing the president and secretary. They also decided how much to collect in dues (usually between 100 and 300 won) and the days for the meeting.

> *Workers rarely had the experience of making decisions for themselves. [. . .] The very act of choosing their own name and rules was revolutionary. [. . .] It was a moment of self-determination, you see. [. . .] That's how you start training yourself for democracy.*[5]

A missioner was assigned to each group to provide all the accommodations that the group needed for its meetings (i.e., preparing the space and materials). This task was high on every missioner's list of priorities. If a group decided to bake, Myeong Noh-seon had to be ready with all the ingredients in the kitchen before the start of the meeting. She worked so closely with each of the groups that she could list the names of almost every member in the nearly 150 groups.[6]

In Myeong-jin had to leave his father's 60th birthday celebration prematurely to get back to Seoul in time for his group's meeting. Workers often met at odd hours, whether at six in the morning after working the night or at 10 in the evening after working overtime. Regardless, the YDP-UIM staff always had to be ready to greet the workers.

> *The workers had all the authority. [. . .] That's fearfully empowering. [. . .] The more the groups met, the more conscious they became. [. . .] Once they've awakened, we simply did as they said.*[7]

After meeting for a while, the groups usually expressed their interest in talking about labor problems at their own initiative. They might ask, for instance, that the missioners explain to them the LSA. The missioners did not immediately oblige and instead pressed the workers to be even more assertive. In Myeong-jin was especially skilled at playing the villain. "What would a factory girl like you do knowing the law? Just do whatever the company says." Statements like that could seem antagonistic, but the workers usually knew the missioners had their best interests in mind. It was also their way of leveling with the workers. The environment in the factory was oppressive as it is. What the young women needed were not pontificating preachers, but family.

Cho Chi Song also took occasional jabs to make a more profound point. He told the workers of Control Data, for instance, that they were just a group of "highly educated fools." As high school graduates, the workers of Control Data were more educated than most of their working peers.[8] The education most of them received, however, was part of a pipeline designed to produce a docile workforce that accepted what it was told uncritically. Cho's challenge to the workers was to go beyond the mere appearance of education and learn how to truly think for themselves. Thus, the missioners of the YDP-UIM in the 1970s were both passionate organizers and minjung educators.[9]

Most groups started their meetings on fairly mundane topics like cooking, marriage, dating, time management, personal finance, and social etiquette. After about three or four months, however, they turned their attention to more serious topics like labor issues, politics, and economics. A knitting club became a group study on the labor laws. Then, once they were awakened to the injustice in their workplace, they became motivated activists.

"I used to have zero sense of individuality," Kim Yeon-ja said, looking back on her transformation through the small groups. "I was just another cog in the machine. [. . .] But the small groups taught me that I, too, am a human. I have the right to live a dignified human life. Workers have the right to live a dignified human life. It taught me that we had rights according to the laws of this land, and we deserved to have our rights protected."[10]

The organizing of small groups began in earnest in early January 1972. By May, 470 meetings had taken place with a cumulative 8,814 participants. By September, there were about 50 groups meeting regularly two to three times a month. Organizing and maintaining small groups became the YDP-UIM's first priority. There were usually 100 to 120 groups in existence at any given moment. Leading up to a major action, the number surged to between 150 and 180. In the aftermath of the struggle, it was nearly halved to 70 to 80, recovering to around 100 as things stabilized.

The most active year for the small groups was 1979, when several major struggles took place simultaneously. About 100 groups met three to four times a month that year, with a cumulative total of 62,400 participants.[11] All this activity was housed in two leased units of the Dangsan-dong Sibeom Apartment. Each was just 21 pyeongs (about 69 square meters). There was always less space than the mission needed. Even the bathrooms had to be utilized to house all the group meetings.

While trying to increase the number of groups, the YDP-UIM continued to invest in the quality of their leadership. There was a group of LAIE leaders who had met since 1970 called the "Pioneer." Cho changed this group into a monthly meeting for small-group leaders where they could share their experience and ideas for running their groups. It also served as a forum to discuss matters that required collective action and provided an opportunity for leadership training.[12]

The small groups became so important that it was impossible to discuss the YDP-UIM in the 1970s without them. Cho believed they were the heart and core of the ministry. "Park Chung Hee's biggest mistake was that he never stopped the small groups. [. . .] Which, for us, was an amazing opportunity. [. . .] The small groups took over the labor unions' role as the workers' church."[13]

Indeed, the groups not only empowered the workers to solve their own problems, but also allowed them to recognize their human dignity. They provided a setting for character growth, allowing the workers to become individuals who could sacrificially serve the needs of the community. They also helped the workers recover the divine image they were created in, which was the ultimate objective of the UIM ministry.

Tens of thousands of working women were awakened to their rights and found a sense of ownership over their lives. That was the key that empowered them to become the agents of social transformation. Soon enough, the women who were once pressed down were fighting for justice in their workplace, creating some of the brightest moments in South Korea's history of the 1970s.

Worship by Coercion?

One frigid day in December, two women visited the YDP-UIM. Cho sat them down next to the furnace and asked how he could help. After fidgeting for a while, the two exhausted women told him, "We want to quit our jobs." The work was too hard and the wages too low. However, the company had told security not to allow them to take their personal belongings out of the dormitory. The women either had to stay or forfeit a month's worth of their wages.

Cho offered to send a missioner back with them to demand that the company lets them go. If it refused, the mission could report them to the authorities. Cho penned a letter addressed to the labor commissioner in their name, just in case they needed it.

During the small-group meetings, Cho asked the other workers if they had experienced something similar. He also asked if their companies had been good about paying severance to the temporary workers when they left. "We thought temps didn't get severance," they said. Cho was the first person to tell them that the LSA mandated severance for anyone who worked for an employer for a year or longer, regardless of their contractual status.

The mission soon discovered that most of the companies hired female workers initially on a temporary basis. They were only switched to regular employment after they had worked for a number of years. When they quit, the company paid severance only for the years the women were on regular employment status. This meant the workers were being robbed of the severance they earned doing the same work for the same number of hours merely because of their "temp" status. Of course, the worst of the employers did not pay any severance at all.

All of this violated the LSA, which mandated that *every* worker was paid a month's worth of wages in severance for every year they worked for the same employer. According to a *Donga Ilbo* report, only 4 percent of employers were compliant with the most basic labor law in the early 1970s.

What was even more astounding was that the workers worried about their employers when the mission said it would report their company for breaking the law. "Wouldn't that put our CEO in trouble," they asked, "or put the company out of business?" Cho was angry and baffled.

Someone made a fool out of these innocent children. Could you absolve the educated, rich, and powerful of their responsibility? Are their sins not to blame for the poverty of these workers, or for their ignorance of their own exploitation?
How could these tragedies continue if the church knew about the plight of the workers? [. . .] How could anyone fault them for refusing to be taken for fools any longer? Yet the world takes away the livelihood of those who try to make an honest living. It throws them in jail and scoffs at them.
It will be Christmas the day after tomorrow. [. . .] I believe this season is the most grievous one to our Lord. [. . .] It is corrupt. [. . .] We stone the blind and ignore the cause of freedom for the oppressed to celebrate our Christmas. [. . .] The sweater factories are working the girls day and night,

making them take caffeine pills to stay awake. O Lord [. . .]
Bless the fools this Christmas. Bless them with the hope of the
New year.[14]

Hope was certainly on its way. Rev. Myeong Noh-seon, another missioner of the YDP-UIM, recounted the transformation of the small-
group workers that she saw over time.

We had the front row seat to witness the many injustices of
our society. The days of persecution and suffering kept stacking
up for us. And yet, we felt the hand of God working in our
lives through these days of trial. Our heart and our flesh
were weak, but our workplace and our world were gradually
changing. [. . .] The march of the fools who had come together
to arrange flowers and sew plush dolls was gradually changing
the course of history.[15]

Both the missioners and the workers knew that the small groups
were just the first step toward transforming the workplace and, ultimately, the whole of society. The goal was to bring peace and justice
into a world that abused its workers. This gave the women a strong
sense of calling and agency in their own activism.[16] The small groups
became the core that allowed the ministry to remain faithful despite
the persecution under the Yushin regime.

Ironically, the first war waged by the small groups was against mandatory worship in the factory. The fact that most members of management
attended Dongshin Church, where Cho Chi Song received his ordination, added to the irony. Daehan Textiles required all 1,000 workers to
attend the monthly service in the cafeteria. Additionally, it required the
400 workers living in the dormitory to attend a weekly Thursday service,
regardless of whether one had just finished a very long shift. The women
who were caught hiding in the bathrooms or closets were punished by
not being allowed to leave the dormitory for over a month.

The issue started when Lim Gyeong-ja, one of the founding members who created the first small groups in Daehan Textiles in 1972, failed to show up to her small-group meeting. It turned out she had been grounded in the dormitory for failing to attend a factory service. This started a discussion in her group. Ko Seong-shim, who did not go to church but was the daughter of an elder, raised a sharp question. "The company is forcing us to attend worship. Is that really what Christ would want?"

The group's conclusion was that there was nothing Christ-like about coercing people into worship. In fact, doing so only made a mobster out of him. Worship was merely a means of exerting psychological control over the workers. If not, they should have been treated as the employer's equals for having been part of it. Whatever the supervisors believed, the factory services were not turning anyone toward Christianity. All they did was create more resistance to the faith.

Moreover, compelling workers to participate in Christian worship without regard for their personal convictions clearly violated the laws and humanitarian principles. For their part, the missioners concluded that while they did not oppose having worship in the factories, workers should only attend voluntarily. Grounding workers to punish them for failure to attend a service violated the LSA regulation on company dormitories.

The YDP-UIM decided to demand correction to Daehan Textiles' dormitory policy. It also decided to use the opportunity to call for a stop to the 18-hour shifts that had been happening every Sunday. The ministry started to spread the word and shared the situation with the other small groups. It launched the campaign in early 1973 after a minimum of 20 small groups had been formed in Daehan Textiles. The first task was to write a petition to demand the most urgent improvements the workers wanted:[17]

- Stop the 18-hour super-shifts between Saturdays and Sundays
- Implement the eight-hour workday and guarantee a day off per week

- Guarantee employee autonomy to decide whether or not to work overtime
- Guarantee legally mandated one-hour lunch breaks
- Stop requiring attendance at the factory worship service

Almost all of the 400 workers in the dormitory signed the petition addressed to the CEO. Management ignored it except to stop the 18-hour super-shifts. It also started retaliating against the signatories through the dormitory staff. In response, 341 workers signed another letter demanding the immediate replacement of the dormitory staff. The company did not respond. The workers voiced their demand again on February 7 in a protest in the dormitory. The company called the police, who took away Ko Seong-shim, Lim Gyeong-ja, Baek Min-jeong, and Jang Cheon-ok. After their return, the company fired the four organizers on February 13, citing company rule violation. Security guards dragged the four out of the building. The workers demanded the four's reinstatement. Faced with mounting pressure, the company relented on all of the other demands. However, it did not reinstate the four. It also continued to persecute the workers who participated in the demonstration, especially targeting the members of the YDP-UIM this time.

The persecuted workers did not take the abuse quietly. They reported the company for breaking the labor laws and filed a request for the labor commission's intervention in a case of wrongful employment practices. They also organized mass prayer meetings, demonstrations, and rallies. The missioners, for their part, reached out to churches to ask for their support in reinstating the workers and stopping the mandatory factory worships.

At some point, somebody suggested taking the struggle to the CEO's church, which happened to be having its revival week. The opportunity seemed right. The revival services were open for anybody to walk in. Cho felt reluctant about starting an issue in the church where he happened to have received his ordination.

However, what was more important was that the workers made their decision. Cho gave them his support. His only caveat was tactical advice for moderation: "Try not to come across as menacing; it's going to work better if you sit down in prayer to appeal to their Christian conscience."

The workers took his advice and went on a quiet hunger strike in front of the pulpit throughout the revival. They sat there day and night, holding signs that said, "can worship be compelled?" or "Elder Kim Seong-seob must stop compelling his workers to attend the factory service." The four also wrote an open letter to churches throughout the country in the name of Lim Gyeong-ja to make an appeal to their reason and conscience.

> *Daehan Textiles forced all of its workers to attend a monthly worship service. It also forced all its dormitory workers to attend a weekly worship service. Even those of us who know nothing about Christianity are forced to attend worship. Even after 12 hours of hard labor, we are forced to attend. We can barely stay awake from exhaustion. All we do sitting there is struggle not to fall asleep. This is no worship at all. It is another painful ordeal, no different than forced labor. Workers who are caught trying to avoid worship are punished harshly. They are not allowed to leave the dormitory for an indefinite period. I was punished the same way for two months from May to June last year, simply because I failed to attend one mandatory worship service. Why should followers of another religion or no religion at all be forced to partake in Christian worship? Is it because our employer happens to be an elder of the church? I cannot understand this practice with my human conscience. [. . .] What I do understand is that Jesus Christ was full of love. Then why does our company insist on using force to make us worship him? I ask the wise leaders of the church and society to answer our question. Can you truly force someone into worship? I plead with you. Help*

us workers choose how we may worship in the freedom of our conscience.[18]

Indeed, there were some conversions to Christianity that happened in spite of the mandatory worships, not thanks to them. Park Deok-hee, one of the workers who went on the hunger strike, later became a Christian after retiring to the country. Ko Seong-shim, who was the only non-Christian in a very religious family, became a practicing Christian after the struggle. Cho believed this was a good example of God reaping for himself a people to worship him in spirit and truth regardless of human failings.

Firing the workers for asking not to be forced into worship started to attract attention from society. Conscientious Christians from all denominations were outraged to discover that the CEO made his employees work 18-hour shifts while he was in church, only to later force them to attend a mandatory service when they had just finished working a shift. Christian activists organized a committee for the reinstatement of the four wrongfully dismissed workers, which issued a statement with nearly 700 signatures, filed a complaint with the authorities, and ran fundraisers and petitions to increase support for the struggle. The committee also wrote to churches throughout the country to ask for their support. Young volunteers from Dongshin Church wrote the address and sealed the envelopes.

The issue came to its resolution on July 26 when agents from the DSC brokered the company's reemployment of the four workers in exchange for their voluntary resignation within a month of returning. In the aftermath, some of the more conservative church leaders started to call the YDP-UIM an unsavory group that purported to be a Christian ministry while going around to pick fights with good Christian business owners who were trying to promote worship in their factories. In other words, the YPD-UIM was guilty of fratricide. A lengthy open letter was sent throughout the churches once again— this time painting a very slanderous picture of the ministry.

The struggle in Daehan Textiles was significant for a number of reasons. First, it was the first struggle organized by the small groups. Second, when confronted with a choice, the YDP-UIM chose to stand with the powerless workers rather than the powerful Christians. Third, the struggle created an adversary to the UIM within the PCK. Many of the pastors supported the workers during the struggle in Daehan Textiles. Their elders, many of them business owners, reacted against them. They became an enduring force of opposition to the UIM in the years to come. Fourth, the employers became decidedly cautious of the UIM. There was no longer any question about which side it was to take. Finally, the incident woke Christians up to their implicit bias. They used to believe, without questioning, that the employers they saw in church are usually right when there was a labor dispute. Now, the Christians knew they had to exercise critical judgment.

Cho believed the fight in Daehan Textiles was inevitable and important. Still, he lamented the fact that it had to happen. The issue was framed as a fight against the UIM and a Christian employer who wanted to promote worship. This divided the church and eroded some of the UIM's base of support while creating an adversary within the PCK. It was a painful pill for Cho to swallow knowing that a handful of pastors had to pay a personal price for supporting the YDP-UIM. Rev. Lee Seong-eui, in particular, found himself having to resign. It turned out that one of the elders in his church was a relative of Daehan's CEO. Despite the cost, the YDP-UIM believed taking a stand was necessary. It would have tarnished the gospel greatly had it remained silent on the abusive practices of Daehan Textiles committed in the name of bringing people to Christ.

Reviled by the World

Namyoung Nylon was a middle-sized company in Mullae-dong that produced women's underwear, pantyhose, and swimsuits. It employed about 1,200 workers in Seoul and another 800 in the Cheonnan factory. Namyoung was also one of the more law-abiding employers that provided the eight-hour workday and a weekly day off as required by the LSA. That said, it paid some of the lowest wages.

Namyoung's workers got connected to the YDP-UIM when they started using its credit union in the early 1970s. Some of the workers then began the small-group meetings. They started by meeting around topics of general interest, initially led by In Myeong-jin. As they became more conscious over time, however, they started to organize action to reform the ineffectual labor union in their company. The women worked hard to grow the small groups. By the end of 1975, all of some 300 workers in the products division were members of a small group.

Reforming the union first required electing a new steward. The delegate assembly was to meet for the election in May 1976. The workers in Seoul were very well organized. As early as a month before the election, they had already elected almost every delegate from among the members of the YDP-UIM.

The problem was in Cheonnan, where there were no small groups. Most of the delegates elected there were supervisors. The deputy steward leading them had next to no knowledge about labor activism. And, of course, the union for the whole company was as good as nonexistent.

Nearing the day of the delegate assembly, the reformists— primarily consisting of small-group workers—decided they will vote for Na Joo-sik as the new union steward. Ra was not a part of the small groups but was previously associated with the YDP-UIM. There seemed to be no other suitable candidate to the small-group workers.

The workers confronted an unexpected roadblock on the day of the delegate assembly. The sitting steward, Moon Chang-seok, knew he was likely to lose the election. To hold onto his position, he declared an indefinite suspension of the assembly, then left the building. The workers had no experience with procedural politics and did not know how to respond. The election could not move forward and what little union functions there were fell into a complete limbo.

Determined to reform their labor union, the small-group workers led a brief campaign to resume the election. The workers wrote letters, wore ribbons, boycotted overtime work, and occupied the union office. Moon Chang-seok and his sponsors in management were impassive. They were equally determined to prevent a reformist steward from getting elected. Eventually, the workers and management cut a deal. Na Joo-sik resigned from the candidacy in exchange for Moon Chang-seok's promise to appoint who the workers wanted for the majority of the members on the executive committee.

The delegate assembly resumed on July 1. The reformists kept their end of the bargain. Moon Chang-seok did not. He reneged on his promise to only choose five of the members of the executive committee and instead handpicked 15. Only five of the 20 seats on the executive committee were filled with people the reformists wanted. The attempt to reform the union failed.

That did not stop the small-group workers from launching another campaign on May 7, 1977. About 800 workers demanded that the company raise their average wage by another 250 won. This was because they were still not getting a living wage after the raise in April, which gave them an average of 3,000 won. The workers also demanded a reform to the pay-setting policy, which had no regard for skills or years of experience and instead rewarded whoever did the most to appease management.

The workers took turns going on successive partial strikes. After three days, the company promised it would give them the raise in about a week. The strikers went back to work, but nothing changed. On the morning of May 17, 200 workers boycotted and they sat down on the lawn to protest. Around 5:00 p.m., the company sent its supervisors and male employees to put on a counterdemonstration. The signs they held said "out with the UIM" and "rabid dogs need the stick."

At some point, the men started assaulting the women and forced them off the lawn. During the commotion, one of the women hurt the attacker with a pair of scissors that she was carrying in an attempt to defend herself. The police who had arrived much earlier and did nothing about the men assaulting the women immediately stepped in. It was blatant partiality.

The workers continued the demonstration the next day as the company continued its violence and the police their inaction. The men beat the women, grabbed their hair, and kicked them on the ground. The detectives did nothing. Some of the passersby saw the barbarism and tried calling for help. Unfortunately, they called the police.[19]

Sixteen demonstrators were arrested. Five of them were immediately discharged, but 11 were detained for between 15 and 20 days. The company began intimidating the workers associated with the YDP-UIM. It mobilized the other workers to chant "out with the UIM" during the company assembly. It also distributed literature in the Cheonnan factory with defamatory charges against the UIM.

About a month after the lawn protest, nearly 30 men from Namyoung Nylon came barging into the YDP-UIM office on June 16. They grabbed In Myeong-jin and Myeong Noh-seon by their collars and assaulted them. One of the men picked up a chair and threatened to beat them with it. The mob warned the missioners to "stay out of Namyoung Nylon," threatening to "bring our knives tomorrow" and accusing the missioners of being "Kim Il-sung's stooges." They also threatened Stephen Lavender, the Australian missionary.[20]

It was past 10:00 p.m. when the mob left with the warning that they would come back the next day. Cho Chi Song happened to be away that night, attending a conference in the Anglican Cathedral to meet Philip Potter, the WCC general secretary. He hurried back as soon as he got In Myeong-jin's phone call, but the situation was already over.

The missioners of the YDP-UIM had heard their fair share of criticism and intimidation since they got involved with labor activism, but this was the first time they had been physically attacked. The mission publicly denounced the company for directing violence against a Christian ministry and made strong calls for legal consequence.

Having seen the issue escalate, Choi Hyeong-woo, an NDP lawmaker provided assistance. He urged the government to protect worker rights and the UIM and JOC ministries during the National Assembly session. He also sued the mob sent by the company; called on the interior minister, director of public security, and city police to take firm action; demanded the dismissal of the managers who directed the persecution and slander; and called upon other Christians to help address the problem.[21]

The YDP-UIM called for a boycott of all Namyoung Nylon products to fight against its worker suppression and smear campaign. Around 60 women's organizations, including the YWCA, answered the call, wanting to stop the company's violence against women. Before the boycott could start, however, the Namyoung's CEO Kim Jae-shik somehow learned about the YWCA board meeting in which the issue was supposed to be discussed. Without missing a beat, he went to the YWCA and presented his *sincere* apologies, promising to rehire any worker who had been wrongfully fired during the row.

This abruptly closed the issue. Regrettably, the YDP-UIM just missed the opportunity to use the most powerful weapon in the ordinary people's disposal.

> *You couldn't ignore the impact of a boycott. [. . .] It could*
> *put a stop to even the most wicked of employers. [. . .] It also*
> *helped raise consciousness across society, since you were getting*
> *other people involved in the workers' righteous struggle.*[22]

Namyoung Nylon's premature surrender ended the war, so to speak, before the workers could claim new territory. This doomed the labor union to remain perpetually ineffective.

This was not the only time the small groups tried to reform the labor unions in their companies. Similar attempts were made in Hanguk Textiles, Daeil Chemicals, Lotte Confectionery, and Haitai

Confectionery. All of them failed except in Hanguk Textiles (later Wonpoong Textiles).

The YDP-UIM believed this was for the following reasons. One, they needed more time to prepare the reformation of the labor unions. Two, they lost the initiative in the fight when the companies turned the labor struggle into a gender war, turning its male workers against the predominantly female reformists. Three, there were very few experienced activists among the young workers of the small groups. Four, the missioners and workers had underestimated the level of corruption they would have to deal with. They were not prepared for how far the established union leaders would go to hold onto their status and privilege. Finally, the climate had become generally more hostile to anyone associated with the UIM.

Having learned their lessons, the missioners began emphasizing the practical skills the workers needed to lead a labor union. Small-group leaders started to learn how to run procedural meetings, lead a discussion, speak in public, and overcome stage fright. The missioners tried to give the workers as many opportunities to practice as possible. They took workers who they thought could become the new leaders of a reformed union to places like the Christian Academy or National UIM Alliance to take the floor and address the audience.

The missioners and workers did not wallow in defeat. They may have lost the battle, but the workers were still winning the war as long as they were accomplishing what they could, given their environment. This was every action's most important premise. Workers had to believe they could win in any fight. The odds were not important in deciding where to take the next action. The workers' cause was righteous, supported even by the laws of the land. As long as they remained steady, the workers had to prevail.

Indeed, the workers took significant risks to themselves in choosing to take action. They were able to do this because of the sense of fellowship and common calling they had developed through the regular small-group activities. The gatherings provided the context in which they could grow a sense of ownership over their own activities. This was critical to enabling them to be resilient in the face of persecution.[23]

Facing Goliath: Pangrim Textiles

Pangrim Textiles was South Korea's largest dyeing company that employed 6,000 workers in its Mullae-dong plant not far from the YDP-UIM. The owner was an expatriate living in Japan and had advanced his business to Korea through well-placed connections after Park Chung Hee's coup on May 16, 1961.

Pangrim was a giant even among the Yeongdeungpo factories and, like most others, had an ineffectual labor union that was incapable of advocating for even the most basic worker rights. Accordingly, workers were apathetic about the union and went without even knowing the steward's name.

The YDP-UIM had paid close attention to Pangrim since the 1960s and believed the only way to solve the workplace problems there was reforming the labor union. Cho had tried multiple times to organize a LAIE branch there but always failed because the workers were simply too busy. Their work was too hard and hours too long to make the time to talk with strangers. It took a decade before the YDP-UIM finally managed to organize a handful of Pangrim workers in 1975. Once it had gained a footing, it only took a year for the small group to multiply itself to 30 members.

The high level of receptiveness to the small groups was likely a testament of the horrid working conditions in Pangrim. Despite the government, management, and union happily singing the praise of Pangrim Textiles as a model employer in the spinning industry, the YDP-UIM identified the following problems.[24]

- Workers only got between 5 and 15 days off per year. This included all the national holidays. Workers got no Sunday leave, monthly leave, period leave, nor annual leave.

- Workers were expected to start their work an hour early. They were also expected to stay an hour late. They were essentially working two unpaid hours of overtime work every day. It was common for first-shift workers to leave at 1:00 or 2:00 a.m., well past their end time at 10:00 p.m.
- The pace of the work was too fast for the workers to take a proper break to eat or use the restroom.
- Workers relied on taking caffeine pills to stay awake. Some had symptoms of addiction.
- The starting wage was 1,120 won in 1977. This was very low for the intensity of the job.
- Workers were physically and verbally abused. They suffered various kinds of degrading treatment.

In February 1977, about 250 small-group workers got their coworkers to sign a 14-point letter to the labor commissioner and CEO demanding the following:

1. Work according to schedule with pay for overtime
2. A weekly day off
3. Monthly and period leave
4. Annual leave
5. Stop the verbal abuse and infringement on human rights
6. Stop the physical abuse committed by the section chiefs
7. Provide meals for the workers
8. No more unpaid work in the form of community cleaning
9. Protected mealtimes for workers living in the dormitory
10. Soundproof the rooms in the dormitory
11. Provide equipment to boil the laundry in the dormitory
12. Permit religious activities outside the company
13. Pay the arrears in overtime compensation
14. Pay overtime for workers who perform quality control

These were all reasonable demands. The workers were asking what could pass as common sense. The company's response, however, was to persecute the workers. Those who signed the letter were dispersed and isolated through job reassignments. The managers then tried to talk them into recanting. The ones who remained defiant were laid off.

The small-group workers fought back and called upon their coworkers to do the following:

- Work on schedule. Do not start early. Do not leave late.
- Stop the supervisors' abuse.
- Get the overtime arrears paid.
- Exercise the right to legally mandated leaves.

In a rare move, the YDP-UIM sent an official letter to Pangrim's CEO on February 28, urging him to meet the demands. It then held a press conference on March 21, going public about the story.

After a few more moves, the workers got a response in April. The company said it faced certain challenges that prevented it from immediately implementing all of the mandated leaves. It also needed to operate overtime a while longer. The company promised to both give the leaves and stop the overtime schedule starting on June 1. It also promised to stop persecuting the workers associated with the YDP-UIM.

After applying more pressure, the workers got all of their grievances addressed with the exception of overtime pay. The company still refused to pay the arrears it had accumulated. The workers continued to press with the demand and succeeded in getting the Seoul Labor Administration involved. The company, however, directed the other workers to respond to the investigator with a scripted message. They were to deny working overtime and claim they only worked six days a week.

The written report said unpaid labor was required of only about 800 workers in certain sections of the company between May 1976 and February 1977. It estimated about 17 million won in overtime arrears for the 800 workers.

The YDP-UIM had a very different estimate. Assuming their experience was the norm, a survey of 100 workers suggested that Pangrim had accumulated 1.575 billion won in overtime arrears to its 5,000 workers over a span of three years.

The gap between the two estimates was far too great, but the bureaucrats in the labor office did not concern themselves with it. They transferred the case to the prosecutors, washing their hands off the matter. They did not bother exercising their authority to issue an administrative order to get the company to pay whatever arrears they did acknowledge. Their message was to say that the workers could go to court if they wanted the money.

The company was practically under the protection of the labor authorities. This emboldened the management in its recalcitrance against paying the overtime arrears. The issue became a stalemate. The inaction of labor unions at all levels—the Federation of Korean Trade Unions, Federation of the Textile Workers Union, and the local Pangrim Textiles Union—defeated the purpose of their existence. This was the sad norm in the Yushin era.

The small-group workers started to feel frustrated by the road-blocks they faced at every turn. Even the labor administration sided with the employer.

The YDP-UIM turned to another ally. It called upon its old friends among democracy activists, legal professionals, academics, conscientious politicians, church youth organizations, and both Protestant and Catholic clergy. The step was to hold three prayer meetings in conjunction with the Korean Christian Action Organization (KCAO). These took place on June 26, July 14, and August 15 and served as a public forum to expose the truth about Pangrim Textiles.

Next, the YDP-UIM began collecting petition signatures to pressure Pangrim to pay the overdue wages. Members from nearly 100 small groups visited churches, factories, and other places throughout Seoul to collect close to 10,000 signatures. Three workers from Wonpoong Textiles (formerly Hanguk Textiles) ran the petition drive in front of Seoul National University, risking arrest.

On September 12, the various allies organized an action committee and declared their support for the Pangrim workers in their fight to get their overdue wages paid. The committee consisted of 106 individuals representing Christians, activists, lawyers, politicians, and academics. Gong Deok-gwi served as the chair of the committee, while Yoon Po-seon and Hahm Seok-heon served as counsels. The involvement of such prominent dissident figures caught the government's attention.

Still, the company was far from relenting. In its meeting with the representatives of the action committee, the company denied having required overtime work without payment and repeated the propaganda that they were a model employer in the entire sector.

At the same time, the company intensified its persecution of the workers. It used a full range of tactics from persuasion, pressure, reassignments, and bribery, even contacting the workers' parents or the brokers who had found them jobs in the company. The experience of Kim Jeong-ja, a small-group worker, is illustrative. The assistant manager called her one day and asked if she thought it was appropriate to ask for overtime compensation. She said, "Yes, because we're only asking to be paid for the work we actually did." Afterward, the company reassigned her to another work section. She refused the order, saying there was no ground for the reassignment. Then, the company fired her for noncompliance.

As the struggle drew out, fatigue caught up with the workers. They started to lose morale, and the underlying lack of leadership and organizational capacity weakened their internal momentum. To compensate, external support continued to grow. Public opinion turned against Pangrim's owner, who was accused of being an absentee owner profiting at the expense of his own people while living abroad. The action committee also got in touch with the Christian women's organizations in Japan to discuss a boycott of Pangrim products. The network of support was widening.

The government began to worry that Pangrim Textiles could start a chain reaction of workers in all the other companies asking for their overdue payments. Negotiations took place behind the scenes between the YDP-UIM and the company, eventually reaching a settlement in which they both agreed to recognize that 450 million won was owed to the workers. The YDP-UIM's rationale for accepting an amount lower than its original estimate of 1.6 billion was that it was better to gain some concessions rather than none, as the workers were becoming too tired to continue the fight. Meanwhile, the company accepted the raise on the condition that it spent most of the money on building a school and hospital for the workers. Direct payments were limited to only about 30,000 to 40,000 won per worker and called "bonus incentives." This was a cover used by the company to avoid having to publicly acknowledge it owed money to the workers.

Nevertheless, the YDP-UIM found it very significant that they at least got a partial victory against a giant like Pangrim Textiles. Conditions did, in fact, improve. At least some of the arrears were now in the workers' hands. The struggle even had some influence on government policy and created ripple effects throughout the industry. Pangrim was the standard that the rest had to catch up with. Workers in Daehan Textiles, located right next to Pangrim, were direct beneficiaries in a similar struggle.

Pangrim was also the proving ground for a number of new strategies, including petition drives, prayer meetings, and coordinated action with workers from other companies. It was also the first time the mission amplified a workplace struggle into a broader social issue, even reaching out to actors overseas to coordinate a boycott campaign.

The gains came at a steep cost. What was most painful for the YDP-UIM was the dissolution of every small group in Pangrim Textiles. It was impossible to coordinate further action within the company. In retrospect, the initial goal for overdue payments had been set too high at 1.6 billion, considering the limited organizational capacity of the workers in Pangrim. The YDP-UIM also placed itself higher on the government's watch list. The authorities could no longer consider the ministry a mere nuisance or anomaly. It had become a genuine threat whose every activity had to be placed under close surveillance.

The Eight-Hour Workday

Manufacturers in the 1960s and 1970s tried to compensate for the limited equipment by running the machines every day for 24 hours. This meant putting workers through extreme schedules with frequent overtime and holiday shifts. Nor did the employers respect the legally mandated days off and leaves.

The law said the workers could only be required to work eight hours a day. Overtime was only allowed if it was voluntary. What the law did not say, however, was that there was a minimum wage. Employers circumvented the limit on the number of hours they could require by setting the lowest possible salary. That way, workers would need the overtime compensation just to make a living. With reliable access to a workforce that was willing to work two 12-hour shifts a day, the employers could save on the cost of hiring more workers to run three 8-hour shifts.

Days off and leaves were frequent topics of labor actions in those days. The mission believed, however, that the most important task was getting employers to implement the eight-hour workday. The rationale was that limiting hours was the key to breaking a vicious cycle that overworked workers who, too busy and too tired to care about matters of freedom or dignity, readily resigned themselves to more slavish labor. The quality of life could go up dramatically for the workers if they could simply live a more balanced life. Spending eight hours to work and eight hours to sleep, they could have another eight hours to study or participate in cultural life. This could help the workers' personal development, while having adequate rest was sure to lead to better health outcomes. Working fewer hours for the same subsistence wages also meant the workers could effectively get a pay raise.

When he was in Chicago, Cho Chi Song used to marvel at the fact that people there could leave their jobs after working exactly eight hours a day. He envied their ability to spend the rest of the day doing whatever they wanted. Some spent it on union activities, some others on personal hobbies, and some others on additional training so they could find better job opportunities.

This was the hard-won fruit of a previous struggle fought by the workers of Chicago. On May 1, 1886, the American Federation of Labor (AFL) called for a national strike of all workers to demand the implementation of the eight-hour workday. Three days later, six workers in Chicago—including a young girl—were shot and killed by the police. People gathered in Haymarket Square to protest the following morning. Confusion and violence ensued in which five labor activists arrested on charge of conspiring to bomb the police. They were found guilty and sentenced to death, despite the lack of adequate evidence. Years later, the day of the general strike that led to the Haymarket Affair became the International Workers' Day, continuing the call for the eight-hour workday.

Learning this history in Haymarket Square, Cho thought about the young workers in the factories of Yeongdeungpo. The eight-hour workday was becoming an international standard. Without it, the workers in South Korea could not be expected to enjoy their full dignity. The balance between work and rest could not be replaced with any amount of pay raise or other workplace improvement. The YDP-UIM placed the eight-hour workday on its long-term agenda. It regularly began the small-group workers and raising the issue in all of its rallies.

The mission was very intentional about finding its first target. Whichever employer first implemented the eight-hour workday had to be large enough to create a national ripple effect, showing workers how good working conditions can be and showing employers a standard they had to catch up with. Most of the factories in the 1970s ran a 24-hour production cycle with two 12-hour shifts. Switching to an eight-hour workday would mean having to hire a third shift of workers to maintain the same output. It was not going to be easy convincing the employers to invest further in the workforce. After carefully considering the options, the YDP-UIM decided to take the struggle to Haitai Confectionery, which was a strategic choice for the following reasons.[25]

- There were already a number of very active small groups.
- It was not one of the heavy industries that was important to the state and its economic policies.
- It produced consumer goods, which made it sensitive to public opinion and could be pressured with a boycott very effectively.
- The workers could use the existence of competitors like Lotte Confectionery to their advantage.

Haitai's workers also worked in two shifts, from 9:00 a.m. to 9:00 p.m. and from 9:00 p.m. to 9:00 a.m. Then they switched their shifts over the weekend. The crew that had taken the day shift the previous week worked an extra six hours before handing off the work to the new day shift very early on Sunday morning. This meant every worker had to work for 18 consecutive hours to switch between the day shift and night shift over the weekend.

As such, the YDP-UIM's goal for Haitai was to first put an end to the 18-hour super-shifts, then implement the eight-hour workday. The organizers took their time, since the workers were not prepared to immediately demand something as dramatic as an eight-hour workday.

The campaign proceeded in phases, the first of which was to stop the super-shifts. About 300 small-group workers decided to refuse work on Sundays starting on February 8. As always, they were discussing their method during the small-group meetings when someone raised the question of what they could do if they were not working. Someone suggested they all go hiking together.

The women kept their word and did not show up to work. Production came to a screeching halt. A panicked management sent supervisors to grab the workers from their homes or streets as they were making their way to go hiking. In the process of forcing women into the vans before hauling them back to the factory, some of the men were seen publicly grabbing the women by the hair. The episode stirred criticism among nonorganized workers and broader sections of society. Cho Chi Song alerted the International Confederation of Free Trade Unions (ICFTU) and asked them to pressure the FKTU to investigate the incident.

The *International Herald Tribune* covered the story on February 13, 1976, lambasting the poor labor conditions in South Korea with the following points.[26]

- Workers have to work between 12 and 14 consecutive hours every weekday, alternating between the day and night shifts. Then, they have to work 18 consecutive hours to switch shifts on Sundays. For all this, they were paid a mere 22 cents an hour.
- South Korea achieved its previous 15 years of economic development by exploiting its workers, whose standard of living and working conditions have not improved at all.
- Worker strikes are forbidden. The labor unions are controlled by the government. Collective bargaining rights only exist in name.
- Employers break the labor laws with impunity as the government gives its tacit approval.
- One worker, known as "Kim," has to work 12 hours a day to make just $82 (40,000 won) in a month. She only gets 15 days off per year.
- The women of Haitai occasionally steal and eat their factory products to stave off hunger.

- The company is profitable. It took the hard work of both labor and management to accomplish this. The workers, however, did not receive a return on the share of value they helped create.
- The five labor laws in the country are as good as paper scraps.
- Workers always work a minimum of 10 hours.[27]

The *Washington Post* also covered Haitai's story. Rumors circulated that the CEO's son, who happened to be studying in the United States, was shocked to discover from the article how his father had made the money that funded his studies. There was a good deal of competition among the foreign press to cover stories like these. To them, they were scenes that came out of the nineteenth century. The fascination of Western journalists with the state of South Korean labor under a military dictatorship spoke of how regressive it was.

The YDP-UIM sent an official letter to Haitai's CEO to protest, which read: "We believe the demands of your workers are justified, and we are committed to supporting them in every way possible until those demands are met."[28] It also petitioned various organizations, urging them to help address the wrongful practices and worker suppression in Haitai Confectionery.

Sensing that the issue was taking a serious turn to their disadvantage, the company took a step back and announced that it would concede to the workers' demands for legally mandated leaves and days off. The first phase of the campaign was a success. The workers no longer had to work on Sundays and had put an end to the super-shifts.

Internally, however, the company struck back. It started monitoring the workers associated with the YDP-UIM and, one day, fired one of them for a very trivial reason. Small-group workers across the different workplaces called for Seo Jeong-nam's reinstatement, flooding the CEO's office with phone calls and letters. Seo herself wrote an open letter exposing Haitai's coercion of workers into long and hard labor, sometimes even with the use of violence. Women's organizations like the YWCA and NOPW publicly criticized the company. After two months of concerted effort, Seo Jeong-nam was reinstated.

The mass calling and writing orchestrated by the YDP-UIM was especially effective. Paralyzed by the incessant phone calls and letters both at home and in his office, the CEO of Haitai had no choice but to concede. The company seemed to remember its lesson bitterly, for it was always very cautious in dealing with the YDP-UIM afterward.

The workers in Haitai spent the next two years on hiatus, focusing on multiplying the number of small groups in their company. Then, during their retreat in April 1979, they discussed the issue of fighting for the eight-hour workday.

It was clear that the campaign would be met with opposition by both the management and the government. The male employees, who tended to need a higher income to support their dependents, were also likely to fiercely oppose the reduction in hours.

On the other hand, the workers were already at the limits of their patience. Now that there were a substantial number of small groups in Haitai, they had the organizational capacity to have a real chance at winning. They could also point to the economic argument that limiting the work hours would benefit the economy, creating more jobs and forcing management to become more efficient. The workers could reasonably expect outside support. The decision was reached to launch the eight-hour campaign in Haitai Confectionery.

Questions still remained, however, about the stance of the male workers. The men, again, typically needed more income than the women. They were likely to perceive the call to reduce their excess hours as a call to reduce their income in overtime compensation. Their support would be unlikely.

Another and more sensitive question was the issue of whether all of the workers would retain their current salary after they start working for just eight hours, a mere two-thirds of the hours they were currently working. The workers were split in their outlook, but the missioners were more confident. Prices were increasing, and the company could not expect to retain a workforce if it paid any less than the subsistence wages it was currently paying. The eight-hour workday was also a very poor pretext for cutting wages. It was, after all, what the law required. The more confident workers reassured their skeptical friends there will be no pay cut. If there was one, the former assured the latter that they would make up for the losses out of their own salaries.[29]

When the confectionery industry entered its off-season in July 1979, Haitai did implement the eight-hour workday. However, it kept a highly irregular schedule, starting shifts an hour early or an hour late at random. This was to prevent the workers from getting used to a predictable eight-hour schedule, for once the workers had a taste of its benefits there would be no going back.

On July 17, some 100 workers rallied in the YDP-UIM auditorium to discuss their grievances against the sham implementation of the eight-hour workday. They also complained about the sluggish speed with which the company was reforming its subcontracting practices. The workers passed a resolution to initiate another campaign to demand a proper implementation of the eight hours. Some 200 workers in the biscuit division led the first move, walking out of their workstations after exactly eight hours.

Management was caught off guard and sent the director of production to negotiate with the workers. He promised to implement the eight hours the way the workers wanted but asked that they give the company more time. "Just help us weather the downturn in sales this season," he implored them.

The workers demanded a date for the change, agreeing to continue working for 12 hours in the meantime. The company never got back to them with a date, so the workers went back to working just eight hours a day. Between 600 and 700 workers in the other divisions joined the biscuit workers in walking out after eight hours.[30]

Starting on August 3, the company began sending an anti-union of about 150 male workers it mobilized from the Seoul and Anyang factories to stop the women from leaving. The men used verbal and physical violence, hurling abusive insults, and throwing every object they could reach. They pushed the women, beat them, and intimidated them, shouting, "You whores! How am I to feed my family?" and "We'll break your necks if you try to leave." This lasted well into September. Despite its complicity, management feigned ignorance once it had manipulated the men into doing its dirty work. It framed the issue as a dispute between male and female employees.

Under orders from the company, the men primarily targeted the workers associated with the YDP-UIM. They became more violent as the days went by. Women were struck on their faces and dragged by their hair. Many were injured and locked inside storage, bathrooms, and fermentation chambers. Kim Geum-soon lost consciousness after getting hit on her head. Kim Choo-ryeon was trampled and hospitalized for 10 days. Ha Myeong-sook broke a finger on her right hand. Kim Soon-rye and Kim Go-man were ambushed and beaten unconscious. They were thrown into storage where they were found comatose, requiring nine days of hospitalization. The violence was so brutal that one worker prayed:

> *Show us, Father, what we are to do. We cannot even weep at this injustice. Give us wisdom, courage, and faith so we won't bow before their violence. Must the weak suffer for asking for what is right? Yet we won't grow feeble, no matter the tribulation. We will trust in the victory and resurrection of our Lord Jesus Christ. We will remember his cross raised on Calvary. [. . .] Lead us in the path of light. In the name of our lord and savior, Jesus Christ. Amen.*[31]

The workers' only source of comfort in the midst of violent persecution was their fellowship with each other and their faith in Jesus Christ. They were powerless in the kingdom of this age, but they trusted in the ultimate deliverance. They took comfort in the fact that

Christ had walked a similar road of suffering on his way to Calvary. This sustained them in their most trying times.

The hospitalization of Kim Soon-rye and the other workers exposed the violence committed within Haitai's walls. To avoid public scrutiny, the company dialed down the use of violence and instead turned to psychological pressure.

It started to call the workers' parents and relatives to come sign their resignation forms. The standard line was something along the lines of "Your daughter got wrapped up with some dangerous folk from the UIM" and might be arrested for "causing problems." The company generously offered to pay their severance if the parents would take the workers home right away.

It also called the brokers who had introduced the women to the company, saying it was their responsibility to make the workers quit for indirectly causing the "massive losses" that the company was taking. This method was very effective. Most of the workers in Haitai were hired by referral from other workers, retailers, and suppliers. It was difficult to resist the pressure that came from hearing that the person who got you the job is now facing backlash for doing it. Battered by violence on the one hand and stressed by personal acquaintance on the other, about 70 to 90 workers quit their jobs by the middle of September.[32]

Missioners also received direct threats. One night, a drunken man from the company barged into the office without his shoes or shirt and shouted, "I'll kill all you UIM ministers!" He called for In Myeong-jin, asking why a "pastor would do such a thing," warning him to "back off or things won't look pretty." Cho also received a good deal of written threats at his home, which his wife tore up without reading.

While the violent persecution continued in Haitai, another issue stole the public's attention. The workers of the YH Trading Company occupied the NDP headquarters on August 9, 1979. The police tried to violently disperse the workers around 2:00 a.m. on August 11. One of the workers, Kim Gyeong-sook, was found dead in the aftermath.

The so-called YH Incident diverted attention from Haitai. Moreover, In Myeong-jin, who was the missioner assigned to the Haitai workers, was charged and arrested as one of the conspirators behind the YH demonstration. The workers of Haitai had to continue a long and lonely fight on their own.

In stark contrast to the savage violence of the anti-union, the workers continued to fight within the bounds of the law. In fact, the rule of law was just what they were asking for. Through the YDP-UIM, they wrote to various religious groups for their support, especially the Christians.

> *To the esteemed members of our society. [. . .] Here we have*
> *a company that is willing to use every inhumane method*
> *to force its workers to work for 12 hours a day (which only*
> *includes a half-hour for a break and lunch each). In its*
> *complete disregard for the Labor Standards Act, the company*
> *used threats, intimidation, and violence. Yet, we refused to*
> *give in. We steadfastly asked for the eight-hour workday. [. . .]*
> *Then the men came back and drove us outside, preventing us*
> *from working. Tell us: What is so wrong about our asking to*
> *work just eight hours a day when it is mandated by the law?*
> *We ask that you help address the behavior of our company,*
> *which would like to treat the workers however it wanted with*
> *no regard for our rights or humanity. We may have hired*
> *ourselves out for wages, but we are not slaves. We will not*
> *accept the trampling of our human dignity.*[33]

The workers reported the names of the men who participated in the assault. The police, however, acquitted every one of them. The workers also tried reaching out to the two main political parties. The Republicans were lukewarm in their response, saying that the LSA—which they had passed—was out of touch with reality. The NDP was too preoccupied with the YH Incident to be concerned with Haitai.

Nonetheless, the YDP-UIM kept pressing on. On August 12, it held a prayer meeting with 2,000 participants to intercede on behalf of the women of Haitai Confectionery. On August 31, it issued a statement through the KCAO calling for a boycott of Haitai products. On September 7, interfaith leaders formed an action committee with the goal of stopping Haitai's violence against its workers. Bishop Tji Hak-soun served as the committee chair.

The public authorities finally responded on August 27. The southern district's labor office sent a notice to the Haitai CEO, Shin Jeong-cha, that he was charged for LSA violations and will be investigated. The company received a fine of about 5 million won. Worried that Haitai might become the second YH incident, the government moved quickly to close the issue. On September 11, it opened the central council of labor and management with representatives from every food company. The council reached the resolution that the confectionery industry would implement the eight-hour workday by the end of the year. *Donga Ilbo* reported the story, which was all well except that they said Haitai had already implemented the policy.[34]

Victory was in sight, but it was too soon to relax. The workers of Haitai continued to press on with the following demands. One, the company had to comply with the council's decision to implement the eight-hour workday by the end of the year. Two, the company had to take disciplinary action against everyone who either committed or directed the use of violence. Three, the company had to reemploy every worker it had forced to quit.

It was anathema to publicly concede defeat. Even when it finally conceded to the workers' demands, the company made sure it spun a different story. In an article submitted to *Hankook Ilbo* on October 4 it claimed, "We found that we could improve our efficiency by raising productivity and lowering manpower requirements by implementing the eight-hour workday starting next March." The story made it look like management had made an independent decision to adopt the eight-hour workday. Not a word was written about the laws it had broken or the violence it had committed to avoid having to implement it.

In any case, the eight-hour workday was now an irreversible change, thanks to the industry-wide decision and the fines against Haitai's CEO. The following year on March 1, Haitai joined the other food companies and adopted the eight-hour workday. As the YDP-UIM expected, it did not cut the salaries. Workers were paid the same for working just two-thirds of the previous hours. This effectively meant they had received 61% raise. Most importantly, the change reverberated throughout the industry. More companies adopted the eight-hour workday while retaining their wage levels. The seeds planted in a single company's struggle were beginning to bear fruit for all 45,000 workers in the South Korean food industry.[35]

At 2:00 p.m. on March 23, 1980, workers gathered in the YDP-UIM auditorium to celebrate the victory in Haitai Confectionery. They received words of encouragement for the hardship they endured and were joined by others to celebrate the historic achievement. Rev. Moon Ik-hwan addressed the audience as the main speaker in a lecture titled "Why the Church is Preferential to the Workers," proclaiming the justice of the UIM's involvement in the labor issues.

Haitai Confectionery was a case of patient preparation that took six years to bear fruit. As the first struggle for the eight-hour day in South Korea, it was a milestone not just for the YDP-UIM but the entire country's labor history. It also set the precedent for a number of tactics for moving public opinion, including open letters, prayer rallies, boycotts, and mass call-ins and write-ins.

Haitai also demonstrated the power of the small-group workers even in the face of intense repression. The victory that the women achieved had an enormous impact throughout the food industry. A good account of the struggle can be found in *For the Eight Hour Workday*, written by Kim Geun-soon but published in Soon Jeom-soon's name to prevent retaliation against Kim who was still working in Haitai at the time of the book's publication.[36]

The YDP-UIM believed whenever it got involved in a labor dispute that the issue of a single company was one day going to affect the entire country.

We didn't pick our fights with the smaller companies. We only took on the big ones. That's how you multiply impact. You had to change all of them if you wanted to change one of them. [. . .] We invested years preparing the one struggle that could make a difference. [. . .] It was the workers who fought those fights. They shed their blood and put their lives on the line. They went into it with the mind of a martyr. [. . .] The one conclusion I reached is that. [. . .] Only the workers could truly solve the labor problems. [. . .] The UIM? We were simply a helping hand.[37]

It took more than just conviction in the righteousness of a cause to fight for it with success. Many labor activists in the day unfortunately waged sporadic wars of attrition. The YDP-UIM tried to be more systematic, preparing each case with careful analysis before launching a campaign that was based on a comprehensive strategy. The success in Haitai Confectionery was evidence of the validity of such method.

The Road to Seoul

We were busy working when the section chief came again. He said there was a lot that needed to get done and that we were going to have to work overnight. Starting tomorrow, we will also have to work in the evenings.

"What am I supposed to do if I'm working overnight?" I asked.

"You just work all night then leave in the morning," The chief replied.

He told me to write down my name, which I did. My sister saw me and approached us. She spoke to the chief, "My sister is new to the factory. She can't work overnight. Take her name off, please."

Then she tried to convince me to not do it, while the chief kept saying that I should. He seemed adamant and was looking at me. So I said I could do it.

"Listen to me! You can start working overnight next time. Just don't do it this time." My sister pleaded with me.

"You don't think I can do it, do you? Everyone else is doing it. There's no reason I can't!" I tried to hold my ground.

"This is different from domestic work," she told me, "you can't leave once you start till it's over, no matter how hard it gets!" Then, she left, looking upset.

I asked the person next to me what we are paid for working overnight. She said we'll get paid more for working after hours and for finishing extra jobs. I was determined to work overnight. That's why I came to the factory, after all. I could do anything if I could make more money.

That was my first overnight shift. It was very, very hard. We didn't get to break for 24 hours except to eat for an hour in the middle of the night. After I ate, I felt unbearably sleepy. I had lied down on a bench for a minute when I fell asleep. It was wooden and hard, but it couldn't have felt more comfortable. Then suddenly, somebody woke me up. It was the night supervisor. He said it was time to go back to work. I felt so embarrassed. Working all night without catching a moment of sleep was extremely painful. I thought this must be what it's like in hell. I finally understood why my sister was so upset.[38]

The text above was taken from a worker's memoir titled *The Road to Seoul*. Song Hyo-soon worked in Daeil Chemicals, which produced bandages and pain relief patches. The workplace she described was quite typical of most other manufacturing companies in the 1970s.

Song was introduced to the YDP-UIM through a personal acquaintance and initially visited the mission to use its credit union cooperative. Then, she noticed there were small-group activities, which she wanted to join. There were no small groups in Daeil, so Song brought some friends together to create the first group.

The conditions in Daeil were appalling. Workers had to work between 12 and 14 hours at a time. Sometimes, they had to work for 24 hours. The supervisors beat the workers and insulted them, driving them as if they were a herd of animals. There was a labor union, but it was so ineffective that the workers did not even know it existed. Cho Chi Song said:

> *Forget about the Labor Standards Act. [. . .] They had no start time. Workers had to show up whenever the company said they had to for morning assembly or cleaning. There was no end time, either. The workers just stayed there doing whatever the supervisors told them. They didn't know they were supposed to get paid higher rates for working after hours or finishing extra jobs. [. . .] I felt very angry. Angry at the government and the company. They were taking advantage of these young, innocent workers simply because they didn't know any better.*[39]

Song Hyo-soon said she regretted discovering the YDP-UIM so late when she found out how much the company had taken advantage of her ignorance. She tried to learn her rights as quickly as she could so she could improve the conditions in her workplace. However, it took a while before she had her first opportunity. While Song and her coworkers were eager to fight, the missioners believed they needed to acquire critical mass before initiating action.

The workers could no longer wait in 1976. Some 80 workers created a list of the following demands and took it to management.

- Stop beating us.
- Cleaning is part of work. Pay us for it.

- Provide weekly, monthly, annual, and period leaves as required by the law.
- Pay us our severance.
- We will not work for 24 consecutive hours.

The supervisors were astonished when the workers marched in. They were no longer the docile girls who could barely make eye contact.

As basic as they were, these were urgent needs. Workers especially needed an end to the overnight shifts. The youthful workers looked deathly ill after working 24 consecutive hours. Financially, they could not afford to lose the extra income with a base salary of just 13,000 to 14,000 won. Yet it made no sense to slowly lose their lives in order to make a living.

The company put forward a managing director to negotiate with the workers. He was a deacon in the PCK Namdaemun Church and had a son who was familiar with the YDP-UIM. Having read the literature that the mission spread throughout the churches of Seoul to expose the workplace conditions of Daeil, the deacon's son warned him not to get entangled with the ministry.

The deacon therefore tried to use dialogue to resolve the issue. He obliged when the small-group workers told him to see them in the YDP-UIM office.[40] "Persuade them," the missioner present told him. "Talk them out of taking action if you can. They are your employees." It was, indeed, best in the interest of both parties to quickly reach an agreement.

Song Hyo-soon and the others laid out a litany of grievances. "You beat us and make us work overtime whenever you want. Then, you don't even pay us. Nor do you give any leaves." The managing director could not refute them on any of the points. Instead, he promised that the company will take appropriate measures to address what it could and discipline the supervisors who hit the workers.

The promise did not amount to much. Management did make a few gestures, but it dragged its feet on making any meaningful change.

By the time it addressed one issue, the workers had already identified more. This made the other executives impatient. They sacked the managing director as the negotiator, chiding him for helping the YDP-UIM grow its presence inside the company.

The company turned to a hardline approach. They took advantage of the fact that the Yushin regime had begun cracking down on the UIMs. Daeil Chemicals also started targeting the small-group workers. First, it reassigned them to unfamiliar and difficult jobs. Then, it started spreading rumors about their association with "dangerous dissidents" to discourage other workers from interacting with them. The small-group workers were literally isolated, moved to seats facing the walls. They were sent to menial posts regardless of their skills but required at the same time to complete absurd workloads. All of this was expected, however, and very few workers left their small groups.

In the summer of 1980, the authorities finally recognized that the illness of workers (due to their dealing with toxic chemicals) was an occupational disease. This sparked another round of intense dispute in Daeil Chemicals, just a year after they had finished a major struggle over the overtime compensation and continued violence against workers. The battle was fierce.

In the aftermath, the company ordered Song Hyo-soon and a handful of other small-group leaders to relocate to its Osan factory. The hope was that the workers would sooner resign than move to another city. Song and her colleagues, however, recognized that reassigning employees to another plant was within the rights of the employer. Resisting it could constitute a valid reason for termination of employment. To avoid giving management the pretext it wanted, Song and the others agreed to get a room together and move to the Osan factory.

This was to the company's great chagrin. As they saw it, the previously pristine environment of Osan was now infected with the UIM. Management sensed it could not afford to let Song and the others become too active and ordered them to be placed on close surveillance. The relocated workers were not allowed to speak to each other. The supervisor constantly watched them through his office window. One day, a manager questioned Kim Deok-soon about whom she talked to that day. Angered by the interrogation, Kim went back to her workstation and taped her mouth as a sign of protest.

The workers still wanted to visit the YDP-UIM in Seoul at least a few times a week. This made them get into frequent arguments with their supervisors over their refusal to stay behind to work late. They once had to run across the snow in their slippers to catch the train.

These workers never allowed the company to intimidate them, even when the company began pressuring them from all sides against the backdrop of the terrorizing rule of the *Shingunbu* (or the new junta under Chun Doo Hwan). Unable to control them, the company eventually fired them.

The workers continued their struggle in the offices of the YDP-UIM. Investigators from the Joint Investigation Headquarters, which Chun Doo Hwan set up to consolidate his power after his coup, came to question them about their protest against the layoff. Around a dozen workers including Song Hyo-soon tearfully shared their stories, unable to contain the years of pent-up emotions.

"Why would you cry in front of them?" Cho Chi Song told the workers when the investigators left. "Don't cry in front of men like them. You did nothing wrong. Hold your heads up." He also reassured them that the fight was not a failure. They had lost, but only after doing their best. He suggested that they process their experience in writing. Everyone agreed that Song Hyo-soon should pen the text, since she had been their leader from the very beginning.

Thus Song Hyo-soon wrote *The Road to Seoul*, detailing their struggle in Daeil Chemicals. Unfortunately, the Shingunbu intensified censorship at the time she completed the writing. The book had to remain in storage for a while even after it had been printed. Once it saw the light of day in August 1982,[41] however, it became every student activist's essential reading.

The struggle Daeil Chemicals remained relatively unknown in its time because of the martial law imposed after the Gwangju Democracy Movement. It looked like a failure at the surface, Yet the missioners believed it was a successful part of a longer journey. Activism did not end with a single fight. Everything started by making the smallest improvements in one's surroundings. As the person grows, so does the depth of action.

The ultimate goal was to edify the inner being of the worker so that they could think and act like their employer's equal, capable of negotiating and even demanding their rights. As long as the workers came out of a struggle more mature than they were before, they were a step closer to creating an equal society. Every fight was worthwhile, whatever the immediate outcome.

Song Hyo-soon and her colleagues were recognized by the state following the country's democratization in the Special Act to Restore the Honor of Persons Associated with Democratization (hereafter the Honor Restoration Act).

The Wonpoong Textiles Union

The YDP-UIM's relationship to the workers in Wonpoong Textiles dated back to 1964 when Cho Chi Song was a newcomer in the area leading the factory worship in Hanguk Textiles. Kim Gap-jun was one of the original members of the LAIE, who later introduced Park Young-hye to the YDP-UIM. Park then led the struggle for severance payments when she quit Hanguk Textiles, which was an important milestone in the company's labor history.[42] The mission and the workers had also built a solid relationship over the course of the struggle, which lasted from May to October.

Hanguk Textiles was the first successful action for both the YDP-UIM and its workers. It set the tone for the coming years of activism for both of them. The ineffective leadership of the labor union was replaced with frontline workers, laying the foundations of one of the most powerful worker-controlled labor union in the 1970s. The workers formally relaunched the Hanguk Textiles Union on August 17, 1972, which changed its name along with the company in 1975. The founding members of the newly branded union included 43 members of the JOC, 70 members of the YDP-UIM small groups, and 50 members of the YDP-UIM credit union cooperative.[43]

The reformed union demonstrated its capability when the company went bankrupt in June 1973. It formed an emergency committee and helped run the company before handing it over to a new management at the end of the year. Recognizing the role the union played, the shareholders who met in February 1974 agreed to give 380,000 shares or 20 percent to the labor union. The steward, Ji Dong-jin, became a senior managing director who continued to help run the company until October. Unions often found it difficult to survive the bankruptcy or merger of their previous employer. This made the Hanguk Textiles Union unique for its remarkable organizational unity and steady leadership that not only survived the bankruptcy of the company but even helped steer it out of a crisis.

Bang Yong-seok, who succeeded Ji Dong-jin as the steward, signed a new collective contract with Wonpoong Industries, which acquired Hanguk Textiles, in January. The union was renamed the Wonpoong Textiles Union. Bang was a graduate of both the LAIE worker education and YDP-UIM union officer training. He was a man of a conservative faith with a background in the Full Gospel Church.[44] His career in the union began as the director of education and publicity on August 17, 1972. After joining the executive board, then serving as the deputy steward, he was elected by the delegate assembly as the steward on June 11, 1974.

The Wonpoong Union survived for nearly a decade under the ruthless persecution of the Yushin regime. Furthermore, it exerted a great amount of influence as one of the few major worker-controlled, democratic labor unions. This feat was possible because the members of Wonpoong Union had developed a very high level of consciousness through the YDP-UIM and JOC activities. It also had several key members and officers who provided strong organizational leadership. The Wonpoong Union was very active even outside its workplace. For instance, four of its members were arrested while supporting the struggle in Haitai Confectionery. Three others were arrested supporting yet another struggle in Pangrim Textiles. Jeong Sang-beom and Bang Yong-seok did not shy away from getting arrested for violating Park Chung Hee's emergency presidential decrees in September 1972. The Wonpoong Union was involved in every major labor or social issue: the prayer meeting for Dongil Textiles in the Korea Christian Building, the combined Easter Service, the protest for In Myeong-jin's release, the Christian Academy Affair, the memorial ceremony for the YH worker Kim Gyeong-sook, the Undercover Wedding in YMCA, and more. It was, indeed, a thorn in the side of every public security agency.

During the Seoul Spring of the 1980s, the Wongpoong Union also led the national rally for basic labor rights and the following occupation of the FKTU headquarters. It sent Bang Yong-seok as a labor panelist for the public forum on constitutional amendment. When hopes for a democratic election were dashed in the bloodbath of May 18, 1980, the Wonpoong Union raised 4.7 million won to send to the citizens of Gwangju. Deputy steward Park Soon-hee personally delivered the money to Archbishop Yoon Gong-hee of the Gwangju Archdiocese. This demonstrated the courage of the Wongpoong Union. Most were reluctant even to mention the name of Gwangju in those days.[45]

The regime, of course, clamped down on the union, naming 191 of its members as targets for "social purification." Almost all of the officers including Bang Yong-seok and Park Soon-hee were arrested or placed on a national wanted list. Under the government's pressure, the central committee of the national Federation of Textile Workers Unions even removed the names of Bang and Park from its roster of union members.[46]

After spending some time in hiding, Bang and Park turned themselves in on April 1981. Agents from the KCIA (later the Agency for National Security Planning or ANSP) offered them jobs in the Anti-Communist League and the Ministry of Health, respectively. The two refused and were determined to rebuild their labor union. The YDP-UIM hired Bang Yong-seok on paper so he could have some income while leading the Wonpoong Union without a job in Wonpoong Textiles. This arrangement lasted for almost two years, which was remarkable since it was risky to even provide tangential support for a labor union in those days.[47]

It took a considerable amount of effort to rebuild the Wonpoong Union, but it came under attack again near the *Chuseok* holidays on September 27, 1982. All the union officers were fired for no particular reason. When the workers protested inside the union office, the company sent enforcers to remove them from company premises. Unable to go back inside, some 80 workers spent the next two years demanding their reinstatement over the course of three different campaigns. They used the YDP-UIM as their office.

Each campaign was fierce. The police arrested 134 people on the first protest and 197 on the second. They also put 12 of the arrested workers on short-term detention. When some 130 people were making their way for the third protest, the police found and arrested the union officers who were hiding. Five of them were placed on a 20-day detention, while five others including Bang Yong-seok were placed on trial while in custody.

The MBC evening news told a distorted version of the story, titled "Labor Extremism in Wonpoong Textiles," angering labor and democracy activists. A total of eight officers were prosecuted and sentenced to 10 months in prison. They were released on special pardon right before they completed the sentence on August 13. The first thing the released officers did was to rebuild the union once again, even if they had to do so outside the factory. Around 80 workers regrouped to carry on their struggle from inside the YDP-UIM.[48]

The story of the Wonpoong Union even after its expulsion from the workplace was quite remarkable in that the members were so strongly united that they managed to stay together for two years even when most of their leaders were in prison or hiding. The cycle of repression and resistance was a fate common to all worker-controlled unions under the military rule. The resilience of Wonpoong, however, showed the power of cultivating a collective sense of justice, democracy, and community through the YDP-UIM small groups and leadership training.

Unfortunately, Chun Doo Hwan's regime was closing in from all directions. The YDP-UIM and Wonpoong Union had to part ways on January 19, 1983. The members of the Wonpoong Union had been camping in the YDP-UIM for nearly two years without their leaders. The YDP-UIM believed the officers had to return, whether to continue leading their union or to call off its struggle. The union leaders disagreed as they were still wanted by the state.

Meanwhile, the YDP-UIM was now waging its very own struggle against the PCK denomination. It had been ordered to revert to the older modes of industrial evangelism, using less activist and more religious means of ministry. Both the mission and union were now struggling for survival. The YDP-UIM simply did not have the resources to provide refuge to the union indefinitely. The two sides agreed that the Wonpoong Union would find a new place to stay and that the two would part ways.

Fortunately, the parting helped strengthen the unity of the remaining members of the Wonpoong Union. They raised 48.4 million won, mostly by claiming the dues they were owed since their expulsion in 1982. Using these funds, they purchased an office where they started an unregistered union in 1984, called the Korean Council for Workers' Welfare. Free from the regulatory reach of the state as an unregistered group, the CWW was able to be very active. It led the struggle against wrongful terminations and the barring of employees under Chun Doo Hwan's regime.[49]

The last steward of the Wonpoong Textiles Union, Bang Yong-seok, later got a proportional seat as a lawmaker for the National Congress for New Politics (NCNP). He then served as the labor minister under Kim Dae-jung then as the president of the Worker's Compensation Service under Roh Moo-hyun.

The 156 Wonpoong Union workers who were fired were later recognized as victims of unlawful union-busting practices and barring employees under the Shingunbu regime. Their honor was restored on August 28, 2010, by the Truth and Reconciliation Commission, some of them receiving the state's monetary compensation.

The Wonpoong Textiles Union was the last worker-controlled, democratic labor union to survive under the Shingunbu regime. It was clearly a major part of a previous chapter in the history of the YDP-UIM, since many of its members had been trained at some point by the ministry. The media and government aptly called it the "seedbed" or "final bastion" of the UIM. After parting ways, however, the YDP-UIM had to find a new way to engage with the workers.[50]

NOTES

1 NCCK, *Testimonies from the Ground: Labor in the 1970s* (Pulbit, 1984), 136–137.
2 Kim and Yoo, *Cho Chi Song's Oral History* (Vol. 2, 2011).
3 Kim Myeong-bae, "Ministry Reports from January–May 1972," Yeongdeungpo UIM Files Vol. 1 (YDP-UIM & Soongsil University Center for Culture and Mission Studies, 2020), 134.
4 In Myeong-jin, "The Strategy of the Yeongdeungpo UIM in the 1970s," *Yeongdeungpo UIM: A 40-Year History* (YDP-UIM, 1998).
5 Kim and Yoo, *Cho Chi Song's Oral History* (Vol. 2, 2011).
6 Sohn Eun-jeong, "Transcribed Interviews: Myeong Noh-seon" (2022).
7 Sohn Eun-jeong, "Transcribed Interviews: Myeong Noh-seon."
8 Yoo Ok-soon, "Building a Democratic Labor Union in Control Data," *I, A Working Woman 1* (Greenbee Books, 2011).

9 Kwon Jin-gwan, "Social Movement As A Collective Learning Process," *Class Culture And Identity Among Korean Workers in the 1960–1970s* (Hanul Academy, 2006).

10 Seo Deok-Seok, Hong Yoon-gyung and Lee Hoon-hee, "Kim Yeon-ja's Interview," *Interviews of Related Individuals for the Biography* (YDP-UIM, June 2011).

11 Kim Myeong-bae, *Yeongdeungpo UIM Files Vol. 1* (YDP-UIM & Soongsil University Center for Culture and Mission Studies, 2020), 128–388.

12 Kim, *Yeongdeungpo UIM Files Vol 1*, 128.

13 Kim and Yoo, *Cho Chi Song's Oral History* (Vol. 2, 2011).

14 Cho Chi Song, "Who Turned Them To Fools," *Yeongdeungpo UIM Files Vol. 1* (YDP-UIM & Soongsil University Center for Culture and Mission Studies, 2020), 192–195.

15 Myeong Noh-seon, "The Unforgettable Memories of the UIM," *Yeongdeungpo UIM: A 40-Year History* (YDP-UIM, 1998).

16 Seo Deok-Seok and Sohn Eun-jeong, "Interviews of the Older Members of the UIM: Park Jeom-soon, Shin Mi-ja, Song Hyo-soon, Park Deuk-soon, Kim Mi-soon, and Han Myeong-hee" (2011).

17 Kim and Yoo, *Cho Chi Song's Oral History* (Vol. 8, 2011).

18 Yeongdeungpo UIM 40th Anniversary Committee, *Yeongdeungpo UIM: A 40-Year History* (1998, 154–160).

19 Kim Myeong-bae "Strategy for the Namyoung Nylon Labor Action," *Yeongdeungpo UIM Files Vol. 1* (YDP-UIM & Soongsil University Center for Culture and Mission Studies, 2020), 337–341.

20 Kim Myeong-bae "Litigation Forms," *Yeongdeungpo UIM Files Vol. 4* (YDP-UIM & Soongsil University Center for Culture and Mission Studies, 2020), 432–433.

21 Kim and Yoo, *Cho Chi Song's Oral History* (Vol. 9, 2011).

22 Kim and Yoo, *Cho Chi Song's Oral History* (Vol. 9, 2011).

23 Seo Deok-Seok and Sohn Eun-jeong, "Interviews of the Older Members of the UIM: Park Jeom-soon, Shin Mi-ja, Song Hyo-soon, Park Deuk-soon, Kim Mi-soon, and Han Myeong-hee" (2011).

24 Yeongdeungpo UIM 40th Anniversary Committee, *Yeongdeungpo UIM: A 40-Year History* (1998), 164.

25 Kim and Yoo, *Cho Chi Song's Oral History* (Vol. 9, 2011).

26 NCCK, *Testimonies from the Ground*, 521.

27 Translator's note: Retranslated from Korean. Original English text could not be found

28 Kim Myeong-bae, *Yeongdeungpo UIM Files Vol. 4* (YDP-UIM & Soongsil University Center for Culture and Mission Studies, 2020), 339.

29 Kim and Yoo, *Cho Chi Song's Oral History* (Vol. 9, 2011).

30 Soon Jeom-soon, *For the Eight-Hour Workday* (Pulbit, 1984).

31 Soon Jeom-soon, *For the Eight-Hour Workday.*

32 Seo Deok-Seok and Sohn Eun-jeong, "Interviews of the Older Members of the UIM: Park Jeom-soon, Shin Mi-ja, Song Hyo-soon, Park Deuk-soon, Kim Mi-soon, and Han Myeong-hee" (2011).

33 NCCK, *Testimonies from the Ground*, 529–530.

34 *Donga Ilbo*, September 12, 1979.

35 Yeongdeungpo UIM 40th Anniversary Committee, *Yeongdeungpo UIM: A 40-Year History* (1998), 176–177.

36 Shin Chul-young, "Ten Years of the Yeongdeungpo UIM," *Yeongdeungpo UIM: A 40-Year History* (YDP-UIM, 1998).

37 Kim and Yoo, *Cho Chi Song's Oral History* (Vol. 9, 2011).

38 Song Hyo-soon, *The Road to Seoul* (Hyeongseongsa, 1982).

39 Kim and Yoo, *Cho Chi Song's Oral History* (Vol. 9, 2011).

40 Kim and Yoo, *Cho Chi Song's Oral History* (Vol. 9, 2011).

41 Seo Deok-Seok and Sohn Eun-jeong, "Song Hyo-soon's Interview," *Interviews of Related Individuals for the Biography* (YDP-UIM, 2021).

42 Kim and Yoo, *Cho Chi Song's Oral History* (Vol. 8, 2011).

43 Kim and Yoo, *Cho Chi Song's Oral History* (Vol. 8, 2011).

44 Kim and Yoo, *Cho Chi Song's Oral History* (Vol. 8, 2011).

45 Kim Nam-il, *History of the Wonpoong Textiles Union* (Samchang, 2010).

46 Kim, *History of the Wonpoong Textiles Union.*

47 Kim Myeong-bae, *Yeongdeungpo UIM Files Vol. 1* (YDP-UIM & Soongsil University Center for Culture and Mission Studies, 2020).

48 Kim, *History of the Wonpoong Textiles Union.*

49 Kim, *History of the Wonpoong Textiles Union.*

50 Yeongdeungpo UIM 40th Anniversary Committee, *Yeongdeungpo UIM: A 40-Year History* (YDP-UIM, 1998), 208.

⁅ 4 ⁆

REPRESSION AND RESISTANCE

THE YDP-UIM DID not attract the attention of the authorities until 1968, likely because all it did in its early days of "industrial evangelism" was to express sympathy for the suffering workers and recommend that they believe in Jesus for their salvation. Even after Cho Chi Song decided the workers could not experience salvation through religious rites alone, YDP-UIM provided at most indirect support for the labor unions in the form of counseling and leadership training from 1968 to 1970.

Targeted by the Yushin Regime

Things changed after YDP-UIM played a pivotal role in addressing the death of Kim Jin-soo in 1971 and helped the former workers of Hanguk Textiles get their severance payments in 1972. Yushin was declared later in October that year, followed by the introduction of a number of anti-labor policies. The YDP-UIM's support for the workers now constituted anti-government activities. The declaration of martial law and a ban on all public assemblies signaled the start of the tribulation for the labor movement. Cho always thought this was going to be a matter of time.

> *Fighting the employers wasn't the hard part. [. . .] It wasn't*
> *the hard part at all. [. . .] Labor issues could be easily resolved*
> *as long as the government kept its neutrality. The problem is*
> *that even this was too idealistic to hope.*[1]

There was no chance the government was going to maintain neutrality. Its leader was a dictator who had taken power through a military coup and had just given himself a slew of extralegal emergency powers. The regime wanted the cooperation of business to ensure its survival, while business had everything to gain by providing it. The government promised tax benefits, access to foreign currency, suppression of labor activism, and other protections as long as the companies were willing to follow orders.

The persecution of the YDP-UIM began a month after the declaration of Yushin. On November 28, the city police came and seized files from the mission office without warning or warrant. This happened again the following night. A month later, a training event for union officers had to be canceled because of the Martial Law Command's ban on public assemblies.

The following year, on February 9, the police came and took Cho Chi Song and Kim Gyeong-nak in for questioning. They were asked about the nature of their involvement in Daehan Textiles and Donga Dyeing Company. The missioners had simply supported the workers' call for an end to wrongful employment practices. The interrogators suggested that the two could in fact be Communists.

The National UIM Alliance protested the interrogation in a public statement on February 28. It also sent a letter to the leaders of the PCK and KMC to ask that their denominations vouch for the UIM missioners and provide them with church-wide support. The Alliance also sent an open letter to Christian business owners.

> *We ask that you understand that the UIM missioners in*
> *Yeongdeungpo must take the side of the working poor*
> *rather than their employers on the question of the wrongful*
> *employment practices in Daehan Textiles (owned by the elder,*
> *Kim Seong-seob) and Donga Dyeing Company (owned by*
> *the elder, Lee Bong-soo). We ask that you respect the freedom*
> *of religion by refraining from requiring your workers to*
> *participate in mandatory worship and help create a just*
> *industrial society by keeping with the Labor Standards Act.*[2]

After the kidnapping of Kim Dae-jung in 1973 and the shooting of Yuk Young-soo in 1974, the desire for political change began to burst forth. Protests against the Yushin regime spread across universities in October 1973. The regime responded with four emergency decrees starting in January 1974. All speech critical of the regime was forbidden. All assemblies were banned. This caused a sharp decrease in union activities. Efforts to improve the workplace had all but frozen.[3]

Nonetheless, a number of young ministers in specialized ministries issued a statement criticizing the Yushin constitution on January 17 in the NCCK building. The government responded by arresting several ministers including Kim Gyeong-nak and In Myeong-jin. In the trial followed in August, Kim and In were each sentenced to 15 and 10 years in prison, respectively. It had been less than a year since In Myeong-jin started his ministry. The YDP-UIM escaped the fate of having three of its missioners in prison simultaneously thanks to Cho Chi Song's refraining from signing the statement.

The mission worked busily for the two's release. The YDP-UIM first called on PCK General Assembly to help protect its ministry from government repression. It organized a prayer for human rights in the NCCK building on December 9, a day before the World Human Rights Day. Then, on December 10, the mission issued an open letter in the name of the UIM Alliance to foreign audiences, calling on them to take action to restore labor and human rights in South Korea. The recipients he addressed included the United States and Japanese governments, foreign business, UNCHR, ILO, and WCC.[4]

This was around the same time George Ogle, the Methodist missionary, was deported back to the United States. Eight individuals were murdered by the state under fabricated charges of sedition and conspiracy of insurrection as part of the *Inhyeokdang* (or People's Revolutionary Party). Ogle, who was serving in the Incheon UIM, openly criticized the government for this and the emergency decrees. One could see how repressive the regime had become in its willingness to even deport a United States citizen.

The YDP-UIM nevertheless did all it could to secure the release of Kim Gyeong-nak and In Myeong-jin. It organized prison visits to keep the issue alive and held fundraisers to send money to cover their expenses while in prison. The two were finally released after much hard work on February 15, 1975.

Unfortunately, it was just the beginning for the missioners of the YDP-UIM. They faced many more interrogations and detentions by the state and were repeatedly accused of being seditious dissidents threatening the integrity of society. To address this, the PCK's Central UIM Committee published a document titled "The PCK's Basic Stance on Urban Industrial Mission," vigorously defending the UIM. It called upon the church to:

- Be proactive in resolving the issues between workers and employers in our industrialized society.
- Give workers priority in all labor disputes and protect them from the tyranny of the companies.
- Support the labor unions so that they can have the autonomy required to advocate for the rights and interests of the workers.
- Strive for even distribution of wealth to resolve the polarization of wealth.
- Strive to improve the housing, health, education, vocation, and other aspects that the urban poor need to live in dignity.
- Strive to correct the violations of human rights that occur in urban and industrial society.
- Place its faith in such actions as the only way to advance our gospel ministry, oppose Communism, and build democracy.
- Carry out such actions as part of the gospel ministry of the church, which is the body of Christ, and not as a social or political movement.
- Raise and spend a considerable amount of church budget for urban and industrial mission.

In August 1976, the second deputy director of the Seoul City Police, Kim Jae-gook, published a booklet titled *Understanding Korean Christianity*. He was an elder of the PCK Youngdo Church. In it, he accused the UIM of being Communists. The YDP-UIM wrote to the PCK General Assembly and requested an investigation of the book's claims. It also sent a letter to the prime minister asking him to stop the slander and libel against the UIM on July 14, 1977. The general assembly responded to YDP-UIM's calls and sent the interior minister an official letter requesting an explanation of the targeted investigations against the YDP-UIM.

Repression was experienced by all of the UIM organizations in Incheon, Cheongju, Gumi, and Daejeon. Men sent by the employer dumped sewage water on the workers associated with the Incheon UIM. Go Ae-shin, the UIM missioner sent to Gumi, was so viciously accused of being a Communist trying to infiltrate the factories that she was forced to leave the area.[5]

On April 17, 1978, In Myeong-jin was invited to preach during a prayer service hosted by the Hwalbin Church of the Cheongju UIM. The goal of the service was to intercede on behalf of the farmers who had recently experienced wrongful treatment. In Myeong-jin chose Micah 2:1 and 7:3 as the Scripture passage. Then, on May 1, the authorities arrested him. The charge was that In Myeong-jin had violated the ninth emergency decree that forbade critical speech against the regime. He was placed on trial in custody. The prosecutor was Lee Jin-woo, a member of the PCK Somang Church.

Apparently, the speech in question was none other than the verse of Scripture that In Myeong-jin quoted. Micah 2:1 in the Common Translation Bible he used described "those who devise wickedness and evil deeds" (NRSV) in everyday terms than the more literary expressions of the New Korean Revised Version, which most churches used. This came across as In Myeong-jin's attack of the government.

The YDP-UIM immediately protested the arrest as the suppression of religious freedom. Not even the colonial authorities arrested a member of the clergy over a verse of scripture during the days of the Japanese occupation. Protestants throughout strongly demanded that the government respect the freedom of religion.

On the same day as In Myeong-jin's arrest, the prosecutors searched the YDP-UIM office. After seizing a pile of documents and accounting files, they charged the YDP-UIM 1.35 million won as overdue payroll taxes for its missioners. This was unusual, given the fact that the clergy was exempt from the payroll tax. Missioners were taken and questioned about the ministry's accounts and finances. Cho was charged with tax evasion, albeit without being taken into custody. Shortly thereafter, on June 17, the finance ministry demanded a full list of the members of its credit union cooperative. The YDP-UIM refused, to which the finance ministry retaliated by canceling its license—the first it had ever given, by the way—as a credit union. The reason cited was resistance to inspection.

Despite the state's repeated attacks, the YDP-UIM continued to organize the workers and their small groups. It also organized efforts to secure In Myeong-jin's release, which included prayers, petitions, and collective action with other UIM organizations. It also tried to raise public support for the opposition to the government's persecution of a faith-based, conscientious ministry. Part of this effort was taking the letters written by In Myeong-jin and the workers Kim Hye-ran, Jang Nam-soo, and Jeon Hye-ja from prison and submitting them to the theological periodical, *Gidogkyo Sasang (Christian Thought)*.

The women in the small groups showed up to every protest, prayer, and trial to show support for the UIM and its fight against the repression. Once, the YDP-UIM missioners went on a hunger strike from March 15 to 20, 1978, in the Korea Christian Building. The CBS office was inside the same building, but it did not cover the story. Indignant at this, the workers marched to the CBS office to protest.

The small-group workers were seasoned veterans in the fight against unjust authority. It was anathema to do nothing when their previous helpers now needed help. The world tried to tell the workers that the UIM missioners were dangerous Communist sympathizers, to which the women responded, "if these good people are Communist sympathizers for the good they're doing, let us join the sympathy!"[6]

The YDP-UIM urged the PCK General Assembly to do more for In Myeong-jin's release. About 150 ministers formed the PCK Committee for the Defense of the UIM with Rev. Cha Gwan-young as the chair. The committee very actively addressed the persecution in various prayer meetings and seminars.

Meanwhile, the PCK Central UIM Committee published a document titled "The Principles and Guidelines for Industrial Mission," which was endorsed by the 63rd General Assembly. The document provided the theological justification and parameters of the UIM. The primary purpose was to protect the ministry from external attacks, but the document also called on the missioners to use an approach that could be better received by a more general audience. As the later pages will discuss, this proved to be a double-edged sword.[7]

The NCCK proceeded to provide a systematic theological support for the UIM against the state's propaganda. In August 1978, it published a booklet titled *Why They Accuse the UIM* to refute the false charges made against the UIM. It featured Cho Chi Song's "The Problems and Features of an Industrial Society," In Myeong-jin's "Labor Issues and Industrial Missions," and Jang Nam-soo's (who was a small-group worker) "A Worker's Prayer." The booklet also featured a worker's testimony that could clear the name of In Myeong-jin, titled "The Reverend In Myeong-jin I know." The NCCK's Committee of Theology and Committee of URM co-hosted a seminar on the theology of the UIM in the Academy House from September 5 to 7. Combining the various theological studies, they issued "The Declaration of Industrial Missiology." Thanks to these multifaceted and consistent support from the church, the YDP-UIM was able to boldly assert the legitimacy of its ministry.

The YDP-UIM also worked to raise support overseas. It made large numbers of pennants and key chains inscribed with the Korean letters for "standing with the oppressed" and sent them to the churches of Australia, Germany, and the United States. This was an effective tool for spreading international awareness about the state of human and labor rights in Korea.

Cho especially believed the partnership with the foreign church was instrumental to countering the state's repression and intentionally tried to expand the YDP-UIM's interactions with foreign actors. For instance, he proposed that the Council of Korean and Japanese UIMs work together for In Myeong-jin's release, to which the churches in the two countries responded positively.

Sensitive to international opinion, the state tried to stop the communication between the UIM and its international allies. On June 17, 1978, the airport authorities denied extending the visa of Steven Lavender, who had been sent to the YDP-UIM from Australia, and deported the missionary in his bare feet. This was to prevent him from coming into the country to leave with additional news of what was really happening in South Korea.[8]

The repression under Park Chung Hee reached its peak with the death of Kim Gyeong-sook during the police's violent dispersal of the YH workers occupying the NDP headquarters on August 11, 1979. The authorities framed the incident as an example of the disorder that the Communist sympathizers in the UIM had been inciting.

Manipulated by the UIM ministers, who believe it is their Christian duty to build a society ruled by the proletariat [. . .] the officers of the labor union at the YH Trading Company caused great social disorder and conspired to subvert both our state and society.[9]

The authorities arrested Myeong-jin, Moon Dong-hwan, Lee Moon-young, Ko Un, and Seo Gyeong-seok along with three union officers under charges of conspiring to incite the YH Incident. The Supreme Prosecutor's Office activated a task force to investigate the "infiltration of industrial occupations by external forces," which lasted from August 17 to 30. The task force said that "while the UIMs are no longer suspected of having links to the Communists, some of the pastors have gone beyond pure religion and the gospel. We found that some incited the workers to unlawful agitation in violation of the labor laws, all under the pretense of doing industrial ministry."[10] Even after clearing their names of being Communists, the UIMs were still being labeled as harmful dissident groups.

The media was instructed to toe the line. MBC led the charge by denouncing the UIM on national television on August 17, 1979, followed by the national articles printed by *Seoul Newspaper* (August 21, 1979), *Joongang Daily* (August 24, 1979), *Hankook Ilbo* (August 28, 1979), and *Kyunghyang Shinmun* (August 28, 1979). Around the same time, Youngnak Church (led at that time by Rev. Park Jo-joon) cut its financial support for Cho Chi Song, caving under pressures from the KCIA.[11]

The YH Incident and the Busan-Masan Democratic Protests on October 15 signaled that the Yushin regime was coming to an end. Ten days later, on October 26, Park Chung Hee was assassinated. Some of the Christian activists called his assassination the "YHWH Incident," alluding to the YH Incident and suggesting that God's judgment had finally fallen upon the ruler who had persecuted so many.[12]

Something curious about Cho Chi Song is that he never served a term in jail. Despite his prominent role in the UIM, Cho was only interrogated or temporarily detained at most. Some might think this was evidence of shirking responsibility and making the other missioners take the fall for the ministry. The truth was that Cho Chi Song simply knew how to avoid unnecessary risks. He had escaped North Korea and survived the treacherous years of war. He had seen both sides of the ideological divide killing each other. It was second nature for him to refrain from saying any more than he had to, especially the things that exposed him to unnecessary risks. Even when facing a seasoned intelligence officer in interrogation, he never said any more than "I only work to support the workers within the boundaries of the law."

This was the exception to the trend. Many of the democratic intellectuals in the 1970s and 1980s were so occupied with the struggle against the dictatorship that they engaged in an abundance of adversarial rhetoric. Cho, by contrast, refrained from saying anything publicly about politics. The only issues he talked about were the rights of the workers and the issues in the workplace. Even with its highly politicized regulations designed to crack down on even the slimmest opposition, the state could not find the pretext for punishing Cho except for violating its repressive labor regulations.[13] This explained why the authorities suddenly required the ministry to pay its missioners' payroll tax, despite the income of clergy not being a taxable category. It was grasping at straws.

The Great Repression under the *Shingunbu*

After the death of Park Chung Hee, a new faction of military officers known as the Shingunbu took power and frustrated the desire for democracy once again. When the people of Gwangju rose up to protest this, the new junta labeled them rioters and violently murdered them. The hope for democracy was dashed from May 18 to 27, 1980.

The Shingunbu issued orders to arrest every democracy activist throughout the country. In Myeong-jin was leading a two-day retreat for the small-group workers when he was taken away on May 17. Cho Chi Song was out of the country, having left for Australia for the WCC World Mission Conference. He was transferring to another flight in Japan when he heard the news of May 18. His associates warned him not to come back to the country.

After delaying his return for a while, Cho came back on July 13. Immediately, agents from the Joint Investigation Headquarters took him away from the mission for questioning. Three days later, Shin Chul-young was also taken by the Yeongdeungpo police for questioning. With three missioners in simultaneous detention, the YDP-UIM was paralyzed.

In Myeong-jin was sent to the Seodaemun Detention Center on July 15. He had suffered severe beatings and torture by the time of his release on August 9. Cho Chi Song was subjected to sleepless interrogations in the basement of a counter-espionage interrogation facility. The interrogators threatened him by saying that he could get himself killed if he was not careful. Shin Chul-young was questioned for an entire week, allegedly for distributing literature about what happened in Gwangju.

Around 70 union officers and workers who had a relationship with the YDP-UIM[14] were also taken away by the Joint Investigation Headquarters. They were part of the 500 "UIM-related" activists who were being investigated. Some were placed on a list that barred them from reentering the factories, some were designated for "social purification" and sent to the Samchung Reeducation Camp.

The mission came under heavy surveillance. Nobody visited the center that once bustled with workers. The DSC, KCIA, central police intelligence, and two different local police branches constantly monitored it from an inn across the street.[15] The small group of workers were also placed on a list that barred them from getting another job. The missioners could no longer directly support the workers in a labor dispute because of the law against "third party interference."

In the face of the great repression and Gwangju tragedy, the YDP-UIM called for 40 days of prayer starting on June 1, 1980. The theme was to intercede for the imprisoned missioners, ministry, workers, and the country. The worship hall was left open every day from 6:00 a.m. to 10:00 a.m. Anyone could come in to pray. A cumulative total of 313 individuals had stopped on July 10.[16] The Yeongdeungpo Labor Church also held a series of special worship services from October 24 to 26, inviting Rev. Go Young-geun as the speaker. They were meant to provide the workers with consolation and courage. About 800 people participated. The YDP-UIM also created a reading room and music room inside the mission center in August to allow workers to find some reprieve through reading, music, singing, cinema, and other cultural activities.

On January 1981, Cho Chi Song decided he needed to send In Myeong-jin away for a while to prevent his health from deteriorating irreversibly. He received the Yeongdeungpo UIM Committee's permission to send him to Australia for his studies, where he could stay in the care of Rev. John Brown, the general secretary of the Australian Presbyterian World Mission (APWM). In Myeong-jin visited multiple congregations of the Uniting Church in Australia (UCA) that financially supported the YDP-UIM. Delivering the necklaces and key chains he had brought from Korea, the missioner asked for their prayers for the workers and missioners back in Korea. He was encouraged to see their enthusiastic support. After two years, In Myeong-jin recovered his health and returned to Korea.

On August 3, 1981, Shin Chul-young was arrested again for his involvement with Lee Tae-bok and the creation of the Confederation of Democratic Workers. He was sentenced to two years in prison. The YDP-UIM called for nationwide worship service to pray for his release on October 25. Shin Chul-young was tortured in the Namyoung interrogation facility before being put in prison. He was released on probation in May of the following year.

On April 18, 1982, the KCAO hosted an ecumenical prayer service to intercede on behalf of the people who were in prison. The participants, however, went beyond the original intent and issued a statement that was critical of the United States government in its response to a fire in the US Cultural Center in Busan. Kim Gyeong-nak and In Myeong-jin had signed the statement and were taken in for questioning. Their involvement also provided additional fodder to fuel the state's renewed smear campaign. The government claimed the statement was the product of "manipulation by the UIM groups that have anti-American and pro-Communist sympathies." Every media outlet was mobilized to launch a month-long attack and distortion against the UIMs.[17]

Conservative organizations like the Veterans Association, War Veterans Association, and Korea Freedom Federation flooded the YDP-UIM with threat mails and phone calls. They issued public statements criticizing the UIMs as "Communist sympathizers, seditious dissidents, and anti-American supporters of a liberation theology that is linked to the guerrilla fighters of South America."

Hong Ji-young, a mysterious writer known to be a former KCIA employee, collected such accusations and set them in a highly readable text titled *The Truth of the YDP-UIM*. The book was distributed to the government offices, banks, schools, media centers, and companies. Hong also wrote several other booklets with similar contents, including *Korean Christianity and Communism, The Logic and Practice of Political Theology, What the UIM Wants,* and *The Problem with UIM.* He also criticized the UIMs in several speaking events for pro-government organizations and businesses.

News stories on the topic often featured the image of the YDP-UIM center with its signage. It thus became the face of all the UIMs in the country along with their infamy. Schoolchildren walking by purposefully took the longer route to avoid going near the "den of Communists."

The workers associated with the YDP-UIM also became targets. They were often ostracized in their workplaces and reassigned to more difficult jobs or locations that were too far for them to commute. They were pressured to leave their unions and denounce the UIM. Those who refused were fired for any pretext the company could find. A list of workers associated with the YDP-UIM and the worker-controlled unions was shared throughout the factories, making it very difficult for them to get reemployed and therefore threatening their livelihood. This kind of persecution was not unique to Yeongdeungpo. The same was experienced in Incheon, Bupyeong, Cheongju, Masan, Changwon, Gumi, and any other area with a UIM.

The layoffs, arrests, and flight of the workers associated with the UIMs weakened the missions' ties with the labor unions. One by one, truly worker-controlled unions were destroyed throughout the country. By the summer of 1982, only two of them had survived the ruthless persecution of the Chun Doo Hwan regime: the Control Data Union and the Wonpoong Textiles Union.

Then, in July 1982, the workers of Control Data also lost their jobs. This was because the company was about to withdraw from South Korea. The government and media blamed the workers and the UIMs for causing the company to fail with their activism, although the truth was that the company was closing its old Korean plants to shift its focus to a different kind of production. To the government, the truth was not important. What mattered was the opportunity to turn public opinion against the UIM. Baseless propaganda coined the memorable phrase "*dosan* (都産, UIM) brings *dosan* (倒産, bankruptcy)."[18] By September, things had taken such a bad turn that even the Wonpoong Union lost its leaders to arrests and was driven out of its workplace.

To counter the assault on the UIM, the NCCK Youth Committee called for a prayer rally on August 5 to intercede for the workers of Control Data and the union leaders in prison. On September 13, two groups of the young and progressive members of the PCK clergy—the Association for New Missions and Association for Current Ministry—held a joint seminar on "The Past, Present, and Future of the PCK UIM." Those present in the seminar expressed their support for the UIMs and urged the PCK General Assembly to demonstrate its resolve to protect them. Toward the end of September, the 67th General Assembly responded, designating Sunday, October 31, as a day of remembering those who were in prison. It also delegated the task of addressing all UIM-related affairs, including the YDP-UIM, to the Committee on Church and Social Issues.

On November 13, the NCCK and its six-member denominations held a combined prayer service for the protection of the UIMs. They gave the Wonpoong Union workers a time slot to speak about their experience under persecution. The hosts also distributed a pamphlet titled *The Field and Freedom of Missions* to help the attendees understand the intent behind the UIM. From November 29 to December 1, the Council of Churches for UIM Policy (CCUP) called for an emergency meeting to resolve the protection of UIM.

The great repression of 1982 was far more coordinated and sinister than before. While the Yushin regime had relied on brute force and intimidation, the Shingunbu regime made heavy use of its media control and propaganda. Prominent conservative figures appeared on television and the national papers to consistently feed the public with a negative image of the UIMs.

The YDP-UIM was struggling to stay afloat, let alone provide support for the workers. Most of the small groups had been destroyed and their members were driven out of the factories. The missioners lost morale when the PCK insisted that they revert to using less activistic and more ecclesiastical means. Cho Chi Song's chronic migraines had also become worse, causing his frequent hospitalizations. In Myeong-jin succeeded Cho as the general secretary. Looking back, he said those years of the great repression under Chun Doo Hwan was "the gloomiest spring in 100 years of Christian missions in Korea."[19]

Bad for Business?

The persecution of the UIM was inseparably tied to the political and economic situation of South Korea. The regimes that took power through military force lacked legitimacy and could only maintain their hold on power through the support of a handful of political generals and capitalists. In return for exclusive access to foreign aid and currency, business owners swore their allegiance to the regime's economic policy and provided the rulers with needed political funds. Therefore, when the UIMs joined hands with the labor movement, both the state and corporations had their reasons to fear the organized discontent at the low wages, poor working conditions, and union suppression.

"Whenever we submitted a complaint," Cho Chi Song said, "the labor authorities were as unhappy as the companies were. Sure, we addressed them as 'the esteemed commissioner,' but none of us really esteemed each other, did we?" [20]

The state originally tolerated the UIMs because their initial goal was to proselytize. They had nothing to do with the labor movement. However, the UIMs shifted focus in the late 1960s. This resulted in the workers gaining more bargaining power. The employers felt their exclusive access to profit was now under threat. The state worried about its means of keeping the businesses disciplined.

From a management standpoint, paying less than a living wage was bad for remaining competitive. In the long term, business survival depended on sharing the profit with the workers who created it. Yet the employers were preoccupied with maximizing short-term profits, mainly because they could. They could always call on the readily available assistance of the state whenever they had to suppress the workers. Of course, the state, in theory, was accountable to everyone in the public. As such, it needed a cover to justify its utter partiality. The excuse it found was that the UIMs were inciting workers to drive the companies out of business. Since it was the government's job to prevent the social confusion of chain bankruptcies, they had every reason to be prejudiced against the UIM and their associates. Cho Chi Song, however, argued the contrary.

> *I actually believe the UIMs helped the companies. [. . .]*
> *Think about it. All you have to do is listen to the rightful*
> *demands of the workers, pay them a living wage, treat them*
> *with respect, and give them a pleasant work environment.*
> *Then productivity would go up as well as society's respect*
> *for your company. Wouldn't that have been much more*
> *profitable?* [21]

The logic is better appreciated today. Investing in people pays off in the long term. Cho's statement indicated that the YDP-UIM had more than just the moral ground compared to the companies; it had a superior business strategy, ahead of its time. Cho used to say "the UIM is not just about saving the workers, it's also about saving their employers."[22] It was baseless to say that the UIM's goal was to cause the bankruptcy of the companies.

Nor was there a single company that had gone bankrupt because of the YDP-UIM or its associated labor activism in the 1970s and 1980s. On the contrary, productivity rose for most of the factories where the YDP-UIM helped organize a worker-controlled labor union. In the case of Wonpoong Textiles, the union even pulled the company out of a bankruptcy.[23] According to the labor ministry, there were about 130 companies at the end of 1979 whose workers had ties to the UIM. Control Data was the only company that blamed the ministry for its bankruptcy, and even that turned out to be a fabrication.

Cho consistently maintained that a mature society should not generalize every labor movement based on the extreme behaviors of a few. Even the extreme behaviors could be understood as instinctive reactions to the constant infringement upon one's basic rights. Cho believed that once the companies started respecting the workers' autonomy and treating the unions as equal partners in a negotiation, most of the extreme behavior would stop.

Because of this, Cho always emphasized the importance of using peaceful methods. Every leadership training in the YDP-UIM included a segment on industrial peace. "Peace is assured by the balance of powers," Cho said, "which means peace in the industrial workplace is only possible when the workers have as much power (through organization) as their employers do (through capital)." Balance was the reason he was preferential to the workers, who were relatively weak.

An angry worker once joked that he would go and destroy the company's production equipment, since the employer was also breaking the laws. Cho immediately jumped at him and reminded him:

Do not even joke about damaging the equipment. We are
here to demand that the employers keep the law. If we start

breaking it, we would be denying the legitimacy of our own
movement. You can despise the owners, but do not despise the
factories. You have to treat your workplace like it's your own
home. [. . .] That is the moral high ground that gives you
your power.[24]

The UIMs fought the charge that they caused business failures, which they believed amounted to gross defamation. The truth was that Control Data was pulling out of Korea because it was closing down its older production lines. It was also doing this globally, not just in Korea. Humored by the slogan, "*dosan* (the UIM) brings *dosan* (bankruptcy)," Cho slapped back with a catchphrase of his own: "*Yeongsan* (the YDP-UIM) brings *Cheonsan* (the kingdom of heaven)."

On March 1982, the Control Data Labor Union sent a letter to the corporate headquarters in the United States, demanding the reinstatement of the union officers who had been wrongfully fired. They also sent the same letter to the president, secretary of labor, and the churches of the United States. Of these, the churches answered the workers' call and protested the layoffs to Control Data's headquarters. As a result, during a general shareholders' meeting, the company dismissed the board director and local executive responsible for Control Data Korea, holding them accountable for the worker suppression and wrongful terminations.

On June 3, company executives from the United States came to Korea in an attempt to discuss a solution to the issue. The union officers and members talked with them well into 2:00 a.m. inside the union office. Mistakenly judging from their prolonged silence that the messengers had been taken hostage, the Control Data headquarters called the South Korean police. Around 40 union members were taken away, and some of them were beaten by the police.

On July 10, about 50 union members gathered to protest the incident and demanded a meeting with the labor minister. The police took them again. Between July 13 and 15, the union officers were locked up and beaten by the custodial workers in the company. The custodians also held pickets against the union, which said "out with the UIM's Han Myeong-hee, we can build our own company." The media raced to cover the story, making it into national news.[25]

The issue began to escalate in the United States as the churches criticized Control Data for targeting unionized workers and allowing the baseless accusations to continue against the Christian UIMs. This compelled the headquarters to publicly clarify that they were closing the South Korean plants because their assembly lines were no longer necessary after their transition to producing computer chips. It also added that the company had laid off 340 workers and placed thousands more on leave throughout the world. The issue was not unique to South Korea, let alone caused by the UIMs. The US embassy followed suit and sent the head of its political section and a labor officer to the YDP-UIM on July 23. The two apologized for the misdirected accusations against the UIMs and gave the missioners copies of the foreign articles that corrected the record.

The damage was already done, however. State propaganda using a submissive media turned out to be a huge success. The phrase "*dosan* (UIM) brings *dosan* (bankruptcy)" circulated the factories like a slogan, as large factories began sharing their lists of workers affiliated with the UIM. They even distributed a checklist to their workers to help them determine whether someone was a *dosan* agent, kindly telling them to stay away from "friendly and well-mannered workers who often talk about what's wrong in the company and offer to introduce you to a good program, leave work exactly on time, or invite you to join their meetings." The vigilance was shared by the supervisors who began monitoring every move of a worker suspected of working with the *dosan*, asking whom they met, what they talked about, etc.

The violence of the reaction was a testament of how deeply UIM and the associated labor movements have challenged the order of the day. This earned the mission both friends and foes. On the one hand, the UIMs were gradually being ostracized by a society that accepted the propaganda at face value. On the other hand, conscientious actors, democracy activists, and the global church recognized and lauded UIM as the final bastion of democracy that was among the last who dared to resist the will of a dictatorship backed by the military.

Under the World's Spotlight

News of the urban and industrial mission's persecution in the hands of the dictatorship attracted the attention of the foreign press.

> *Journalists dispatched to Korea or Japan from American outlets like* The Washington Post *or* New York Times *frequently covered our stories. I believe it was because the things that happened around here (in the workplaces) seemed like things from a century ago. They felt responsible to tell the world that these things still happened somewhere on the face of the Earth.*
>
> *Did the foreign journalists come here themselves?*
>
> *They came, they took our public statements then translated them. [. . .] Foreign journalists came by our center quite frequently.*
>
> *So that's how it was back then.*
>
> *The UIM got itself on the daily papers of many different countries. [. . .] It's just that our own never had a good word about it.*[26]

The foreign press was a source of great support as seen from Cho Chi Song's perspective. It usually had a better understanding of the truth about the UIM and often wrote articles that were positive about it. It also helped that Cho could articulate the position of the YDP-UIM directly in English. At a time when it was still rare to find an article about Korea within its pages, *TIME* magazine printed the following article about Cho Chi Song on the January 3, 1977, issue under the title, "A Song for the Workers of Seoul":

Chang Hyang Soon, 22, has just lost her job as a bus conductor. Dressed in a simple blue suit, she sits worriedly in a tiny office in Seoul's grimy industrial suburb of Yongdungpo [sic], telling her story with mounting bitterness. It seems that she left her company dormitory to buy skin cream for an allergy, but failed to ask for her employer's permission. She was not only summarily fired from the $60-a-month job, she says, but was physically abused by a superior who roughly twisted her arms. As she speaks, a slight figure in a worker's blue shirt and trousers sits perched on a desk, swinging his stockinged feet to and fro while he listens. He will support her complaint to a government labor office, he promises. If that fails, as it usually does, he will mount a campaign—petitions to the company, letters, phone calls—in the hope that the company will relent.

The listener is the Rev. Cho Chi Song, 47, a mild-mannered Presbyterian minister who for the past ten years has run the Yongdungpo Urban Industrial Mission amid the factories, the shanties and the mushrooming concrete apartments across the Han River from Seoul proper. Cho's mission is a few ground-floor rooms in one of those gray slab walk-ups, rooms that are rarely empty. Each month more than 5,000 people most of them not formally Christian, come to the mission for some kind of help or encouragement. Last week alone the mission had 72 scheduled meetings on subjects ranging from labor law to flower arranging, birth control to the Bible. The mission also had its usual three or four harassing calls a day from the Korean Central Intelligence Agency.

The KCIA seems to think that the Rev. Mr. Cho is a labor agitator. In the circuitous manner that seems prudent for social change in South Korea these days, he is. Though the Yongdungpo [sic] mission provides such mundane services as a credit union and consumer-goods cooperative, its main

energies are devoted to labor reform—a difficult process in a
country where President Park Chung Hee's emergency decrees
forbid strikes. Cho uses public protest instead. "We always
have three or four labor-management disputes going," he told
TIME Tokyo Bureau Chief William Stewart. "Last year there
was a company with a 90-hour week. We asked the managers
to change, but they never listened. So we organized our
workers. One thousand wrote one letter each to the company
every day. One thousand others made 1,000 telephone calls to
the company every day. We sent out about 10,000 pamphlets.
Then the Washing Post wrote an article, and the manager's
son telephoned from the US. Now the company has an eight-
hour day and gives holidays as well. The KCIA didn't like
that."

Though his social gospel is often called communistic
by his critics, Cho is a refugee from North Korea, where his
family were prosperous Christian farmers. He fled south in
1950, worked at odd jobs while putting himself through
Seoul's Kyonggi College and Presbyterian Theological
Seminary. It was at the seminary that some American
missionaries from Japan introduced him to the need for
industrial missions. He joined work projects in coal mines
and textile factories and became enraged at the long hours
and harrowing working conditions in those places. Now, says
Cho, South Korean workers are becoming more and more
impatient for their share of the country's burgeoning economy.
"There are all kinds of pressure from the police, the KCIA,
and business. But the workers' power is growing, and it
cannot be destroyed."

Cho acknowledges that his own denomination is "very
conservative" in South Korea and that he receives scant
outside support: $1,500 a year from US Presbyterians,
some help from a few sympathetic local churches. Many of
the workers close to Cho would like him to start his own

congregation, but he resists that idea. "I don't talk about the church and religion," he says. "I don't even pray in the same way anymore. I listen to people's problems and I ask God, "How can I find a way?"[27]

Compared to the domestic press, which repeated the misinformation and negative characterization supplied by the government, the foreign press demonstrated a higher commitment to discussing the facts about the UIM. It gave a much more accurate description of the mission's activities, as well as a much fairer assessment of the role it played. It also gave the YDP-UIM a platform to talk about the local workplace, raising international awareness of the labor conditions in South Korea. Influential outlets like *The Washington Post, New York Times, L.A. Times, NHK,* and *Chrismon* gave the Korean UIM and its persecution an equal amount of coverage as the broader democracy movements, making the UIM a symbol of democratization in South Korea. This was partly why the regime turned to the press and propaganda as its preferred means of repression. It was risky to use physical force when the entire world was watching.

Foreign missionaries to Korea were another important channel for sharing the truth with the outside world. In fact, relaying information from Korea became the primary task of the missionaries assigned to the YDP-UIM. Foreigners were exempt from body searches in the airport, making the missionaries the ideal messengers to carry important reports and photographs out of the country. The missionaries were also very helpful in translating a variety of documents from Korean to a foreign language and vice versa. Steven Lavender, among others, considered it an honor to spend his days in the cramped basement of the YDP-UIM.

The difficulties of my life were trivial compared to trials endured by the workers I saw. It was inspiring to work with the courageous workers and local missioners who acted on

behalf of justice despite the dangers they or their families
could face. That memory still moves me to this day.[28]

In Cho's memory, the missionaries provided the critical strength
necessary to withstanding the repression. In particular, he remembers
the help of Robert Hoffman from the United States, who was given the
Korean name Hahm Boo-man, and of Richard Wootton and Steven
Lavender from Australia. Cho also regretted the fact that while George
Ogle was later awarded the Civil Merit Medal for his contributions to
Korea's democracy, Steven Lavender, who like Ogle was subjected to
deportation for his service in Korea, was never recognized and honored
likewise.

The nexus through which the global church sent its support
to the YDP-UIM was the World Council of Churches (WCC).
Specifically, the WCC was the organization that first introduced and
later sustained the Korean UIM through the CCM-UIM. At first,
churches in the United States sent a monthly gift of $1,500 through
the WCC, enabling the PCK IEC to begin its first activities. Most of
the operational expenses of the YDP-UIM were also funded by the
money raised by the WCC. The WCC also laid the bridge for the
YDP-UIM to meet the special envoy for human rights sent by Jimmy
Carter shortly after his inauguration to share the state of labor rights
in South Korea.

There were actually many different groups and individuals who
were willing to support the YDP-UIM financially. In the interest of
total financial transparency, however, Cho directed all of them to send
their gifts through the WCC, no matter how large or how small they
were. Even the collection of one or two dollars raised by an elderly knitting club in Australia were sent to the YDP-UIM through the WCC.
This was the outgrowth of Cho's experience serving on the WCC's
UIM programs review board. He had learned then that a relationship
with the council could easily expand into a relationship with the many
churches of the world.

The YDP-UIM was generally trusted by its foreign supporters including the CCA and WCC. Most of the funds that Cho Chi Song requested were sent without objection. Such confidence was the product of the YDP-UIM's long and deliberate effort to nurture its partnerships.

For instance, the YDP-UIM was very thorough in writing its program reports, covering not only the purpose and amount of expenditure but also the number of people who participated, a detailed description of how it proceeded, and anything else that helped the givers paint a picture of what was happening on the ground.

The givers, in turn, practically gave the YDP-UIM total latitude with how it spent the money, foregoing the requirement of receipts. That did not stop the YDP-UIM from collecting them.

I would like to take this opportunity to thank our Christian brothers and sisters for keeping our mission in your hearts and sharing our burden in our Lord from overseas. I thank God for granting me to partake in this industrial mission and to stand strong with your churches, united in faith and spirit. [. . .] Though we can offer nothing else in return, we give you our word that we will humbly keep our place amid this suffering, strengthened by your warm support and continued prayer. I thank God for the kingdom that will come at last [. . .] which shall not crumble even in the history of tribulation in the 1970s. [. . .]

Our future likely lies not on the wide and easy, but on the narrow and difficult path (Matthew 7:13–14). Yet, we will not stop the march. If we do not reach the destination, our successors will. The journey has already begun for the Korean UIM.[29]

Cho sent countless English letters like the foregoing asking for prayer and support to Christians outside the country. He also built a network of contacts in foreign government agencies, the ILO, UNCHR, worker support organizations, and any other group he could call upon to write the Korean labor authorities to protest a certain action or inaction. This proved very helpful in the critical moments. Thanks to the early lessons in the importance of building a broad network of solidarity, the YDP-UIM was able to call upon their friends without when they were most isolated within the country. The overwhelming support that flooded in was able to counteract many of the disadvantages that had followed.

Building the YDP-UIM Center

Cho Chi Song had wished for very long that the YDP-UIM could be housed in its own mission center. Building a "Christian Labor Center" was, in fact, a long-term objective he had put in the pamphlets introducing the YDP-UIM ever since he arrived. The need for space was especially accentuated when he stopped leading worships in the factories and began meeting the workers outside. They needed somewhere they could meet consistently to learn and train. YDP-UIM had proposed raising 20 million won to build a new mission center as early as in 1968. When the PCK and KMC merged their UIM ministries in Yeongdeungpo the following year, the need for a proper center became even greater. The two denominations agreed to raise funds for the project.[30] The Korean churches did not have resources to spare, however. It was not easy raising the target amount. When the small-group movement began in the early 1970s, the rented space used as the YDP-UIM offices became too crowded. The need to build an independent center became more urgent.

> *The flats were just 18 pyeongs (60 square meters), maybe 20 (70 square meters). [. . .] It wasn't much space, and we tried to have 16 small groups a day. It got so crowded that the workers had to meet inside the bathroom. It was a packed can of sardines. We had to house 200 meetings a month with a cumulative traffic of 5,000 people. [. . .] That was why I thought we needed to build our own building.*[31]

The workers also needed space for assembly when the flurry of labor disputes began. The rented apartments just would not suffice. Nor could the mission rent a proper office. Most of the building owners were reluctant to house the YDP-UIM because of the propaganda.

At first, the YDP-UIM was met with strong opposition when it first brought up the building project to the WCC and the UPCUSA. Their UIM staff believed a group could not focus on social activism when it became the owner of a building. Movements were driven by organizing and uniting people. Building ownership was a distraction from the efforts to reach out and could create complacency. George Todd, who at the time was leading the UIM in the WCC, was especially vocal. He asked how the YDP-UIM planned on maintaining a building in the tiny, urban area of Yeongdeungpo and insisted the project will do its social mission no good. He went so far as to say that raising a building will be the death of the mission and its concrete walls the walls of mausoleum.

The YDP-UIM responded by pointing out that his correspondents already were housed in a decent office. He tried his best to help them see the situation in Korea, sending photographs of the tiny offices that were already full with a few desks and a conference table. They also explained the general lack of sympathy for the UIM in the locale, making it difficult to rent a space. Those who initially opposed the construction eventually relented at Cho's persistence. The WCC decided that the YDP-UIM was deserving of its own center, given its track record, and gave the project a green light.

The WCC-UIM connected the YDP-UIM to the churches in West Germany, which in turn sent surveyors from the government's finance ministry and Protestant Association for Cooperation in Development (EZE, Evangelische Zentralstelle für Entwicklungshilfe) to determine the necessary level of funding. The YDP-UIM submitted a proposal endorsed by 18 different organizations with which the YDP-UIM had a relationship, including the PCK General Assembly, FKTU, and ILO. The German church officially announced its intent to support the project and received a blueprint of the three-story mission center to review. The original plan was to build a total of seven stories to provide the YDP-UIM staff with lodging, but Cho gave up the idea when it became apparent the cost would be prohibitive.

Oh Jae-sik, then the WCC's director for development and CCA's director for UIM, connected the YDP-UIM to West Germany's EZE. Thanks to the connection, the YDP-UIM secured additional funding for the project when Cho Chi Song stopped by Germany on his way back from Chicago in the spring of 1971.[32] As a strong believer in Christian activism as the key to Korea's democracy, Oh was very proactive in raising foreign support for the Korean industrial and urban mercy ministries. Oh always provided the amount of money Cho Chi Song requested for the YDP-UIM. Cho, however, did not like getting more than what was necessary. Once, when the WCC sent an additional sum of money, Cho sent it back, saying the YDP-UIM never requested it.

Fundraisers were organized throughout the world. Members of the global church raced to show support for the Korean UIM. It became apparent how deeply they had been affected by the stories. They saw in the UIM a biblical resistance to the unjust powers and wealth to which all Christians were called but so few actually reached. The respect and admiration were palpable.

The project went into a hiatus when two missioners on staff, In Myeong-jin and Kim Gyeong-nak, were imprisoned in 1974, which was followed by the KMC's break from the YDP-UIM in 1975. This created the question of who retained custody of the construction project. The KMC decided it will build its own center in Incheon while the PCK continued to be responsible for the center in Yeong-deungpo. The process left Cho disillusioned about the construction, and he almost gave up on the project. As his successor as the general secretary, In Myeong-jin finalized the construction talks with the German church in the fall of 1977.[33] The German church had promised its support for the construction. The problem was purchasing the land. The funds by the denomination came up short. The YDP-UIM missioners sold their homes and got additional support from Youngnak Church. Still, the mission needed just a little more money. This gap was covered by individual contributions from the workers associated with the YDP-UIM and members of the Labor Church.

The workers were motivated by the fact that a complete reliance on foreign aid for the construction of their mission could weaken the organization's sense of agency. Reasoning that the center will be used as their own home, they resolved to contribute as much as they could. The "offering of the workers" was thus inscribed onto the bronze plate of recognition at the entrance of the center when it was completed.

Construction started with Rev. Lee Jeong-hak appointed as the project director by the YDP-UIM Committee. The original plan was to purchase the land in the name of one of the missioners, but the owner said they were too well known to sell the land to them. The missioners barely managed to get the owner to sell the land in the name of Rev. Lee Jeong-hak, who was the chair of the project committee. This was thanks to the slightest oversight in surveillance by the KCIA and its attempt to obstruct the project. Stories were later told of a certain detective being lambasted by the KCIA for failing to prevent the land purchase. The detective, to be named only by his alias "Dahm Go-gil," had actually developed something of a relationship with the YDP-UIM, having been its overseer for a very long time. The missioners hosted him for table tennis in the first-floor lobby, trading insignificant bits of information for his occasional service in delivering money to the prison for inmates related to the YDP-UIM. They even received discreet warnings when there were orders for an arrest. Once, Detective Dahm warned Cho Chi Song and Shin Chul-young that there was an order for their arrest for their involvement in the YMCA "undercover wedding." Cho said he would stay behind to watch the YDP-UIM, but told Shin to go seek refuge. Dahm offered to keep him in his house for one night.

Shin Chul-young was a student in the College of Engineering in Seoul National University when Kim Jin-soo died in 1971. He volunteered to staff the funeral service as part of this industrial social studies club and later spent one of his breaks working undercover in Fujika's oil furnace factory with the help of Cho Seung-hyeok of the Incheon UIM. Years later, the YDP-UIM hired him as a labor expert to help maneuver the very tight corner the YDP-UIM had found itself amid the intense repression of 1978. He was also the only construction expert on the YDP-UIM staff with a degree in mechanical engineering and relevant work experience in the Hanyang Housing Company. As such, as soon as he arrived in Yeongdeungpo on July 18, he was tasked with overseeing construction.

The project started in the midst of many difficulties. All of the YDP-UIM account books and files had been seized by the authorities on May 1. Each of the missioners was called in for questioning and In Myeong-jin was put in jail. Then, Steven Lavender was deported in June. Nevertheless, construction began on October 23 with a worship service.

In order to supervise the project directly, the YDP-UIM limited the floor space of the building to 245 pyeongs, right below the regulatory threshold of 250 pyeongs (826 square meters) above which it would have had to contract the work out to an external construction company. The missioners concentrated on getting the building up. In Myeong-jin started overseeing the project, but he was arrested. Cho Chi Song, who had taken a sick leave, came back to take his place. He stood next to the mixer and wrote down the exact ratio of cement, sand, and gravel that went into the concrete. He told Shin Chul-young to do likewise, telling him to go around with a ruler to measure every brick according to measurements on the blueprint. If they were off, Shin had to take the bricks apart before the concrete cured to lay them again. Thanks to this level of attention to detail, the YDP-UIM center avoided the fate of many other buildings that had been built hastily and carelessly in the

1970s. It has been a sturdy fixture of Yeongdeungpo for 43 years at the time of this writing. Agents of the police, KCIA, and DSC watched the whole process from an inn across the street. At the behest of the state, the press railed about a building going up in the middle of the capital that was funded by Communists through the WCC. The missioners of the YDP-UIM ignored the noise and concentrated on completing the project, even if only to defy their oppressors. Every brick was laid with the urgency of a soldier who was building a fort.

Toward the end of construction, the YDP-UIM sent an invitation to the German ambassador to attend the opening ceremony, fixing the date as July 8, 1979. This was a move to ensure the authorities would not sabotage the safety inspection required to open the building for use. One last wrench was thrown into the timeline when the accountant suddenly refused to sign the papers that needed to be submitted to the German EZE to declare the project complete. Fortunately, Shin Chul-young personally knew another accountant. The papers were signed and submitted, passing the ball to the other side of the court.

Now the district office had an emergency. The center had been built according to its blueprint. The German ambassador was going to attend the opening ceremony. Unless the district office completed the required inspections before July 8, it would have to suffer the public humiliation of having a foreign dignitary attend the opening ceremony of a perfectly fine building that it failed to give a permit. For once, the public authorities bent over backward to help the YDP-UIM get its permit before the ceremony. This demonstrated the broader irony of a government that was authoritarian within but submissive to the opinions without for their lack of legitimacy.

Two-thousand people gathered at the opening ceremony on July 8, 1979. The German ambassador expressed congratulations for the new center and took the opportunity to refute the propaganda: "Don't believe the baseless rumors that this center was built with money from a Communist state [. . .] it was our government and church of [West]

Germany who sent the money, and not a penny of it has come from a Communist."[34]

Despite the troubles that happened in the process, the YDP-UIM center was one of the finer buildings for an urban industrial ministry both by Korean and international standards. Some of the outside observers publicly commented that having become the owner of a luxurious building, the YDP-UIM would take a turn to the right, becoming too complacent to take action like it used to.

One of the dentistry volunteers later asked why the mission had installed such a large, expensive screen and projection equipment on the third-floor auditorium. The implied message was that it was an unnecessary luxury. Cho and the other missioners disagreed. "The workers are always too busy to even watch a movie," Cho said. "Our center needs to be a place where they can have a proper cinema experience that is no less than what they would have in the theaters. [. . .] We don't do our mission to make people poor. We do it to allow the workers to flourish as much as their employers."[35]

Cho Chi Song believed that even an impoverished worker ought to be able to enjoy as sophisticated a cultural life as the rest of society. Only then could the least among us dream and strive for progress and transformation in their lives. Designing the center to be as comfortable and well-equipped as possible was part of his ministry of serving the whole of the worker's being.

It was true that the project was already tight on funds. Nevertheless, the YDP-UIM invested in recreational features and making the center as comfortable as possible out of the belief that even the poorest workers needed to access the same kinds and quality of cultural life as the rest of society. This was what oriented them toward transformation and progress.

Even so, upon its completion, it was Cho who most regretted starting the project. He was so focused on finishing the job that he failed to notice how much time had passed. Now that the work was done, Cho felt he had spent far too much time and energy on raising a slab of concrete. He said he felt shame at not having directed the same effort to organizing more workers. He felt he could have organized a few thousand more if he had.

Despite Cho's worries, the center became a positive legacy. It continued to serve its original role as a space for supporting the workers. The landmark fight for the eight-hour workday in Haitai, for instance, was planned, launched, and sustained in the YDP-UIM building. Except for the period when the center was virtually in lockdown because of the *Shingunbu*'s "social purification policy," the YDP-UIM center in the early to mid-1980s was one of the few places where workers could gather in massive assembly. It was the home of the democratic movement of workers before the legalization of the Korean Confederation of Trade Unions. It even predated the gathering of the Korean Teachers and Education Workers Union. In 1986 alone, for instance, it served as the headquarter for the thirteen mid- to large-size labor rallies including the Labor Day rally, protests against the unjust barring of employees, a pay raise action, denunciation of wrongs, Gwangju commemoration, and a worker's culture festival.[36]

One of the landmark accomplishments made possible by the existence of a new space was the creation of the Korean Federation of Christian Workers (KFCW) at a time that the labor movement was heavily suppressed in the mid-1980s. A number of local churches in Yeongdeungpo where a LAIE branch organization had existed still had young workers who gathered as part of the church's industrial evangelism ministries. When some of them began participating in the labor movement, they needed someone to train and organize them. The YDP-UIM united with the successors of its old affiliates to provide timely support. The young Christian workers then held their founding ceremony and first general assembly in the YDP-UIM center, electing Yoo Dong-woo (author of *A Stone's Cry*) as the president and Han Myeong-hee (fired worker of Control Data) as the secretary general. Thus, the KFCW was born.[37]

As a church organization, the KFCW was relatively free to go in and out of the mission center to organize its training and assembly. It was a rare gift at a time when most worker rallies had been banned and they were allowed to organize nearly 2,000 workers, including many non-Christians, for a Labor Day rally. Later on, when Shin Dong-wook became the president, the KFCW held a weekly Wednesday Bible study in Yangpyeong-dong Church. Its leader, Lee Geun-bok, later compiled the materials and published a worker's Bible study guide titled *Meeting Jesus in the Workplace* (Nanumsa).

The YDP-UIM continued to use the center to serve those who had been marginalized in the changing labor environment after the democratization in 1987. To list some, the center was home to the Asian URM Diakonia Training, support for the irregularly employed workers including those in the E-land Group, therapeutic counseling for emotional laborers, and a homeless recovery community. It continued to house its holistic ministry, including the consumer cooperative, credit union, and Seongmunback Church (formerly Labor Church) among others.

Even so, after years of use, the structure came to require renovation to maintain its utility. The initial search for options in the 2000s gained renewed impetus in 2010 when Sohn Eun-jeong was the general secretary. The PCK designated the center as a historic Christian site, while the Korea Democracy Foundation (KDF) raised a large memorial stone there to recognize its role in bringing democracy to the country. The city of Seoul also recognized its historic value by designating it a "Future Heritage" site in 2013. Modern renovation became imperative if only for the sake of historic preservation. The ninth general secretary, Rev. Jin Bang-joo, sent a proposal to city hall offering to share the space in the mission with a public worker welfare center in exchange for financing the bulk of the building's renovation. The city of Seoul approved a special grant for the project in 2018. After three more years of raising the support of the Yeong-deungpo Presbytery, churches, organizations, and individuals, the mission finally started the project in February 2021 and reopened on November 11.[38]

The renovated center now houses a gallery of the ministry's history on the basement and first floors. The first floor also houses the consumer cooperative, the used goods store of the *Nonumaegi* cooperative for homeless recovery, and a dining area. The second floor houses the worker missions division, the *Shwim* therapy center, *Squirrel Fellowship*, international solidarity office, and pastor's office for the Seongmunbak Church. The third floor houses the worker support center's conference room and auditorium, which also serves as the worship space of Seongmunbak Church. The fourth and fifth floors house the worker support center's office, book café, and counseling rooms.

The Death Sentence

The PCK was the first among Korean Protestants to start an urban industrial ministry. As such, it was one of its heaviest investors, having built a nationwide network of UIM organizations and a very rigorous program for training their staff. Indeed, the PCK had a proud place among all of the nation's UIM ministries. The very capable individuals serving in the UIM also helped diversify the denomination, helping it to forge a thicker ecumenical network with the global church.

Cho Chi Song maintained a positive relationship with the higher denominational organizations, mainly the YDP-UIM's two presbyteries and the General Assembly Department of Evangelism. He also continuously created seminars and training programs for both the clergy and lay of the church to enhance their understanding of the UIM. Thanks to his hard work in trying to raise support among the church, there was a group of ministers that served as steadfast financial and moral supporters of the YDP-UIM. The National Organization of Presbyterian Women also provided the salaries for the UIM missioners in Yeongdeungpo, Gumi, and eastern Seoul. Such support was a testament to how much the church initially cherished the UIMs as one of the frontier missions and a way to share the burden and suffering of the working poor.

The most difficult challenge for the YDP-UIM was facing the opposition from inside the church. The persecution by the state and media were well within expectations. The stronger the wind of the storm, the deeper the roots of the YDP-UIM could grow. But when the very church (or rather, denomination) that was supposed to be the YDP-UIM's shield began repeating the same baseless accusations, it was more than enough to demoralize the missioners.

The YDP-UIM first clashed with the church during the struggle against mandatory worships in the companies. To remind readers, the workers of Daehan Textiles submitted two written requests to end the company's mandatory worship policy and a number of other wrongful employment practices in 1973. Four of the workers associated with the YDP-UIM were fired in retaliation. The workers responded by organizing an action to press for their reinstatement by petitioning a variety of outside groups. They also took their protest to the CEO's church.

At the YDP-UIM's suggestion, a group of young ministers of the PCK also organized an allied action for the reinstatement of the four workers. The CEO of Daehan Textiles struck back by printing and distributing leaflets across the country's churches accusing the YDP-UIM of obstructing Christian worship within its factories. This signaled the tension between the UIM and the PCK. The fact that the CEO of Daehan was also an elder of Dongshin Church, where Cho Chi Song had received his ordination, further exacerbated the issue.

When the issue became public, a group of ruling elders who were also business owners joined the fray on the side of their compatriot. A counter-movement began in opposition to the UIM. The unity among owners and supporters of capital who rallied around the CEO of Daehan proved to be quite powerful. Their concerted criticisms of the UIM later morphed into the mainline opposition movement within the PCK to the UIMs in the 1980s.

The more progressively oriented members of the clergy were fewer in number. They were, however, the denomination's opinion leaders as the most vocal spokespeople on all issues of ecumenical or social interest. The anti-UIM movement among the conservatives within the church would not become very salient in the 1970s. The PCK, therefore, was generally protective of the UIM even under the repression of the Yushin regime throughout the 1970s.

Part of this manifested in the adoption of a document titled "The PCK's Basic Stance on Urban Industrial Mission" by the 60th General Assembly in 1975, reaffirming the legitimacy of the UIM and issuing the following calls to the church. In keeping with the statement, the PCK showed strong support for the worker actions in Daehan Textiles, Pangrim Textiles, Namyoung Nylon, and Haitai Confectionery, all of which were key UIM-affiliated labor actions in the 1970s.[39]

When In Myeong-jin was arrested over the translation he used for Micah 2:1 in May 1978, the PCK vigorously defended him by criticizing the state for its politically motivated persecution of a Christian minister who was administering a religious ceremony.

The authorities who prosecuted a Christian minister preaching the word of God with the charge of breaking the ninth emergency presidential decree ought to realize that they can just as easily fall into the error of arbitrarily deciding what counts as the proper scope of Christian mission according to selfish political interests as they can fall into blasphemy.[40]

One can sense a slight change, however, in the denomination's stance in "The Principles and Guidelines for the UIM" adopted by the General Assembly in 1978. This, too, was a document that was meant to protect and support the UIM, which it does at a theological level, proclaiming the legitimacy of the UIM as an organ of the church for preaching the gospel that carries out public activities according to the constitution, creed, and theological beliefs of the PCK. The document, however, also prescribes a narrower scope and practical guidelines, seeking to place the UIMs under the tight control of the Central UIM Committee and their respective presbyteries.

> *The organization of an urban industrial ministry must receive confirmation by the UIM Committee of the Department of Evangelism of the General Assembly. The members of its staff must recognize the principles of industrial mission [laid out in this document]. [. . .] The ministry's main activities will be worship, Bible study, evangelism, counseling, instruction of the workers, and the like. Guidance may be provided to the workers for dealing with workplace issues as long as it remains within the boundaries of the law, but all solutions must be pursued after reporting the matter to the superior committee. [. . .] Petitioning to foreign recipients will only be allowed with permission with the Department of Evangelism of the General Assembly. The UIM missioners must not break with the constitution of the General Assembly. The rules for the employment, education, and training of the UIM ministry staffs shall be determined by the Central UIM Committee of the Department of Evangelism.*[41]

The purpose of such strengthened control was to prevent the UIM from providing anything more than the sentimental support for workers with which the average Christian could sympathize and prevent the ministries from becoming a direct part of a labor dispute, resulting in a conflict with the employers and the state. The YDP-UIM did not fully agree with the principles and guidelines. Even so, as an organization under the auspices of the denomination, they could not disregard what was adopted by the resolution of the General Assembly. The extent of the YDP-UIM's activity began to decline.

Then one day in the winter of 1978, the board of directors of the General Assembly called the YDP-UIM missioners for a meeting. "We believe it would best for you discontinue the UIM. It's creating noise in the PCK. It's not something for the church to do." Cho countered, "I have never worked outside the boundaries of the Presbyterian doctrine. If you believe I am in the wrong, you should cancel my ordination."

The directors further charged, "We are not saying you're in the wrong. We're saying you should change course and just focus on proclaiming the gospel." To which Cho countered, "But I am proclaiming the good news, nothing more. Unless you cancel my ordination, I will continue with the ministry." Cho was adamant about staying the course with the UIM.

Not too long afterward, Rev. Lee Eui-ho, the head of the DOE, expressed his concerns to Rev. Cho, sharing that Youngnak Church was about to cut its financial support for Cho and part of the YDP-UIM operational expenses. Apparently, there had been an emergency meeting between the leadership of Youngnak Church and a KCIA agent in the Sejong Hotel over the question of the YDP-UIM. The agent reportedly told the pastor of Youngnak that it was the responsibility of his church to stop the YDP-UIM, since it had enabled it to grow into the problem that it is with its financial support. Of course, the agent asked politely. Cho stood up enraged. "You should discuss everything about PCK's evangelism with the KCIA, then!" Park Jo-joon, who had succeeded Han Kyung-chik at Youngnak, called Cho to explain his position. "We're in a bind, Rev. Cho. My congregation is about to be divided over the issue of urban industrial ministry. Please, couldn't you take a more moderate approach?" "We were never immoderate in our approach," Cho said. "And doing anything other than what we've done would do nothing to serve the working people."[42]

Youngnak sent its last support for the YDP-UIM in December 1978. A relationship of 14 years had come to an end. Youngnak also cut its support to the rest of the UIMs, including the salary for Lee

Geung-ha in Changwon. It was hoped that losing a major supporter like Youngnak would cause the YDP-UIM to run too dry to persist in its ways.

The power of externalities, however, was put on full display, as churches from around the world rushed to YDP-UIM's assistance upon reading in the news that Youngnak had cut its support. Finance never became a problem. As a matter of fact, too many different givers were willing to send a gift that Cho had to ask all donations sent through the UIM office of the WCC to streamline the bookkeeping.

To its credit, even as it tried to convince the UIMs to change their ways, the PCK still demonstrated a firm resolve to protect them from the unjust attacks of the state and media. In particular, indirectly alluding to the government's actions following the YH Incident in 1979 and the *Shingunbu's* great repression in 1981, the General Assembly publicly stated:

We are outraged at the one-sided reportage from the authorities that make it seem industrial missions are Communist sympathizers and dissidents who only pretend to be Christian [. . .] let it be very clear that our urban industrial missions are absolutely not pernicious, communistic dissidents. [. . .] We cannot contain our anger at the state for accusing the UIMs of being seditious Communist sympathizers in the disguise of Christians through the very one-sided coverage by the press. [. . .] Let it be known very clearly that the urban and industrial ministries of our denomination absolutely are not seditious Communist sympathizers.[43]

We are confident that the hardships the UIMs had to endure in past years were a suffering for the sake of the gospel. We call upon all who are in the church to take a keen interest in urban industrial mission of the PCK [. . .] to proclaim the good news to the industrial population.[44]

Although the language of the statement did not get any more specific than this, it was a daring show of public defiance for the representative body of an entire denomination in those days of the junta's dictatorship.

The final rupture between the General Assembly and the YDP-UIM happened after the KCAO issued a statement denouncing the United States government for its actions following the fire in the US Cultural Center in Busan in April 1982. The General Assembly did not take to the criticism of the United States very well. Moreover, as the authorities used the statement as a pretext for another barrage of attacks, the General Assembly also began denouncing the UIM. This was the first anti-American statement released from a religious group. As such, it had a tremendous social impact. Cho Chi Song was actually opposed to the idea of including anti-American contents into the statement. Nevertheless, he had to add his name to what the others in the KCAO had drafted as the general secretary of the council Cho Chi Song and In Myeong-jin both got into legal trouble for their involvement in the statement. The Shingunbu used the event as ammunition for more of its smear campaign. The general opinion in the denomination began to slant against the UIM.

Whereas the NCCK expressed support for the KCAO, the more conservative leadership of the PCK sent a letter to every PCK church in the country in the name of the moderator, Rev. Go Hyeon-bong, which said, "We are grieved by the shock and controversy that the [KCAO's] statement caused to society. [. . .] The social missions organizations ought to renew themselves as members of the church and work to establish themselves in their faith. [. . .] Our denomination will continue to ever strengthen our friendly relationship with the United States, a country with which we share a long history of missions." It was an explicit display of preference for the United States. Some of the members in the Gyeonggi, South Seoul, and Southeast Seoul Presbyteries, which had supported the YDP-UIM financially, went so far as to accuse the UIMs of having "a faithless, leftist political ideology that incites labor agitation, having been co-opted by Communism" and demanded the removal of Cho Chi Song and In Myeong-jin from the denomination. The PCK stopped short of doing so because of the vehement opposition by Bang Ji-il, Lee Jeong-hak, Cha Gwan-young, and Lee Soon-young, who were former chairpersons of the YDP-UIM Committee. They stated that expelling the UIM from the PCK would be as grave a mistake as when it bowed before the colonial authorities and agreed to participate in worships in Shinto shrines.

The most vocal opponents of the UIM within the General Assembly were mostly pro-government owners of businesses and a number of retired military officers. They included Seo Jeong-han (PCK accounting), Choi Chang-geun (President of *Kidok Gongbo*), and Yoo Chee-moon (president of *Jangrohoebo*), who were ruling elders, and Rev. Koo Haeng-mo (a former supervisor from the labor administration). A number of prominent conservative ministers also joined the fray. Together, the detractors relentlessly attacked the UIM in the local presbyteries and General Assembly. They also went on to become members of the DOE and Central UIM Committee to neutralize the UIM by changing the relevant policies and exercising institutional control.

At last, at the persistent call by the anti-UIM forces, the 67th General Assembly in 1982 passed a resolution to delegate the search of a solution to the UIM question to the Committee on Church and Social Problems. Comprising six individuals, the committee returned to the assembly with the following six recommendations.

1. The term "urban industrial mission" will be changed to "industrial evangelism."
2. The UIMs will no longer receive foreign aid.
3. Every member of the current UIM staff will be replaced.
4. The YDP-UIM Committee will be dissolved by December 1983.
5. Each presbytery will create an IEC.
6. The PCK will look for a new policy of industrial ministries.

Outraged by the suggestion that the denomination should revert on its proud UIM history, the young ministers, seminarians, members of the national Youth Association, workers, and lay associations launched a powerful protest against the committee's recommendations. The Association of Ministers for a New Generation, Association for Current Ministry, and Association for Contemporary Theology opened several public forums and discussions on the topic of the PCK-UIM's past, present, and future, seeking to create broader support for it. The young clergy members also worked together with seminarians and lay organizations to amplify their voice in public statements and protests. Met with vehement opposition, the General Assembly tabled the six recommendations for a year and discussed it again in the 69th General Assembly in 1984. Even then, only the first recommendation to change the name of UIM back to industrial evangelism was passed with the fairly evenly divided votes of 305 against, 405 for.[45]

That one change in name, however, was still a significant defeat for the YDP-UIM. Reverting back to the anachronistic name of "industrial evangelism" symbolically and practically meant that the YDP-UIM could no longer be involved in workplace disputes. The contents of its activity had to be strictly spiritual. Even the YDP-UIM, defiant in the face of the state and the press, was powerless before the attack from within. The very forces that should have protected the UIM had turned against it.

This caused Cho to be deeply disillusioned with the church. "We used to face a twin-headed dragon called the state and corporations when we got involved with a labor issue," he said. "Now we had a triplet, the third head being the church. The workers had nobody left. [. . .] That's when I lost hope of the church. [. . .] That's when I realized this organization can't save anybody who was a laborer."[46]

The YDP-UIM had already tried and despaired of the method of industrial evangelism in the 1960s. Telling him to go back to doing nothing more than keeping the workers in his thoughts and prayers meant he should now resign from the UIM. Myeong Noh-seon had already resigned in January 1983. Cho, perhaps sensing the PCK's decision to come, had also submitted his resignation in October that year, citing his illness as the cause. The central committee did not accept it, however, and instead filing him for leave. Even so, after retiring to Okhwa-ri in North Chungcheong Province, Cho never came back. In Myeong-jin succeeded him as the general secretary of the YDP-UIM for a short while before resigning in May 1984 and leaving for a school in Australia. The leadership that took over afterward were the second-generation UIM missioners who Cho had trained. In successive order, Lee Geun-bok, Jin Bang-joo, Sohn Eun-ha, Park Jin-seok, Shin Seung-won, and Sohn Eun-jeong took up the mantle.

NOTES

1 Kim Yong-Bock and Yoo Seung-hee, *Cho Chi Song's Oral History* (Vol. 2, 2011).

2 NCCK, *Testimonies from the Ground*, 622–624.

3 NCCK, *Testimonies from the Ground*, 425.

4 Kim Myeong-bae, *Yeongdeungpo UIM Files Vol. 4* (YDP-UIM & Soongsil University Center for Culture and Mission Studies, 2020).

5 Koh Ae-shin, "A Report on the Persecution of the Gumi UIM," unpublished text, 1979; Yeongdeungpo UIM 40th Anniversary Committee, *Yeongdeungpo UIM: A 40-Year History* (YDP-UIM, 1998), 197.

6 Kim and Yoo, *Cho Chi Song's Oral History* (Vol. 4, 2011).

7 Yeongdeungpo UIM 40th Anniversary Committee, *Yeongdeungpo UIM: A 40-Year History* (YDP-UIM, 1998).

8 Kim Myeong-bae, *Yeongdeungpo UIM Files Vol. 1* (YDP-UIM & Soongsil University Center for Culture and Mission Studies, 2020), 366.

9 NCCK, *Testimonies from the Ground*.

10 Yeongdeungpo UIM 40th Anniversary Committee, *Yeongdeungpo UIM*.

11 Kim and Yoo, *Cho Chi Song's Oral History* (Vol. 2, 2011).

12 In Myeong-jin, "The Government's Attack on the YDP-UIM," *Yeongdeungpo UIM: A 40-Year History* (YDP-UIM, 1998).

13 Seo Deok-Seok and Sohn Eun-jeong, "Interviews of the Older Members of the UIM: Park Jeom-soon, Shin Mi-ja, Song Hyo-soon, Park Deuk-soon, Kim Mi-soon, and Han Myeong-hee," 2011. The workers involved with the YDP-UIM said they never heard Cho Chi Song say anything political other than when he commented, "good riddance," after the death of Park Chung Hee on October 26.

14 Cho Chi Song, "For A New Step Forward," *Freedom for the Oppressed* (Dongyeon, 2020), 396.

15 Shin Chul-young, "Ten Years of the Yeongdeungpo UIM," *Yeongdeungpo UIM: A 40-Year History* (YDP-UIM, 1998), 485.

16 Kim Myeong-bae, *Yeongdeungpo UIM Files Vol. 1* (YDP-UIM & Soongsil University Center for Culture and Mission Studies, 2020), 386.

17 Yeongdeungpo UIM 40th Anniversary Committee, *Yeongdeungpo UIM: A 40-Year History* (YDP-UIM, 1998).

18 Yeongdeungpo UIM 40th Anniversary Committee, *Yeongdeungpo UIM*.

19 In Myeong-jin, "The Government's Attack on the YDP-UIM," *Yeongdeungpo UIM: A 40-Year History* (YDP-UIM, 1998).

20 In Myeong-jin, "The Government's Attack on the YDP-UIM."

21 In Myeong-jin, "The Government's Attack on the YDP-UIM."

22 Kim Yong-Bock and Yoo Seung-hee, *Cho Chi Song's Oral History* (Vol. 8, 2011).

23 Kim Nam-il, *History of the Wonpoong Textiles Union* (Samchang Books, 2010).

24 Kim and Yoo, *Cho Chi Song's Oral History* (Vol. 8, 2011).

25 Yeongdeungpo UIM 40th Anniversary Committee, *Yeongdeungpo UIM: A 40-Year History* (YDP-UIM, 1998).

26 Kim and Yoo, *Cho Chi Song's Oral History* (Vol. 3, 2011).

27 *TIME* (January 3, 1977).

28 Steven Lavender, "To the Friends in the Yeongdeungpo UIM," *Yeongdeungpo UIM: A 40-Year History* (YDP-UIM, 1998), 470–473.

29 Cho Chi Song, "An English Letter Requesting Prayer."

30 Kim Myeong-bae, "Ministry Reports form October–November, 1968," Yeongdeungpo UIM Files Vol. 1 (YDP-UIM & Soongsil University Center for Culture and Mission Studies, 2020), 79, 82.
31 Kim and Yoo, *Cho Chi Song's Oral History* (Vol. 2, 2011).
32 Kim Myeong-bae, "English Communication Records," *Yeongdeungpo UIM Files Vol. 4* (YDP-UIM & Soongsil University Center for Culture and Mission Studies, 2020).
33 Kim Myeong-bae, "Minutes from the 37th Committee," Yeongdeungpo UIM Files Vol. 3 (YDP-UIM & Soongsil University Center for Culture and Mission Studies, 2020), 130.
34 Kim, "Minutes from the 37th Committee," 130.
35 Kim, "Minutes from the 37th Committee," 130.
36 Shin Chul-young, "Ten Years of the Yeongdeungpo UIM," *Yeongdeungpo UIM: A 40-Year History* (YDP-UIM, 1998).
37 Seo Deok-Seok and Sohn Eun-jeong, "Lee Geun-bok's Interview," *Interviews of Related Individuals for the Biography* (YDP-UIM, 2021).
38 "Program for the Opening Ceremony," Yeongdeungpo UIM Files (2021).
39 In Myeong-jin, "PCK's Attack on the YDP-UIM," *The Story of Seongmunbak's People* (Christian Literature Society of Korea, 2013).
40 63rd PCK General Assembly, "Statement On Current Affairs" (1978).
41 63rd PCK General Assembly, "Statement On Current Affairs" (1978).
42 Kim and Yoo, *Cho Chi Song's Oral History* (Vol. 2, 2011).
43 Yang Myeong-deuk, "The 63rd General Assembly's Statement," *Freedom for the Oppressed* (YDP-UIM & Dongyeon, 2020), 29.
44 Yang Myeong-deuk, "The Position of the General Assembly on UIM Activities," *Freedom for the Oppressed* (YDP-UIM & Dongyeon, 2020), 30–32.
45 In Myeong-jin, "The Challenge from the Church," *The Story of Seongmunbak's People* (Christian Literature Society of Korea, 2013), 123–128.
46 Jeong Yeong-cheol and Sohn Eun-jeong, "Cho Chi Song's Interview," *Documenting the Oral History of the Democracy Movement* (Korea Democracy Foundation, 2002).

❧ 5 ❧

THE WARMER DAYS
OF YEONGDEUNGPO

DESPITE WHAT THE state and media's propaganda said, the YDP-UIM did not take the side of workers in the labor disputes because of some "leftist ideology" or "Communist sympathies." Rather, it was born out of Cho Chi Song's lived experience when he participated in the work projects in the mines as part of a summer program with the Institute of Industrial Evangelism. Mining for coal in Jangseong, Dogye, Cheolam, and Hwangji, as well as for iron ores in Yangyang, Cho felt his human dignity vanish under the sludge of sweat and dust. Then he was enraged again at the corporations and society as he saw the young women of Yeongdeungpo driven to take drugs to stay awake through the incredibly long hours that were forced upon them.

They, Too, Are Human

So many workers were sacrificed to change such simple things.
[. . .] They paid a much greater cost than any of us missioners
did. [. . .] All we did was share in their indignation.[1]

Cho felt called to take the side of the workers in fighting against the tyranny of capital and avarice of employers through the UIM as the clerical call to "love your neighbor as yourself," as Christ taught. He therefore thought that industrial workplaces were corrupt and abominable in their insubordination to God's good design, against which he felt righteous anger. His thought process is evident in the ministry reports he wrote in the early days of the YDP-UIM.

Capital and technology are considered more important than human character in today's reality. One cannot get rid of the sense that people now commonly believe that the laborer belongs to a lower class than a university professor or member of the clergy. [. . .] The church should not expect anyone to respond to its calls as long as the teaching of Christ that a single soul was worth more than the entire world remains unrealized in our society.[2]

The laboring mass is bound to see every issue through the lens of resentment in our society. How could they not, given how hard they are worked and how little they are paid. [. . .] How will the church, as slaves for Christ, share in their burden and serve them?[3]

Cho reached the conclusion that it was incumbent upon the church to resolve and act for the creation of a humane working environment that accorded the workers their dignity. If anyone asked what Cho believed was the goal for the UIM in the 1970s and 1980s, he would have said that it was not to bring more workers into the churches nor to make more Christians within the workplace. It was, rather, to bring workers to the realization that they, too, were humans so that they could start fighting for their own dignity. Cho had said, "workers are humans, too." Embedded in this statement was the idea that just as the Israelites had to escape from slavery before they could worship God fully, workers also had to recover their basic level of human dignity before they could engage in a truly religious life.

Many of the workers Cho met did not, at first, have the notion they deserved a certain level of respect for their human dignity. The first task of the YDP-UIM, therefore, was to help the workers recognize their own identity. Cho engaged in countless conversations, always steering them toward the point that "workers are humans, too." For instance, when talking to workers about what they thought was an appropriate wage, he would not ask whether they made as much as the others but rather how much they needed to live with dignity. Indeed, the YDP-UIM defined an appropriate wage level as one that could afford a dignified lifestyle and instructed workers who were about to begin wage negotiations to always include the amount the average member of the middle class would spend on cultural activities such as music. Korea did not even have the concept of a minimum wage at the time. Workers were inspired by the proclamation that they ought to be paid for dignified lifestyles beyond mere subsistence.

One of the things that broke Cho Chi Song's heart was the fact the young women often sent all of their hard-earned money back to their hometowns without ever properly taking care of themselves. The money the women made were often appropriated for their brothers' schooling. "Your brothers have their lives," Cho often reminded the women, "and you have your own." He repeatedly encouraged them to stop sending all the money back home so they could spend or save some for themselves. Spending on oneself was such a novel concept for many of Yeongdeungpo's female workers that it became a meeting topic for a number of small groups.[4] The YDP-UIM also carefully crafted a number of self-respect and interpersonal skills development programs to empower the workers to make their own reasoned decisions. What often started off as amusing acts of play led the workers to the realization, by design, that they, too, were human.

Many of the women who spent their younger days in the YDP-UIM shared that they came to understand their own worth through the small-group activities. Only then did they realize the injustice of their treatment in the workplace and become bold enough to demand that their dignity be respected.

The mission felt as comfortable as my own home. [. . .] I couldn't have been more excited walking to the center to meet with my small group, even after a long, hard shift. [. . .] Rev. Cho felt like a father, the other missioners my sisters and brothers.[5]

It was only natural that the women felt the YDP-UIM was like their family, when the mission was the one place that greeted them with warmth in stark contrast to the disrespect and abuse that they endured in a workplace that was governed by regressive labor-management relations. Those bonds and powerful sense of fellowship must have shown up during the struggles in the form of unwavering loyalty to each other. For instance, none of the workers gave up the names of the missioners to the authorities. Most of the petitions, complaints, and petitions were penned by the YDP-UIM missioners in the names of the workers. Giving up the real authors could have reduced the amount of pressure that fell onto the workers. Yet none of them caved to the investigators because of the deep confidence and loyalty they had for the missioners.

> *When we reached the peak of the movement in the late 1970s, the workers had grown so mature that there was nothing that ministers needed to tell them to do. [. . .] The clergy, in fact, seemed pitiful by comparison.*
>
> *I've met tens of thousands of workers who didn't go to church. They had me confessing, "you are what a follower of Jesus looks like, you are better than I am as an ordained minister."*[6]

Cho's philosophy was that the UIM was a process by which the workers recognized their own worth as human beings and fought to preserve their rightful dignity. The role of the missioners was to assist that process from the side. This became a source of inspiration and model for many theologians and educators, enriching what came to be known as minjung theology and minjung education in the 1970s and 1980s.

The Miracle of a Single Coin

Cho Chi Song had been deeply impressed by the labor unions of Gumi and Japan in the early 1960s, which had a number of very good programs organized to serve the needs of the workers. These ranged from the more public services like health and unemployment insurance to the private interest activities like hobby or sports clubs. What especially caught Cho Chi Song's eyes among them were the cooperatives, and among them, the credit union cooperatives. The cooperative movement began in the same country where the industrial revolution took off in the nineteenth century when the toiling textile workers of the United Kingdom started a consumer cooperative among themselves. They purchased food collectively for their store, selling each item to the members at a cheaper unit price than in the market. Whatever profit the store made was then saved up as all the members' collective asset.

Cho was drawn to the idea that even the individually powerless workers could exercise common ownership of a democratically run business to generate and evenly share in the profits. Running a cooperative could be a way of exercising self-determination and democracy. The principles of equality, fairness, and common interests could also benefit the workers' sense of solidarity and growth needed in the other aspects of their organized movement.

Cho Chi Song began sharing ideas for a consumer cooperative with the workers, beginning with a group of LAIE members from Yangpyeong-dong Church in August 1965. Then in October 1968, the YDP-UIM introduced the cases of consumer cooperatives during a lecture as part of the eighth LAIE educational program.

> *You buy consumer goods every month. Where do you think the profit from the sale goes? The economic activity of the poor ends up enriching those who are already rich. That is why we need our own bank and our own department store. We need them to make the profit our own.*[7]

Cho declared that it was injustice for the workers to gain none of the profit they helped create: first the share in production that they lost to their employers, then the share in consumption that they lost to the banks and distributors. Then he emphatically stated that the cooperative model could be a good alternative through which the workers could reclaim their share of profit. He also added that the cooperatives could create a savings effect that was equivalent to a wage increase of 10 percent.

> *If you can save 10 percent through the cooperatives, you can increase the worth of your money. [. . .] The labor movement and cooperative movement are essentially the same. [. . .] One is a fight to increase the wages, while the other is a movement to make each penny count for more. They both improve the standard of living for the workers in the end.*[8]

He then explained that the following conditions were necessary for the success of a cooperative.

- The members must be able to trust each other.
- There needed to be a spirit of coexistence, in which one was for all, and all were for one.
- The members of the cooperative must work together on the foundation of common fellowship and solidarity.
- The cooperative must be run democratically according to reason.[9]

In February 1969, the YDP-UIM hired Kang Haeng-nim to handle the cooperative and sent Kang to train in the Institute for Cooperative Education. From May 26 to 29, prospective members were brought in for membership instruction. On August 11, around 50 founding members pooled about 14,000 won to start a credit union cooperative[10] for the following purpose:

- To enable a more robust UIM ministry through the workers' economic organization
- To provide financial support for the workers who experience unexpected hardships

- To provide workers with livelihood security by providing access to a lump sum of money they otherwise would not have
- To practice concrete love for our neighbors through the collective use of individually small sums of money

The YDP-UIM credit union launched with the modest "save one won" campaign. The first to participate were those who joined through the concerted membership drive among some 30 small groups in Hanguk Textiles. Park Young-hye collected the money and account books from her coworkers in the dormitory on paydays. Kang Haeng-nim processed and recorded the deposits. The workers trusted Park Young-hye very highly with their money that she was virtually the branch of the credit union within her company.

Within four months of its creation, the credit union grew to 200 members and 400,000 won in net deposits. It now had enough assets to give out loans that were large enough to be meaningful. The workers took out these loans at a monthly interest rate of 2 percent to pay back over 10 months, using them primarily as lease deposits for housing. The credit union thus played a significant role in improving the workers' housing security. After the passage of the Credit Union Act in 1972, the YDP-UIM credit union, formally the "Yeongdeungpo Industrial Development Credit Union Cooperative," received its license as South Korea's very first credit union in January 1973. It had 714 members with net deposits of 7.99 million won. The following year, the deposits more than doubled to nearly 17 million won.[11]

Cho handled the membership education personally, never stopping to emphasize the value and importance of working together.

In a capitalist society, those who have access to large lump sums of money are the winners, and those who don't are the losers. [. . .] Let's say that you could buy a box of grapes for 10,000 won, with each box carrying 10 bunches. That means you should be able to get a bunch for 1,000 won, when in

reality, the stores sell only half a bunch at that price. [. . .]
So if you can get 10 people to buy a box together, you can
get double the value you would have for the same amount of
money you would have spent in the stores. [. . .] It saves you
both money and time. By working together as a cooperative,
we can break the framework imposed onto us by capitalism.[12]

Cho Chi Song took the membership education very seriously and allowed no one to join until they had attended every session. He was also very disciplined about the handling of money. If there was even a penny's worth of discrepancy in the books, the missioner responsible had to pay out of pocket to fill the gap. Cho himself made sure he got a receipt for every dime.

He was also very strict about sticking to the rules of the credit union as illustrated by a particular episode. Shin Mi-ja, a laid-off worker who was fighting her former employer Lotte Confectionery, needed a court deposit to proceed with her lawsuit. She applied for a loan from the YDP-UIM credit union. Cho declined without hesitation, saying that those who were not members of the credit union were not allowed to borrow its money. Shin Mi-ja, understandably, was very upset, as she found herself fired from her company because of participating in a labor action as a member of a YDP-UIM group but without access to the help of its credit union.[13]

Cho, for his part, said he had no choice. The rules of the credit union needed to be respected to maintain its credibility, and there were no provisions yet about providing loans or legal aid to nonmembers. Recounting this episode after his retirement to Okhwa-ri, Cho often said he hoped there could be some kind of "labor funds" that could finance the strike funds of a labor union or hardship relief for the laid-off workers in addition to a membership-based credit union.

Once it took off, the credit union continued to gain a great response from the young working women of Yeongdeungpo for its lending of housing deposits. Despite their higher cost in the long run, women often had no choice but to pay a monthly rent for housing. Through the credit union, they could now borrow enough money to pay a much larger but fully refundable deposit in a type of housing lease called the *jeonse*. This was far more economical in the long run. Many workers thus joined the credit union, often expanding the scope of their participation to the YDP-UIM's labor organizing or church activities. Song Hyo-soon of Daeil Chemicals was one such example. The credit union and the consumer cooperative, along with the small groups, thus became the main pillars of the YDP-UIM's ministry. One of the workers recounted:

> *When we opened the door to come in, the missioners would greet us with a smile. Out of habit, we pulled out every bill and coin out of our bags and pockets, giving them to the staff with our account books. [. . .] Later on, we left our account books and our seals (a stamp of which is equivalent to a personal signature) with the staff. We never had to check if the balance added up. [. . .] That's how much we trusted the missioners.*[14]

The commercial banks were much more difficult to access by the young women; they were happy to take deposits in return for low interest but rarely willing to approve a loan for the women. Moreover, the banks were usually closed by the time the women got off their shifts. The YDP-UIM credit union, by contrast, was always open whenever the workers could visit and lent enough for a *jeonse* deposit to anyone who was a member. The credit union also practically served as the school of personal finance for the women, most of whom had previously sent all the money back home without saving any for themselves.

By 1976, the YDP-UIM credit union had grown to 965 members and nearly 35.5 million won in assets that enabled it to give out 2,133 loans in a year. It gained in popularity among the churches of Yeongdeungpo as well. In 1972, 27 ministers of the Gyeonggi Presbytery received the membership education and joined the YDP-UIM credit union. A number of others, like Dorim Church, created their own.

The credit union had reached around 1,000 members by April 29, 1976, when the YDP-UIM gave birth to the consumer goods cooperative. This one started with 134 members using a loan of 10,000 won for each of the 17 founding members of the credit union plus 600,000 won donated by the Presbyterian Family Service.[15] It was a case of fruit multiplying fruit, with the credit union supplying part of the capital required to start a consumer cooperative business. Shin Young-hee, who had been very active in her small-group activities, was hired as the manager. The store started inside the space that used to be the kitchen in old YDP-UIM office in the leased Dangsan-dong Apartment, where Shin brought the bulk-purchased items that were commonly used among workers.

The transaction was designed to return the profit to members. For instance, a bar of soap that was purchased by the store for 100 won was sold for 120 won. The difference of 20 won was recorded as the purchasing member's credit. The expenses of running the store were then subtracted from the credit that all members had accrued. The remainder was given back in cash to the respective holder of credit. The goods were sold more cheaply than the market price but only to the members of the cooperative. This ensured the members could share the profits without subsidizing the discounted price for nonmembers. Yet, despite the growth of membership, the sales profit of the consumer cooperative never grew large enough to even pay the salary of the store manager. When the repression created additional difficulties for the ministry, the YDP-UIM gave up on keeping a manager and switched the store to unmanned sales. At seeing this, the visiting head of the Asian region in the International Cooperative Alliance expressed concern.

"This isn't a good way to run this, Reverend."

"Why not?"

"It creates unnecessary temptations for good folks."

"That shouldn't be a problem with our workers. They aren't capable of deceit."[16]

It was not uncommon to find someone in society or the companies disparaging the workers as being uncultured and prone to petty thievery. Cho, however, was confident in the women who frequented the YDP-UIM. The unmanned sales continued without becoming a problem. In fact, the store ended up with more, rather than less, money than it should have had according to the books. This was because the workers had been taking less change than they were entitled to. Some of them may have simply skipped the trouble of calling for someone when there were not enough coins in the cash box for the smallest units of change. More of them were deliberately donating the change, since they considered the cooperative to be their own. It was a miracle created through the spirit of cooperation among workers who were so poor they were often hesitant to even take the bus. Cho testified:

I couldn't have been more joyful than I was getting to do ministry with those workers. [. . .] I will bet you no other Korean minister has known such quality people.[17]

Of course, such remarkable display of character and the solid relationship of trust did not form out of a few educational sessions or worship services. Rather, the character of Christ demonstrated through the action of the YDP-UIM missioners seeped into the workers themselves.

By 1980, the membership of the store grew to 450. Sales were low, however, because most of the members were single and did not purchase very many items.

They just didn't spend all that much money. [. . .] Families bought a lot, even if they had to do so on credit. But the single women working in the factories were always reluctant to spend. [. . .] In exchange, it was a boon for the credit union cooperative.[18]

Those were the times when it was considered a virtue for young women to toil in the factories in order to send their younger brothers to university or buy their parents a plot of rice paddy. Naturally, the women barely spent any money for themselves while saving very diligently, showing up as low sales in the store and a steady increase of deposits in the credit union. Nevertheless, having saved the cost of hiring a manager, the unmanned store continued for another eight years and only closed per the vote of the members in May 1982 when the great repression was at its peak.

The credit union was targeted by the authorities right after In Myeong-jin's arrest for his sermon on Micah. First, the prosecutors searched the YDP-UIM's offices and seized its files on May 1, 1978. Then, the tax offices of both Yeongdeungpo and Guro took turns going through the books that the prosecutors confiscated. They were bent on finding some pretext for clamping down on the ministry, but there were no laws broken. The best they could do was charge the YDP-UIM for unpaid payroll taxes for its missioners, despite the fact that members of the clergy are exempt from payroll taxes.

It was not long before the finance ministry sent a notice to the YDP-UIM to demand a full list of all its members. Autonomy from government was crucial for a credit union. There was the obvious concern, too, that giving up the list would allow the government to target the individual members. The YDP-UIM refused to submit the list in no uncertain terms. The finance ministry then tried to pressure the National Association of Credit Unions to make the YDP-UIM give up the list. Cho continued to refuse, saying the YDP-UIM had no such obligation according to the law. All that the association could do was to say the finance ministry wanted it, who in turn could only say that "somebody higher up" wanted it. When Cho prodded who that might be, he finally got the name: KCIA. This knowledge gave the YDP-UIM all the more reason not to give up the list.

The ministry of finance called the YDP-UIM's refusal a resistance to inspection, using it as pretext for revoking the license for the

Yeongdeungpo Industrial Development Credit Union. The YDP-UIM fought the payroll tax charge and the revocation of license in a lengthy court appeal, but could not reverse the decision on the revoked license in the end. As such, it voluntarily dissolved the registered credit union status and instead retained an informal cooperative to retain the same functions, calling it the "Squirrel Fellowship."

The credit union cooperative model of the YDP-UIM was adopted by the UIM organizations of other denominations as well as the labor unions. The Wonpoong Textiles Union especially created and made good use of its own credit and consumer cooperative union to manage the union dues and save for future strike funds. The cooperative movement of the YDP-UIM provided concrete benefits to the workers as well as help them cultivate their capacity for self-governance and democracy. Taking their cue from the YDP-UIM, the labor unions of Yeongdeungpo also began training leaders to head their own cooperatives.[19]

The legacy of cooperatives still continues nearly 60 years after Cho Chi Song had started them in the Squirrel Fellowship, an informal credit union cooperative; the Seorosallim Consumer Cooperative; Bright Society, an educational cooperative; Nonumaegi, a cooperative of those recovering from homelessness; Seoul Medical Consumer Cooperative; and more.

Also, the Squirrel Fellowship, still sustained by the workers who studied the cooperative movement under Cho Chi Song, now plans to launch a "labor fund" or "social solidarity bank"[20] at the time of this writing. Thus, the seeds of the cooperative movement that Cho had planted in Yeongdeungpo are still growing into a broader alliance with the local community and the broader forces for progress.

Living Together

Cho Chi Song encouraged the workers to try communal living whenever he had the opportunity. Cho proposed communal living as an alternative. "Two or three of you," Cho recounted his pitch, "could rent or lease a place together, instead of trying to pay for a place individually."[21]

YDP-UIM followed through on its recommendation and got a kitchen in Mullae-dong to allow the workers who lived alone to come together to eat higher quality meals. It also acquired two flats in 1968 to provide up to eight women who had just arrived in Seoul with temporary housing until they could enter a dormitory or find another place to stay.[22] It also launched a lending program, separate from the credit union, that financed the workers' *jeonse* lease deposits at zero interest and a two-year repayment plan. Of course, these housing programs were meant to improve the workers' housing security, not generate revenue. Cho also talked about Kibbutz, the intentional living community in Israel, countless times to emphasize that the only hope an impoverished, powerless worker had for advancement was to live together in a community. Some of the workers still remember the photographs he used to show.[23]

Cho also experimented with alternative models of business. The Mission Tire Company, created in 1968, was his first attempt at starting a manufacturing cooperative. The tire recycling company was meant to provide jobs and generate income for the UIM ministries without resorting to exploitative labor practices. It was a social enterprise, in modern terms, except for the fact that it had none of the institutional support its equivalents have today. The company was founded with the counsel of Eugene Adams from the United States. Cho Seung-rae, a former technician in Hankook Tire, served as the technological consultant. Seventeen people invested a total of 3 million won and created a tire recycling plant. Kim Dong-hyeok, the president of the Lay Association for Industrial Evangelism, was appointed as the general manager to start working with five employees.

The recycled tires were of such excellent quality that Hankook Tire and Samyang Tire complained that the new tires they manufactured were not being sold. For whatever reason, the local tax officials and traffic police came by to pick an argument almost every day. Cho had established two ground rules for the business. One was to pay not a single penny in bribes. The other was to abide by all the labor regulations, including the Sundays off. Kim Dong-hyeok eventually stated that he could not continue to run the business while keeping all those rules. This was in no small part because of the environment. Although the state would be eager to nurture Mission Tire as a social enterprise, the odds were stacked against a completely honest business at the time.

The 17 investors voted to close the recycled tire business and instead explore the production of new tires for intercity buses. They gave up the idea after being met with strong opposition by the existing tire companies. In its place, they decided to start a prostheses company. Attracted by its association with the UIM, Preston offered to invest significantly in the young prostheses company in exchange for the original 17 investors' agreement to buy Preston shares with their dividends once the company was past breaking even. The company was told it had to relocate to the export-free zone in Masan to receive the full tax benefits for its exports. Despite looking for a suitable location in Masan, the company was met with too many local restrictions on factory operations that they could not even begin to worry about production or sales. Preston concluded that they could not conduct normal business as they knew it in South Korea and gave up on the project. The investment was returned to the investors.[24]

Cho began to understand why the employers were always so eager to appease the government authorities. The survival of their business depended less on the rationality of management and more on their social ability to parlay the various external actors in their favor. There was no concept of ethical management or fair trade. Having the right connections in the right places of power was the most important business skill in the 1960s. In other words, ethical employers could not stay in business.

In 1974, Cho launched a housing cooperative. Most of the loans from the credit union were taken out to pay for a housing lease deposit.

Cho believed the workers would fare even better if they collectively bought land and built their own homes. Cho had seen a precedent of this when he visited Germany to discuss funding for building the new YDP-UIM center. The labor unions in Germany organized workers who were not homeowners to build a common house. Seventeen YDP-UIM workers and missioners who did not own their homes formed a cooperative and purchased 3,200 pyeongs (2.6 acres) of land in the outskirts of Seoul. Before construction could begin, however, the land was designated by the authorities as part of the greenbelt, no-development zone.

The next cooperative purchased 1,400 pyeongs (1.1 acres) next to Coca-Cola in Doksan-dong. This time, the obstacle was presented by the families and relatives who used to hold onto the workers' money. They did not react well when the women came asking for their sums to pitch into the project.

> *"You crazy girl! This is hard-earned money. Why would you try to give it away to some church minister?"*
>
> *"Where is the receipt? You can't give money without a receipt. [. . .] You're naive, and they're trying to take advantage of you."*[25]

Some of the parents came to Cho Chi Song's house to demand that they see the papers to the land that their daughters said they bought.

After a considerable amount of drama, the cooperative managed to scrape up enough funds to pay for the land. They then needed money to start the construction. Fortunately, the American Christian Business Men's Connection (ACBMC) had been financing various self-advancement programs for the poor. Through the introduction of George Todd, the cooperative successfully applied for a long-term loan with 20 years for repayment at an 8 percent annual interest rate.

The only requirement that was left was to get a local government official to vouch for the program to meet the regulatory requirements for United States lending agencies. The loan officer from the ACBMC, a man by the name Adams, accompanied Cho Chi Song to the Korean Housing Bank.

> *"It's a great program," the bank representative said, adding, "you'll just have to give our bank 1 percent of the loan."*
> *"What are you talking about," Cho retorted. "Shouldn't your bank be providing us with an additional 1 percent so our people could own their homes?"*
> *"If you don't pay us, we can't vouch for you."*[26]

There was no way to ascertain if the bank representative was speaking from an actual policy or his own judgment. For all Cho knew, the bank wanted a cut of the precious assistance for the poor, much less to help them. So in April 1975, Cho gave up on the project, saying it was not worth giving up one's dignity before the greedy Housing Bank. The land was distributed among the members so they could individually decide whether they wanted to sell the land or build a house. Thirty-nine of them chose to build a home in 1976. Eighteen of them sold the land and bought a home elsewhere. Cho sold his share of land to pay for a part of the plot that was later used to build the new YDP-UIM center. When the center was completed, Cho traded the plot for the Dangsan-dong apartment that used to be the old office.

Self-government cooperatives were not entirely new in Korea, but they had been completely squashed during the Japanese colonial occupation. With his imagination and speed of action, Cho managed to bring them back to life in Yeongdeungpo in the credit union, consumer goods, and housing cooperatives. He also implemented similar principles in the Mission Tire Company, housing lease lending program, Mullae-dong kitchen, etc. Cooperatives were successful in the YDP-UIM because of Cho's strong conviction and understanding about their underlying philosophy, the strong level of organization among the small-group workers, and the natural necessity to work together in an under-resourced environment.[27]

Unfortunately, the repression of the authoritarian government led to the revocation of the formal license of the credit union and smothered a number of other projects before they even started. Had the politics allowed more liberty, the YDP-UIM's cooperatives may have been able to mature into a full-fledged community with an alternative economy.

It is now recognized in the twenty-first century that the cooperative model may provide one of the only feasible alternatives that can overcome the limits of capitalism. Although the experiments of Cho and the YDP-UIM experienced failure more often than success, each of them was a very meaningful attempt. The cooperatives and social enterprises also likely inspired workers to see that they could hope for greater advancements in life that they could not accomplish through waged labor alone. The cooperatives also provided an additional context through which the YDP-UIM staff could earn the trust of the workers that would prove helpful in organizing them for the later and more adversarial struggles.

Hand in Hand

There were many helping hands that enabled the workers and the YDP-UIM to overcome the various internal and external challenges, including the government's persecution, to leave behind a clear mark in the labor history of the 1970s. Workers were always at the forefront of any struggle, but they were always backed by the many layers of supporters who joined them in the fight against injustice, organizing successive days of mass protest, prayer rallies, court battles, and more against the large corporations.[28] The struggle was fought across a massive and complex front that comprised more than just the workers.

At the core, again, were the small-group workers. Their leaders, like Kim Yeon-ja, Park Jeom-soon, Yoo Ok-soon, Lee Ok-soon, Moon Gye-soon, Song Hyo-soon, Jang Seok-sook, Kim Bok-rye, Kim Bok-sil, Kim Mi-soon, Kim Geum-soon, Kim Soon-hee, Shin Mija, Han

Myeong-hee, and Park Deuk-soon, made labor history by struggling in companies like Pangrim Textiles, Lotte, Haitai, Namyoung Textiles, Wonpoong Textiles, and Daeil Chemicals. Many of them were barred by the employers and persecuted by the Shingunbu regime in the early 1980s for their activism, having their honor restored years later through the Special Act to Restore the Honor of Persons Associated with Democratization. Some received monetary compensation along with it.

The next layer of the concentric circle was the missioners of the YDP-UIM. They were the ones who laughed and cried with the workers, and alongside them. The missioners working with Cho Chi Song served the workers as they would have served Jesus Christ. Kim Gyeong-nak, In Myeong-jin, Myeong Noh-seon, and Shin Chul-young even endured intense persecution at the hands of the military dictatorships. It was gut-wrenching for Cho Chi Song to watch the missioners under his leadership suffer many imprisonments and threats to their lives.

Kim Gyeong-nak worked with Cho Chi Song from 1968 to 1974 as the Methodist representative when the YDP-UIM was a joint ministry of the PCK and KMC. The two of them worked together beyond denominational differences, with Cho focusing primarily on education and training while Kim focused on the labor issues and support for the unions. Kim was a man of action, often leading the activities from the most visible forefront at the price of going to prison. Cho would then take care of matters while he was gone.

In Myeong-jin maintained a close and long partnership with Cho Chi Song, eventually succeeding him as the leader of the YDP-UIM. He tended to the mission's internal affairs as its general secretary while Cho was away leading the PCK's Central UIM Committee training. In could also form new friendships very quickly, which he used very well to build relationships with the workers who were new to the mission. He also endured four prison sentences and many more arrests. Those in the YDP-UIM endearingly called him the missioner "in charge of prison duty."

Myeong Noh-seon was the face of hospitality in the Yeong-deungpo mission, being a mother to the young workers and keeping the space of the mission warm and inviting. Shin Chul-young was the cool-headed theorist who helped keep the ministry on a strategic footing, making sure there were more than just sentiments grounding its activities.

Despite the significant change in method since their days, credit should also be given to the missioners of industrial evangelism ministry in the 1960s. These include Kang Gyung-goo and her staff of Kim Seong-hye, Min Young-seon, Sohn Poong-ja, Lee Seung-boo, Lim Eui-joo, Hwang Tae-joon, and Kang Haeng-nim. Then, those like Koh Jae-shik, Ji Shin-yeong, Myeong Noh-seon, Park Sang-hee, Park Young-hye, Chang Ae-shin, Kim Jeong-ran, Shin Young-hee, Lee Shin-sook, Gwak Yeong-soon, Lee Jeong-ja, Kim Young-hee, Kim Yong-sook, and Shin Cheol-young joined the fray in the 1970s to fight alongside the workers in the second iteration of the ministry. In the 1980s, Jeong Gang-ja, Shin Cheol-young, Shin Soon-cheol, Wang Chae-sook, and Song Jin-seop, among others, worked with Cho Chi Song and In Myeong-jin until they retired in 1983 and 1984. This was followed by a generational shift as Lee Geun-bok, previously trained by Cho Chi Song, took up the mantle of general secretary. Lee Geun-bok was joined in the latter half of the decade by staff missioners such as Sohn Eun-ha, Park Jin-seok, Lee Yeong-woo, Yoo Goo-yeong, Han Myeong-hee, Yoon Cheol, and Jin Bang-joo. Together, they continued to explore the YDP-UIM's path forward amid the changes in the labor environment.

The missionaries of the UPCUSA played a very important role in planting and nurturing the UIM in South Korea. Henry Jones had visited the country nearly 10 times since 1957 as the head of UIM in the CCA, playing an integral role in starting industrial evangelism. He also helped the PCK IEC receive financial support from the UPCUSA and sent its missioners for training overseas.

Robert Urquhart, named Eo Ra-bok in Korean, was originally sent as a missionary to Daegu but was later also appointed to be a partner missionary for the PCK IEC. The PCK also hosted many topical experts to educate its missioners in industrial evangelism, including John Ramsay, a church elder and labor organizer in the steel industry; Epianiah Castro; Rev. Ackle; Alfred Schmidt; George Todd; Calderon; and Marshall Scott, moderator of the UPCUSA.

There were also missionaries who were sent to serve specifically with the Yeongdeungpo UIM. These were Robert "Hahm Boo-man" Hoffman from the United States and Richard "Woo Taek-in" Wootton, Steven "Na Byeong-do" Lavender, and Anthony "Ahn Do-seon" Dawson from Australia. They played important roles in bridging the YDP-UIM and the global church.

Professor John "Byeon Jo-eun" Brown, who taught in the PTS, also helped connect the YDP-UIM to the Uniting Church in Australia (UCA) as an eager supporter of the UIM. Hoffman and Wootton were good partners in laying the foundations for industrial evangelism by sharing the stories of industrial evangelism from overseas. The Australian missionaries who followed continued to be great partners for the YDP-UIM. They acted as messengers who wrote the English newsletters that shared the truth of what was happening in Korea with the global as well as the Australian church and also as couriers carrying funds and documents in and out of the country, sustaining the network of overseas support for Yeongdeungpo.

Often when he shared the story of the YDP-UIM in international settings, Cho Chi Song was asked whether he really was a Presbyterian minister. This was because the PCK was a conservative organization in the minds of many foreign observers, who found it an anomaly that such a denomination would so passionately lead the charge with the UIM. There were many people who thought the Catholics and PROKs were the only ones with a remotely similar ministry.[29]

Cho returned all credit to his forerunners in the PCK who first accepted industrial evangelism (and later the UIM) and then nurtured it. He also credited the supporters he had among ordinary church ministers who formed the Yeongdeungpo Industrial Evangelism (later UIM) Committee as part of the Gyeonggi (and later Yeongdeungpo) and Hannam (later South Seoul) Presbyteries.

Indeed, the midwives who delivered the newborn industrial ministry were the leaders in the PCK DOE and Central Industrial Evangelism Committee. Rev. Lee Gwon-chan, the head of the evangelism department, even defended the YDP-UIM from earliest allegations of Communism through his in-law relationship with the KCIA director, Kim Gye-won. Although he was a conservative evangelical, Lee Gwon-chan remembered Cho so fondly that he wanted to see Cho one last time in his later years even as he suffered from dementia. Sohn Eun-ha, then the YDP-UIM general secretary, took him to the old missioner who had retired to Okhwa-ri. "I went to and came back from heaven," the elderly Lee said. "I met Christ while I was there. I asked him to provide you with a house, because you don't have one." It was a reference to the time when the YDP-UIM did not yet have its current building. "Don't you worry," he reassured Cho, "Jesus promised to give you a house made of gold."[30]

Rev. Oh Cheol-ho laid the foundations for the UIM as part of the staff of the PCK-IEC under its first director Hwang Geum-cheon. He was also the one who took special notice of Cho Chi Song as he participated in the IEC's training program, eventually raising Cho to be the first minister ordained to serve in industrial missions specifically. His *Industrial Evangelism Handbook* was also the very first textbook for the topic.[31] Oh formed a mobile industrial evangelism team, going around the country to organize an industrial evangelism study among the ministers in each of the industrial areas. Oh was also instrumental in cultivating the cultural base of support for the UIM, pushing for the adoption of Labor Sunday, printing the industrial evangelism tracts, and distributing industrial evangelism songs.

Han Kyung-chik played a leading role in sending Cho Chi Song to Yeongdeungpo as a minister for special ministry. While he remained the senior pastor and session moderator, Youngnak Church continued to financially support Cho and the YDP-UIM despite the claims of its elders that they should end the support given the controversy surrounding the UIM. Youngnak also helped purchase the land for the new YDP-UIM center and supported the other UIMs in places like Gumi and Masan.

Bang Ji-il was a part of the Yeongdeungpo Industrial Evangelism Committee when Cho had just arrived in the area as the director of evangelism in the Gyeonggi (later Yeongdeungpo) Presbytery. He remained a consistent supporter of the YDP-UIM as he continued to progress to higher positions of leadership like the Yeongdeungpo Presbytery's moderator, head of the PCK DOE, and moderator of the General Assembly. Even when the government started its crackdown of the UIM, he considered the experience a part of suffering for the sake of the gospel and was not easily given to political prejudice, advocating for the UIM as a genuine mission of the church. Born in North Pyeongan Province, Bang also cherished Cho like he would his own son because of their shared experience of leaving their homes in North Korea. Fearing that Cho might lose his life when the repression reached new heights in the late 1970s, Bang advised Cho to leave the country for a while to go study in the United States. Cho declined the offer, saying he could not leave behind the workers.

The Yeongdeungpo IEC (later the YDP-UIM Committee) supported Cho from the side. Its chairpersons included Rev. Gye Hyo-eon (Myeongsoodae Church), Rev. Bang Ji-il (Yeongdeungpo Church), Rev. Yoo Byeong-gwan (Dorim Church), Rev. Cha Gwan-young (Siheung Church), Rev. Lee Jeonghak (Yangpyeong-dong Church), and Rev. Lee Seong-eui, each of whom acted like a protective fence for the YDP-UIM.

Lee Jeong-hak, in particular, played a very important role in defending the YDP-UIM, having served as a chairperson from 1974 to 1990, which included some of the most trying years for the ministry. His consistent support, both financial and moral, came despite the calls from some of the elders of his own church to stop associating with the UIM.

The non-chair members of the Yeongdeungpo UIM Board were also a reliable source of support during the repression, especially the more reform-minded ministers like Lee Jeong-gyu, Koh Hwan-gyu, and Cho Nam-gi. One would be remiss not to acknowledge that their consistent support was given despite the pressure this created in their own lives and ministries. Thanks to their taking the risk, Yeongdeungpo was able to write one of the brightest chapters in the history of UIM.

One minister sent donations, asking to keep his church anonymous to prevent any backlash against the congregation. Some others, whom the YDP-UIM had never met, left wads of cash wrapped in newspapers at the ministry's doorsteps. The more conservative churches and ministers who were less interested in social missions also showed a considerable amount of support, such as through the sacks of rice donated to the rural churches. Even when the government's repression reached new heights between 1978 and 1979, a survey indicated that 83.5 percent of the PCK's ordained had a positive assessment of the UIMs and their methods.[32]

The PCK may have been a conservative denomination, but it was still the broad base of support from fellow ministers that sustained the growth of the UIM. As such, the YDP-UIM always sought to make sure he was investing adequately into the relationship with the rest of the church and wrote the ministry reports with sufficient detail so that the supporters, presbyteries, and other denominational organs could visualize what was happening on the ground. The steady work of organizing seminars and study groups for ministers interested in the UIM also helped create a broad base of support. The UIM had allies within the PTS, including influential professors like Park Chang-hwan, Moon Hee-seok, Joo Seon-ae, and Maeng Yong-gil. By teaching the biblical, ethical, and educational basis the church has for doing its urban industrial ministry, they helped raise financial and moral support for the mission among the PCK clergy even in times of repression.

The YDP-UIM also had allies among the non-PCK UIMs: the PROK UIM (Lee Gyu-sang, Lee Guk-seon, Oh Jae-sik, Jeong Tae-gi), KMC UIM (Cho Seung-hyeok, Kim Gyeong-nak, Cho Hwa-soon, Ahn Gwang-soo), Anglican UIM (Bishop John Daly), Salvation Army UIM, and JOC (Lee Chang-bok, Yoon Soon-nyeo, Jeong In-sook). These ministries coordinated their policies and action plans in the face of repression together through the National UIM Alliance and UIM Staff Conference. They also trained their staff together through the ecumenical frameworks. For about five years from 1969, the YDP-UIM was a joint ministry of the PCK and KMC.

The progressive Christian organizations were reassuring allies for the UIM. These included the National Council of Churches in Korea (NCCK), NCCK Human Rights Board, Young Men's Christian Association (YMCA), Young Women's Christian Association (YWCA), Ecumenical Youth Council (EYC), Korean Student Christian Federation (KSCF), Seoul Metropolitan Area Special Ministries Committee (Park Hyeong-gyu, Cho Seung-hyeok, Kwon Ho-gyeong, Kim Dong-wan, Heo Byeong-seob, Lee Hae-hak, Jeh Jeong-gu, and Sohn Hak-kyu), Catholic Farmers' Movement, and Christian (Protestant) Farmers' Association, among others. Church leaders like Kim Gwan-seok, the NCCK's general secretary; the Roman Catholic Bishops Kim Sou-hwan and Tji Hak-soun; Kim Sang-geun, the general secretary of PROK; and Kim Jae-joon, president of Hanshin University, also lent their support to the UIM as a matter of allying with the democracy and human rights movement.

Christian student organizations like the EYC and KSCF had several members who directly participated in various struggles of the YDP-UIM. These included Ahn Jae-woong, Jeong Sang-bok, Song Jin-seop, and Park Joon-cheol. The YDP-UIM, in turn, supported the KSCF Student Social Development Corps (SSDC) by arranging labor experience projects for its willing students. A number of research organizations like the Christian Institute for the Study of Justice and Development (CISJD, Cho Seung-hyeok), Christian Academy (Kang Won-ryong), Yonsei Institute for Urban Studies, Sogang University Institute for Labor Studies, and Korea University Institute for Research on Labor and Employment allied with the YDP-UIM on select issues. Dr. Shin In-ryong of Ewha Women's University volunteered as the expert for labor laws. Dr. Kim Yong-bok, Vice President of the CISJD, was one of the few theologians who supported the UIM directly through his academic theology. The Christian press, including the CBS, *Gidokgyo Sasang (Christian Thought)*, and *Ssial Sori (Sound of the Seed)*, tried to fight against the distortions and false accusations of the government with the truth about the UIM.

The churches farthest from home were often the ones that provided the most concrete support. Missionaries like George Ogle, Linda Jones, Bae Chang-min, Rice,[33] Sart,[34] and Father Sinnott spread the news overseas about the state of human and labor rights in South Korea. Indeed, they did quite a bit more to raise awareness about the governments' persecution of the UIM than the domestic press ever did. George Todd, who was the head of the WCC-UIM the UPCUSA general secretary, also held the YDP-UIM in high regard and provided much material and psychological support. The same was true of Oh Jae-sik in the WCC and Ahn Jae-woong in the CCA, who very helpfully employed the resources of their respective international organizations to raise funds, petition for the release of the imprisoned, arrange contacts with the press, exercise influence on other overseas networks, and much more.

Cho never forgot the way George Todd organized churches worldwide to send critical financial and moral support that let the YDP-UIM survive the great repression of the late 1970s. Without it, the ministry could have died, having been cut off from the major domestic sources of support. This also meant there were several files going from the YDP-UIM to George Todd's office. Kim Yong-Bock once remarked that more files were safely stored in the latter than in the YDP-UIM center from the most intense period of the repression.[35]

Cho Chi Song had organized countless public prayers and rallies when petitions alone did not convince the authorities to release the workers and missioners who had been imprisoned. He was very grateful to whoever showed up despite the surveillance of the state to show support for the workers and missioners.[36] These included Cho Yeong-rae, Lee Don-myeong, Han Seung-heon, Hong Seong-woo, Lee Seok-tae, and other human rights lawyers who provided free legal support; the priests, nuns, and ministers in the UIM ministry in other sects or denominations; the dismissed professors (Lee Moon-young, Kim Chan-gook, Han Wan-sang, Baek Nak-cheong, Seo Gwang-seon), poet (Ko Un), and conscientious intellectuals (Ham Seok-heon, Baek Gi-wan) who provided moral support in every trial; independent politicians (Chang Chun-ha, Yoon Posun, Gong Deok-gwi) and social and labor activists who sent their messages of encouragement; the women's ministries who remembered the imprisoned in their tearful prayers; the Christian students who cried that justice would prevail; and the countless workers whose names Cho never learned but faces he never forgot. Park Han-sang, who was the representative of Yeongdeungpo in the National Assembly (also the secretary general of the NDP), also showed his support for the UIM as part of a broader support for workers' rights. He happened to be the brother-in-law of Lee Jeong-hak, the longtime chair of the YDP-UIM Committee. Thus, the YDP-UIM was surrounded by friends even in the midst of its persecution in the 1970s.

Another group of people who joined the YDP-UIM to make history were the volunteers. Several intern pastors and seminarians volunteered to fill in for the missioners who had been arrested or detained for questioning, coming from churches both near and far. Students from the PTS also lent a helping hand by choosing to complete their internship for credit at the YDP-UIM. Student clubs from Ewha University also sent a steady stream of volunteers. All of them diligently provided the much-needed help, whether it be running the worker education programs, distributing literature, cleaning the offices, or something else.

College students from Saemoonan Church, Yeomcheon Church, and Choong-hyun Church served for a long time as teachers in the night school. The students of Saemoonan, in particular, partnered with the YDP-UIM very intentionally under the influence of their pastors Hong Seong-hyeon and Kim Jong-ryeol as well as Professor Kim Yong-Bock. Growing among them were future general secretaries of the YDP-UIM, Lee Geun-bok and Jin Bang-joo.

Right after Cho's arrival in 1965, the YDP-UIM had also been working to connect victims of industrial accidents to the Church World Service and other Christian service organizations so they could receive support for coping with their injuries or the resulting disabilities. The YDP-UIM also invited Professor Hong In-sook from Myongji University, who had been trained in the United States, to speak during its worker education programs on labor health and safety. The YDP-UIM began providing medical services within its offices in 1965, as the workers could not afford to get medical attention for lack of a national health insurance policy. The quality of care was pretty good even by general standards. For instance, Dr. Sohn Jeong-gyun from Paik Hospital provided workers with free eye checkups using one of the few state-of-the-art optometers available in Korea in 1972.

The type of medical care the YDP-UIM offered for an especially long time was dental care. "The workers couldn't go to the dentist even if their teeth hurt," Cho Chi Song said. "If they did, they could end up paying a year's worth of wages. They could lose all their hard-earned money in a single visit."[37]

One of the elders in Bang Ji-il's church had a son who was a student in the Seoul National University School of Dentistry and a student leader in its InterVarsity Christian Fellowship. The YDP-UIM reached out to him, and Lee agreed to volunteer to provide the workers with dental care. Next, the mission needed dentist chairs, which were costly. Thanks to the support of the Family Service Committee of the Women of the Church in the PCUSA, the YDP-UIM acquired two dentist chairs, a cot, and dentistry equipment. The clinic was set up for the first time in June 1972, opening once a week on the first floor of the UIM from 7:00 p.m. to 10:00 p.m. on Tuesdays. It was illegal for students to provide care on their own, so one of the professors volunteered to be the necessary presence. The volunteers initially offered tooth extractions but gradually advanced to providing dental fillings for just the cost of the materials. When Lee Gwan-young himself became a professor of dentistry in Yonsei University, he enlisted his students as additional volunteers. The YDP-UIM dental clinic was now able to offer a much more systematic care even to the family members of the workers. If a case ever needed more equipment than was available in the YDP-UIM, Lee arranged for the workers to get the care in a schoolmate's clinic for a reduced cost.

Cho was very cautious not to allow the volunteers to treat the workers out of some sense of pity or superiority. "Do not take your knowledge and skills for granted," he would constantly tell them. "You are indebted to these workers. Serve them to pay the debt. Do not act like you are teachers. Serve them like you are their students."[38]

Once, a team of volunteers delayed the entire schedule by arriving 10 minutes late. Cho Chi Song reprimanded them for three hours. "Do you know how much 10 minutes are worth to a worker? You signed up for a duty, not the right to serve a group of insignificant people whom you can keep waiting. Don't bother coming back unless you're going to serve the workers like you would the paying clients of your practice." Nobody was ever late again in the dental clinic, and the students appreciated the hard lesson on the true meaning of sincere service.

Volunteering continued to be a strong tradition among the IVCF students in the SNU School of Dentistry. When Cho Chi Song opened the One Home retreat center in Okhwa-ri, they occasionally visited to provide dental care to the rural population nearby. One of the volunteers later became the vice dean of the school and began regularly taking a group of students to volunteer in a particular rural area. Some other students of dentistry went on to experience work in the factories while others started to support the labor movement after starting a private practice. These students formed the Yonsei University

Association of Dentists for Democracy, merging later with the Association of Young Dentists in 1987 following the democratization of the country to form the Dentists for a Healthy Society (Gunchi), becoming one of the many pillars of the democratization movement.

Around 1975, the YDP-UIM began offering a more comprehensive healthcare service, hiring a nurse, Kim Jeong-ran, and enlisting the support of the German "Dr. G," who was a professor at the Catholic University School of Medicine and doctor in Yonsei Severance Hospital. The clinic provided a simple checkup every week for the workers and referred those who needed additional care to a larger hospital. It also periodically offered informative presentations on health, focusing mostly on preventive medicine across the broad range of issues like workplace safety, occupational disease, environmental pollution, oral hygiene, women's health, children's education, health facts, and health counseling. Some others who were instrumental to running the clinic included Dr. Kim Rok-ho, who later began a private practice in Sadang, and Dr. Hong Yoon-cheol, a professor of preventive medicine in Seoul National University.

In the late 1970s, when In succeeded Cho as general secretary, the YDP-UIM began studying specialized care for industrial accident victims with its medical volunteers with the ultimate goal of providing free industrial accident care. They reached the point of creating concrete plans for a hospital, for which they were about to request funding once again from the EZE. Unfortunately, the hospital never materialized as a result of the *Shingunbu's* great repression in the early 1980s.

Songs of Bread, Freedom, and Equality

There was a distinctive culture in the YDP-UIM in the 1970s and 1980s. For instance, unlike most other activist organizations whose office walls were covered slogans calling for struggle, the YDP-UIM center always had an air of simplicity and depth. This was because of the paintings, photographs, and calligraphy that were hung up in its halls. Imitations though they were, they were imitations of quality art.[39]

The missioners played tapes of classical music. This created a relaxing atmosphere that helped workers enter a state of rest after spending their days in the loud, restless factories. The workplaces would play music too, but they usually were popular tunes that added to the overall cacophony. The simple change in what they heard in the background helped the workers find some sense of tranquility. This was by Cho Chi Song's deliberate design. He hoped the contact with visual and auditory art in the YDP-UIM center, even if momentary, could help the workers rest from their labor.

The more activistic side of the YDP-UIM's ministry had to enter a hiatus following the Gwangju Democracy Movement in 1980, limiting its ministry to the explicitly religious activities of worship, prayer, and Bible study. As such, the YDP-UIM shifted the focus of the rest of its programs to activities that enriched the workers' cultural and emotional life, such as flower arranging, music, reading, and cinema. This was partly a design to help the workers recover some sense of psychological security after the great shock of Gwangju, and partly a recognition that the mission had been so fixated on externally organizing the workers for action that it had fallen short in taking care of their inner beings.

Cho Chi Song believed the workers needed to enjoy a musical life. Since the industrial evangelism days in the mid-1960s, he had organized programs to either listen to or make music, ranging in genre from liturgical music to Korean folk music, choral music to famous foreign music. For joint gatherings, he invited musicians from the local church choirs, vocal music majors from Ewha University, the Pilgrim Mission Choir, and the Air Force Band to provide high-quality musical programs. As a result of this groundwork, the YDP-UIM Labor Church later held many of its Easter, Christmas, and Labor Sunday services in mostly musical worship, featuring the choral performance of workers from across different workplaces. The importance Cho placed on music is palpable in the fact that he spent every penny he could buying LP records with classical music because of their scarcity in Korea.

Then right after the Gwangju Democracy Movement in 1980, Cho created a music listening room in the YDP-UIM center. He had taken so much interest in classical music that he took it upon himself to provide the spoken commentary during the listening sessions.

Cho also looked for labor activism songs that the workers could learn and sing along with ease. He also had the workers write their own lyrics and music. The most significant example was the "The Road to Freedom" (Figure 5.1) that was often sung as the song of commitment at the end of the Labor Church worship services starting in 1978.

The mission was also very interested in cinema and reading. The YDP-UIM built a library of major cinematic works whose films were not very common in Korea in the 1970s and often screened them for the workers' enjoyment. These included popular films like *Butch Cassidy and the Sundance Kid*, *The Bridge on the River Kwai*, and Charlie Chaplin's *Modern Times*, as well as artistic short films. The YDP-UIM also screened documentary films about the labor movement overseas and Christian-themed films such as *Faithful Unto Death*, *A Church Without Walls*, and *The Ten Commandments*. The YDP-UIM tried to use these to create community activity by having viewers share their thoughts and feelings after a screening. During the construction from 1978 to 1979, the YDP-UIM made a point of adding thick shades, a projection room, and large screen in the third-floor auditorium. This enhanced the quality of the movie screenings. The YDP-UIM had collected a very impressive library of films by the mid-1980s, which the other labor organizations and minjung churches often borrowed. This was before the widespread use of video tapes.

The YDP-UIM did not originally encourage reading. This was partly because the workers found reading to be rather laborious. It was also because Cho worried the workers may become distracted from real action by the indirect experience gained through reading.

Long and hard though the road to freedom may be,
Holding hand in hand, we will walk onto that path
Crying out, with no justice there's no peace
We'll call for peace in all the lands

Long and hard though the road to freedom may be,
Following our Lord, we will walk onto that path
Crying out, we'll raise justice in this world
We'll call for justice in all the lands

Long and hard though the road to freedom may be,
Walking as one, we will walk onto that path
Crying out for the workers' human rights
We'll call for human rights in all the lands.

Figure 5.1. The Road to Freedom.

As such, the YDP-UIM originally had a small library. Its only books were those used by the small groups or specifically requested by the workers. Reading became a major activity only after the Gwangju Democracy Movement in 1980, when the great repression restricted many of the other activities. The YDP-UIM added a reading room and ordered a large number of new books. It also added a reading club to the Workers' Culture School Program, having workers share what they thought after reading a book.

In contrast to his attitude toward reading, Cho emphasized the importance of writing. He used to pen even the simplest letters and petitions on behalf of the workers in the early days of industrial evangelism. He saw that the workers needed to intentionally learn how to demand their rights with their own voices through writing. This was a challenging task, since most of the young women in the 1960s and 1970s had received limited formal education. Nevertheless, the YDP-UIM tried to offer as many opportunities as possible for clear, logical writing. Workers got to practice writing public statements for their small groups or public prayer during the worships. When a magazine or newspaper asked for a written interview with the YDP-UIM, the missioners encouraged the workers to write and send their own stories. Some of them were published.

Thanks to this deliberate effort, the workers became skillful writers by the late 1970s. The missioners did not pen their petitions, letters, or reports any longer. In fact, there was greater power in the raw voice of the laborers. The workers also went on to author a number of books, including *The Road to Seoul* (Song Hyo-soon), *The Robbed Workplace* (Chang Namsoo), and *For the Eight-Hour Workday* (Soon Jeom-soon). These joined the ranks of essential readings for university students who wanted to join the scenes of labor activism, which include revered titles like *A Stone's Cry* (Yoo Dong-woo), *A Single Spark: The Biography of Jeon Tae-il* (Cho Young-are), and *The Dwarf* (Cho Se-hui). *The Road to Seoul,* written by Song Hyo-soon at Cho Chi Song's recommendation while she was protesting her layoff from Daeil Chemicals, was a milestone work in that it gave rise to the genre of workers' memoirs of the factories.[40]

Another distinctive element of the YDP-UIM's culture were the *nogabas* or well-known songs whose words were changed for the purposes of the workers' gathering. What is now known as the labor culture had not been formed as of the early 1980s. There were very few songs written for the labor movement, so workers often had to sing the songs of student activists even in their rallies. These included titles like "The Cry of the People," "With a Burning Thirst," "The Evergreen Tree," and "We Will Not be Shaken," all of which were unfamiliar to the workers new to the scenes of demonstration. Nogabas were the YDP-UIM's solution to this issue of unfamiliarity.

By adding context-appropriate words to the tunes of popular songs and well-known hymns, the YDP-UIM Labor Church could create an atmosphere in which every worker, both new and old, could easily participate. The nogabas gained great traction. The Wonpoong Textiles Union made and sang a number of them in its struggles against the employer and government, including "The Last Cross," "A Fighter's Song," and "The Day We Won't Forget."

"The Last Cross" was a nogaba set to the tune of "Because the Heart Is Weak," by the popular group Wild Cats. Readers will note that the text had been changed to express the workers' resolve to continue struggling.

> *There is no victory without unity.*
> *We the Wonpoong Textiles Union,*
> *We must stand in unity.*
> *Who could solve our problems for us?*
> *Money and power stand united against us.*
> *We must unite to solve our problems.*

I must bear that last cross.
Quick! Resume our normal operations.
Abide by the terms of our negotiation.

We have suffered much, we have suffered long.
Stop the persecution of workers.
Provide us with a living wage.
Give us the rule of law.
Tell us whom we work for.
Our hot blood is rising.
Quick! Resume our normal operations.
Abide by the terms of our negotiation.

The YDP Labor Church changed the lyrics of hymns like "What a Friend We Have in Jesus" or "Amazing Grace" so they could speak to the workers more directly. These were sung during the YDP-UIM's worship and prayer rallies along with the lyrical activism songs like "Jesus of the Gold Crown" or "The Father of the Minjung."

True Friend (adapted from What a Friend We Have in Jesus)

What a friend we have in Jesus
A true friend who has workers saved
    (Chorus) Can we find a friend so faithful, who
    will all our sorrows share?
    Jesus knows our every weakness, true friend to the
    laboring one.

Though we're weak and heavy-laden, a true friend have
we in the Lord
Precious Savior, still our refuge, a friend to the meek
and weak

*Have we sickness and ailment, a true friend have we in
the Lord
Precious Savior, still our healer, a friend to the ill and
weak*

*Have we chains that keep in bondage, a true friend
have we in the Lord
Precious Savior, our deliverance, a friend to the chained
and weak.*

Amazing Grace That Saved a Worker Like Me (adapted from Amazing Grace)

*Amazing grace, how sweet the sound, that saved a
worker like me?
Hope once was lost, but now it's found, new life I've
now received
2) Freedom
3) Courage
4) Peace*[41]

Cho also changed the lyrics of "Mine Eyes Have Seen Glory" in the early 1970s and titled it "The Song of a Female Temp Worker"— for the women of Donga Dyeing Company to sing during their rallies. This caused the authorities to take him and Kim Gyeong-nak away for 24 hours of questioning regarding the "seditious" content of the song, which said, "after paying rent and buying a few blocks of briquettes, all I have left of my paycheck is the debt." This song was translated and shared with audiences overseas.

Cho explained the rise of the genre:

*Kim Gyeong-nak first changed the lyrics of the song
"Pioneer." It was in the late 1960s. After that, we started*

singing different lyrics to the tune of the hymns. For example,
instead of saying, "what a friend we have in Jesus, all our sins
and griefs to bear," we'd say, "what a friend we have in Jesus,
a true friend who has workers saved." We changed quite a
few songs that way, making hymns the workers could follow
along. [. . .] Then the workers started making their own
adaptations. How should I put it? They were more radical,
more expressive than when we ministers changed the lyrics.[42]

The words of the nogaba hymns offer a glimpse into the faith and lives of the people who labored in our society at the time. Student activists also adopted the practice of changing lyrics of famous songs toward the later days of Yushin. This spread the nogabas into the broader genre of activist and minjung music. In Cho's memory, the student activists only began singing nogabas about a decade after the YDP-UIM had started.

Of course, the detractors used the practice of changing the words to liturgical music as additional fodder for slander. "The Communists in the UIM pretend to worship God, but in reality, they flip the hymns and flip the prayers to blaspheme the Lord."[43]

Hong Ji-young, who wrote several books and led the smear campaign attacking the UIM with the support of certain organizations, made this claim during a speech to the workers of Control Data: "Why are you stirring divisions using a complete fabrication?" An indignant Han Myeong-hee fought back. "Come see for yourself. See if we flip the hymns during our worship in the UIM."[44]

Around 40 of Control Data's workers actually showed up the following Sunday, joined by the detectives of the southern district police, all to see if the accusation of blasphemy was true. There were many other baseless accusations made against the UIM. One rumor, for instance, had it that the small groups were Communist cells whose members wrote their death wishes, which the missioners kept, before beginning their dangerous operations.

It might not have been obvious what the labor movement had to do with the arts and culture. The former was characterized by intense struggle, the latter by sensitivity and refinement. However, the artist and activist shared much in common in that they both acted out of love for humanity and anger against injustice. By engaging with art, workers could realize that they were dignified humans and that the discrimination and injustice they suffered in the workplace were an affront to humanity. This empowered them to resist the injustice in righteous anger. Such was the function served by labor poetry including the works of Park No-hae, the paintings hung up during strikes starting in the mid-1980s, and the labor activist songs that were sung in every rally. For the YDP-UIM, however, the arts and culture had more than just an instrumental value as a tool for labor activism.

"Don't let people think of you as mere factory girls just because you happen to work in the factories," Cho often said. "The people of the world may judge you for your external appearance, but you ought to focus on filling up your inner being. When you do, you will be confident wherever you go. What do you lack, anyway? If we didn't have workers to build the bus, everyone would have to be walking."[45]

Arts and culture were essential for letting workers enjoy the full extent of human flourishing. They could help enrich the workers' inner lives and thus promote the cultivation of their characters, growing their ability to love the others in their community. The workers' affections enlivened through the arts and culture combined with their gritty courage in action to create some of the most beautiful moments in YDP-UIM's history.

Prayer for Strength, Worship for Unity

Throughout the years of intense repression from 1977 to 1979, the YDP-UIM came under constant attack from those who accused it of being a group of secular agitators who were not truly interested in doing Christian missions. This could not have been further from the truth. The YDP-UIM's more activist ministry was, after all, born from the evangelism in the factories that consisted primarily of worship services. Even after it transitioned to a new emphasis in its ministry, the YDP-UIM maintained its worship and Bible studies on Saturday and Monday every week. The contents of these activities were strictly religious. Cho Chi Song was quite faithful in carrying out the dormitory visits, Bible studies, and pastoral counseling as he inherited them from Kang Gyung-goo, his predecessor.

It was only because Cho realized the importance of voluntary participation for the success of Christian ministry that he started to tailor the content of the YDP-UIM's meetings and activities to the workers' needs. The labor rights education and cooperative movement were all offshoots of a genuine attempt to perform Christian ministry.

Starting in 1965, a year after his arrival, Cho implemented a very distinctive way of leading the Labor Sunday and Thanksgiving Sunday services. First, he held them in the form of a joint, inter-community service. For the first Labor Sunday he led on March 14, 1965, he invited members of the LAIE from across all workplaces to the Yeongdeungpo Church. A crowd of nearly 500 had gathered. Bishop John Daly (also named Kim Yohan) preached. The Pilgrim Mission Choir was invited for a special performance. In his ministry report, Cho described the service as having been "an event in which the workers, previously alienated by society and the church, came to worship God while discovering the biblical value of work and their true identity."

The same year, on November 21, a crowd of around 400 had gathered again in Yeongdeungpo Church for the Thanksgiving Sunday service. Dr. Koh Hwang-kyung, the president of Seoul Women's University and a women's activist, was invited as the preacher. In an unusual move, the organizers of the service had the workers bring the products they made in their factories as their thanksgiving offering and charity. Products from a total of 14 different companies were offered on the altar, ranging from the confections of Haitai to bicycles of KIA

Industries. The items were sold at factory price, and the proceeds were sent to those who were in need.[46] Despite the fact that the people of Seoul no longer lived in a rural society, it was still common for the churches to decorate their altars with grains and fruits for Thanksgiving. The YDP-UIM created a variation of this worship format, having the workers instead bring what they actually made. This made the point palpable that the workers could, indeed, please God and serve their neighbors with the work of their hands. It was also a way of affirming the value and dignity of the workers, countering the dominant narrative that often disparaged the factory laborers as being mere *gondgoris* and *gongsoonis*. Indeed, the act of bringing the products of their labor as church offerings was a tangible way for the workers to demonstrate that the image of God was within them: "My Father is still working, and I also am working" (John 5:17).

According to its reports, there were 22 worship services that the YDP-UIM hosted from November 1966 to October 1967, with a cumulative number of 2,109 attendees. The mission also hosted 23 Bible study sessions, with a cumulative number of 292 attendees. This meant that there were nearly two worship services and Bible study sessions each month. In 1968, this number grew to a monthly average of eight worship services and six Bible studies. The number of attendees in the Thanksgiving service that November also grew to about 700, who brought the products of 26 different companies as their thanksgiving offering. Rev. Kim Jeong-joon, the president of Hanshin University, was invited to preach. In the fall of 1970, the missionary Robert Hoffman began holding an English Bible study twice every week. On May 14, 1972, Yeongdeungpo Church celebrated its 14th anniversary in the borrowed space of Kyeongwon Cinema owned by one of its deacons, Lee Gi-yeon. The theater could not seat the nearly 1,200 workers who attended, and some had to stand throughout the service. The members of the LAIE also organized their own weekly worship service in each of their factories, inviting the YDP-UIM missioners as the preachers.

In October 1973, the YDP-UIM began offering a Saturday evening worship service for the workers who could not attend the Sunday service. These services also accommodated the attendance of non-Christians. The Saturday services were a deliberate initiative in keeping with the recommendation of the YDP-UIM's evaluation meeting that took place from October 1 to 2, 1973. The recommendation reads: "Since the YDP-UIM is currently focused on indirect ministry, it ought to create an occasion in which it can teach the Scriptures directly and lead the workers in worship."

The Saturday services were then moved to Mondays in the fall of 1974. They were now dubbed the "Exodus," in which workers met for worship, prayer, and Bible study. It also became far more open to the attendance of those who were not Christians. For the Christians, the Exodus was meant as an alternative to the Sunday services that the weekend workers could still attend. It was also meant as an alternative in substance that allowed the workers to break out of the narrow mold of religion that was often imposed.[47]

In the reports of the YDP-UIM, the purpose of Exodus was to seek out "a way to resolve the tension between religion and faith" and create "biblical, faith-based discussions about the various social issues, including the labor issues, that take place in our industrial society." Cho hoped such dialogue would inspire the workers to initiate their own *exodus* from the trappings of received religion and grapple with the issues in their current contexts. In later years, he assessed that the Exodus meetings were the catalyst that led to the creation of a spirituality of liberation within the YDP-UIM. He also added that while the number of participants was very low, the level of their fervor and discipleship was very high.

As more and more workers tasted the fullness offered by Christianity, the number of participants in the Exodus meetings start to grow. In September 1976, the YDP-UIM had to split the meeting into three groups. Those working the night shifts met at 9:30 a.m. The missioners and those on leave met at 3:30 p.m. Those who worked the day shifts met at 7:30 p.m. Participation averaged about 100 every week. In January 1977, the YDP-UIM wrote in its report to the YDP-UIM Committee:

> *The workers will not find the courage to transform their lives unless they can be convinced of the relationship between the word of God and their day-to-day realities. The participants of the Exodus want a church for workers just like themselves. As such, we need a labor church.*[48]

It was therefore clear that the YDP-UIM still had its roots and core in Christianity. This did not stop the state and other detractors from slandering the UIM as being nothing more than an organization that was bent on stirring discontent among the workers in an attempt to drive a wedge between the mission and the rest of the church. The missioners could have shrugged off the attacks as ignorant talk by ignorant strangers if their sources were merely external. The problem was the eye of skepticism with which some of the clergy and elders of the PCK viewed the UIM. This was a source of genuine pressure for the missioners.

Again, worship and devotional activities were a consistent part of the YDP-UIM's ministry. They were less conspicuous because of the comparatively large growth in the labor education and intervention programs. Nevertheless, the YDP-UIM decided it needed to make its Christian roots very clear so it could avoid unnecessary suspicion. There was also a need to establish the YDP-UIM's identity in Christian martyrdom so it could persevere through the mounting repression. Finally, there seemed to be a pragmatic need for the additional layer of protection of the YDP-UIM from forming an institutional church.[49]

In Myeong-jin was the one who stated the necessity of a church with the greatest emphasis. He carried out most of the tasks required to start the Yeongdeungpo Labor Church, which held its first worship service at 4:00 p.m. on Labor Sunday, March 13, 1977, in the borrowed hall of Dangsan-dong Presbyterian Church. There were about 120 workers in attendance who confirmed the following founding statement of their congregation:

- Only a worker can register as a member of the congregation.
- We politely decline the registration of someone who is already a member of another church.
- We welcome any worker who wants to pray and work with us as we study the question of how the word of God may be applied and the will of God may be realized in our workplace.
- We will gather every Sunday in worship to pray about the issues in our workplace, seeking and acting to implement the will of God in our workplace.[50]

The format of the Labor Church services was just like that of any other church. Their substance, however, whether in the sermon or prayer or liturgical professions, were all of and for the workers. The songs were chosen from hymns, gospels, and activism songs that spoke to the workers. The collection was printed and given the title *Hymns of Victory*, for use in the church and families. Myeong Noh-seon made the music sheets by hand and bound them in a cover with the workers' favorite color: red. Hong Ji-young, who wrote propaganda literature against the UIMs, purported this to be evidence that the UIM was Communist.[51]

Cho was haunted by the memory of the workers who were forced to sit through the factory worships with no respect to their volition or conscience and despite their incredible exhaustion. He was glad that in the new church, the workers were free to worship without the coercion he was an unwitting part of in the 1960s.

The Labor Church was a source of great consolation in times of dire need. Its encouragements came in the form of sermons, intercessions, testimonies, and warm shows of solidarity. Both the workers and missioners could renew their spiritual resolve through the worship services. Workers prayed for the justice of God whenever they were in the midst of a struggle or in preparation for a new one. They took heart in the conviction that they would overcome, for their struggle was aligned with the purposes of God to bring salvation to the workers. The women who stood up to pray on behalf of the congregation shared that they often experienced such a raw surge of emotion that the tears welling up in their eyes prevented them from reading the rest of the text they had prepared.

The emotional charge of the fellowship and prayer is especially palpable in the text of the public prayer for the fourth Sunday of July in 1979, when the repression had reached a new peak.

> *Our father in heaven [. . .] forgive us our shortcomings and*
> *use us as your workers. There are so many around us who*
> *are pressed down and suffering. They are exhausted, hungry,*
> *beaten, imprisoned, watched by the authorities, hated by the*
> *companies, and otherwise exhausted.*
>
> *Father, give us greater faith. Give us more courage. If*
> *you do, we won't live for ourselves but for the deliverance of*
> *all people from their suffering.*

Then, the prayer on August 12 indicated the workers' confidence that regardless of the persecution, they would overcome.

> *How long, O Lord, will you allow the liars and the*
> *unrighteous torment the righteous? How long will you allow*
> *this tragedy? They throw curses at us and trample us with*
> *their feet. They mockingly ask us, "what is justice, what is*
> *freedom, what are human rights?" Countless workers tremble*
> *in fear at the intimidation of the devil's servants.*
>
> *How long will you allow the roots of evil continue their*
> *violence? Give us faith. Give us courage. Grant us to become*
> *your soldiers for righteousness, so we may fight and prevail*
> *against the forces of injustice. Grant that every laboring*

*hand will break the forces of evil and build your kingdom of
justice, freedom, and peace.*[52]

The sermons Cho Chi Song preached during this period include
"The Justice of God" (Job 29:8–17), "God with Us" (Matt 28:18–20),
"The Rich and the Poor" (Eccl 5:9–16, Prov 23:4–5), "Power Corrupts"
(Mic 2:1–6, 7:1–6), "When They Utter All Kinds of Evil Falsely"
(Matt 5:1–12), "How Then Shall We Live?" (Jas 4:15–17), "The
Earthquake That Opened the Prison Doors" (Acts 16:16–20), and "A
New Wineskin for New Wine" (Mark 2:21–22).[53] Then, following
the fall of Park Chung Hee at the hand of his subordinate and the
subsequent demise of the Yushin regime, Cho proclaimed that the
workers would soon be able to find peace in their workplace and
experience the restoration of God's justice.

Han Myeong-hee, who was a leader of a small group in Control
Data, said the Labor Church services were a source of encouragement
and strength for the YDP-UIM's workers.

*In retrospect, the Labor Church of the Yeongdeungpo UIM
was a very valuable place where I made one of my most
important commitments in those very difficult days. [. . .]
We each came from a different workplace, but all of us had
to struggle and experienced hurt. So when we worshiped and
prayed together, we found great strength and encouragement.
[. . .] Through worship, we became bold enough to tell
ourselves, "if things go wrong leading the fight, we can just go
to prison for a few years and come back again."*[54]

The Labor Church provided a context in which the workers
organized through the YDP-UIM could feel they, too, were proper
members of the church. It also provided some level of "sanctuary" from
external attacks. Even a dictator was careful not to give the impression
that it was happy to launch a wholesale persecution of Christians.

The Labor Church originally had to hold its services on Sunday afternoons in the borrowed space of Dangsan-dong Church. After the completion of the new YDP-UIM center on July 8, 1979, the church could meet on Sunday mornings at 11:00 a.m. in the third-floor auditorium of the center. This added greater energy to the congregation. A total of 1,500 people gathered in the first service in the new center; around 22 were baptized in the first communion. In the aftermath of Gwangju in 1980, the Labor Church called for a 40-day prayer to intercede for the UIM, workers, and nation. This lasted from June 1 to July 10. A total of 313 people took turns praying in the third-floor worship hall, always occupying it during the open hours from 6:00 a.m. to 10:00 p.m. every day. Thus, the Labor Church shone a light on a turbulent chapter of history with the prayer and faith of its members.[55]

The missioners hoped that the Labor Church would continue to be the front that could outlast the government's persecution, into which they could absorb and sustain the other parts of their ministry. Unfortunately, the use of the framework of an institutional church did not produce the outcome they had hoped. Most of the small-group workers were dispersed by the *Shingunbu*'s repression following 1980. Organized activity in the workplace came to a full stop. The members tried to regroup in the Labor Church for some time, but their numbers steadily decreased. Despite the goal of reaching 500 regular congregants, the number continued to decrease from the initial figure of between 250 and 300. It was a tangible lesson for Cho Chi Song that a church without walls was far more effective than one that had the institutional walls in sharing the good news of salvation and deliverance with the workers. Indeed, a church that could exist without walls may have been the only thing worth calling a true church.

Starting the Labor Church thus became one of the initiatives Cho regretted from his ministry, despite the spiritual comfort it had provided to the workers and missioners. In Cho's mind, the true church of the workers was whichever community in which hope was made real in context. At first, this was the labor union. Then, it was the small groups. Cho had only opted to use the form of an institutional church to protect and preserve the essence the former two carried. Yet, in the end, the higher organs of the institutional church in the PCK eventually chose to abandon the essence. Cho also believed the second generation of UIM missioners he trained was too eager recreating the form of the Labor Church without the essence of the worker-driven activities.

> *I thought to myself, "we shouldn't have started a church."*
> *Because now that it was there, all that anyone wanted was*
> *to go back within its walls. I regretted it. All the people who*
> *were trained for urban industrial ministry went out to plant*
> *more churches. [. . .]* What should we have done instead?
> *you might ask. I think we should have let the UIM die.*
> *Because if it died, it would have truly lived.*
>
> 　*There is a time for everyone to die. You don't want to*
> *contrive life beyond that. The Bible says so. "Even though they*
> *die, they will live." Jesus had to die and then come back to*
> *life because there was no other way. The UIM's mistake was*
> *trying to catch up to a church that had already lost its grasp*
> *on salvation. The fault is mine for sowing the seeds of that*
> *mistake.*[56]

Indeed, Cho had hoped the younger missioners he trained would have focused on the kind of ministry that he had spent his younger years doing. The reality, nevertheless, was that it was very difficult to sustain any targeted ministry for the workers without the protective walls of the institutional church during the *Shingunbu*'s reign up to the late 1980s. For their part, the juniors of Cho Chi Song were trying to be strategic in keeping the UIM of the 1970s alive along with the rest of the minjung ministry within the walls of the only space that the law now permitted. In the eyes of the veteran missioner, this seemed to be a sellout that prioritized the survival of the church over the substance of the ministry. In any case, the Labor Church continued to survive, changing its name to Seongmunbak Church in 1983, which means "the church outside the gates of the city." The younger missioners used the Seongmunbak as a model to plant a church ministry for workers in every major industrial area throughout the country.[57]

In any case, the YDP-UIM was able to endure the days of persecution and stay its course for as long as it did because of its workers' tearful prayers. Bringing their weary selves to worship, the workers gave themselves up as living sacrifices. They became hardened soldiers of Christ in the struggle against injustice, powerfully united in a self-sacrificial commitment to one another. This especially showed up inside the interrogation rooms, where the investigators barked at the workers to give up which of the UIM ministers had "incited" their strikes or demonstrations. "None of them," the young women replied, armed with the spiritual depth they gained in the Labor Church. "Jesus told us to fight the injustice. What's the matter with that?"

NOTES

1 Kim and Yoo, *Cho Chi Song's Oral History* (Vol. 12, 2011).

2 Kim Myeong-bae, "Ministry Reports from January 1966," *Yeongdeungpo UIM Files Vol. 1* (YDP-UIM & Soongsil University Center for Culture and Mission Studies, 2020).

3 Kim Myeong-bae, "Ministry Reports from January 1966."

4 Kim and Yoo, *Cho Chi Song's Oral History* (Vol. 5, 2011).

5 Seo Deok-Seok and Sohn Eun-jeong, "Interviews of the Older Members of the UIM: Park Jeom-soon, Shin Mi-ja, Song Hyo-soon, Park Deuk-soon, Kim Mi-soon, and Han Myeong-hee" (2011).

6 Jeong and Sohn, "Cho Chi Song's Interview."

7 Cho Chi Song, "Why Cooperatives & How" (unpublished text, YDP-UIM).

8 Jeong and Sohn, "Cho Chi Song's Interview."

9 Cho Chi Song, "Why Cooperatives & How."

10 Kim Myeong-bae, *Yeongdeungpo UIM Files Vol. 1* (YDP-UIM & Soongsil University Center for Culture and Mission Studies, 2020).

11 Kim, *Yeongdeungpo UIM Files Vol. 1*, 164.

12 Jeong and Sohn, "Cho Chi Song's Interview."

13 Seo and Sohn, "Interviews of the Older Members of the UIM."

14 Park Jeom-soon, "Beautiful Memories," *30th Anniversary of the Squirrel Fellowship* (YDP-UIM, 1999).

15 Kim Myeong-bae, "Workers' Consumer Cooperative Reports from 1976," *Yeongdeungpo UIM Files Vol. 1* (YDP-UIM & Soongsil University Center for Culture and Mission Studies, 2020), 306–308.

16 Kim and Yoo, *Cho Chi Song's Oral History* (Vol. 3, 2011).

17 Kim and Yoo, *Cho Chi Song's Oral History* (Vol. 3).

18 Kim and Yoo, *Cho Chi Song's Oral History* (Vol. 3).

19 PCK Department of Evangelism UIM Committee, *The Church and UIM* (PCK Education & Resourcing Ministry, 1981), 113.

20 YDP-UIM, *30th Anniversary of the Squirrel Fellowship* (unpublished reports, 1999).

21 Seo and Sohn, "Interviews of the Older Members of the UIM."

22 Kim Myeong-bae, *Yeongdeungpo UIM Files Vol. 1* (YDP-UIM & Soongsil University Center for Culture and Mission Studies, 2020).

23 Seo and Sohn, "Interviews of the Older Members of the UIM."

24 Kim and Yoo, *Cho Chi Song's Oral History* (Vol. 3, 2011).

25 Kim and Yoo, *Cho Chi Song's Oral History* (Vol. 3, 2011).

26 Kim and Yoo, *Cho Chi Song's Oral History* (Vol. 3, 2011).

27 YDP-UIM, *30th Anniversary of the Squirrel Fellowship* (unpublished reports, 1999).

28 Cho Chi Song, "A Brief History of the UIM," *Yeongdeungpo UIM: A 40-Year History* (YDP-UIM, 1998).

29 Kim and Yoo, *Cho Chi Song's Oral History* (Vol. 10, 2011), 10.

30 Kim and Yoo, *Cho Chi Song's Oral History* (Vol. 2, 2011).

31 Oh Cheol-ho, *Industrial Evangelism Handbook* (PCK Education and Resourcing Ministry, 1965).

32 PCK Department of Evangelism UIM Committee, *The Church and UIM* (PCK Education & Resourcing Ministry, 1981), 259.

33 Translator's note: could not confirm English spelling.

34 Translator's note: could not confirm English spelling.

35 Seo Deok-Seok and Sohn Eun-jeong, "Kim Yong-Bock's Interview," *Interviews of Related Individuals for the Biography* (YDP-UIM, 2021).

36 "Kim Gap-jun's Interview," Interviews of Related Individuals for the Biography (YDP-UIM, 2011).
37 Kim and Yoo, *Cho Chi Song's Oral History* (Vol. 3, 2011).
38 Kim and Yoo, *Cho Chi Song's Oral History* (Vol. 3, 2011).
39 Seo Deok-Seok and Sohn Eun-jeong, "Chang Seok-sook's Interview," *Interviews of Related Individuals for the Biography* (YDP-UIM, 2011).
40 Seo and Sohn, "Interviews of the Older Members of the UIM"; Kim and Yoo, *Cho Chi Song's Oral History* (Vol. 4, 2011).
41 Yeongdeungpo Labor Church (unpublished songbook).
42 Kim and Yoo, *Cho Chi Song's Oral History* (Vol. 4, 2011).
43 Seo and Sohn, "Interviews of the Older Members of the UIM."
44 Seo and Sohn, "Interviews of the Older Members of the UIM.".
45 Seo and Sohn, "Interviews of the Older Members of the UIM.".
46 Kim Myeong-bae, *Yeongdeungpo UIM Files Vol. 1* (YDP-UIM & Soongsil University Center for Culture and Mission Studies, 2020).
47 Kim and Yoo, *Cho Chi Song's Oral History* (Vol. 4, 2011).
48 Kim, *Yeongdeungpo UIM Files Vol. 1.*
49 In Myeong-jin, "The Minjung Church As A New Strategy," *The Story of Seongmunbak's People* (Christian Literature Society of Korea, 2013).
50 Kim, *Yeongdeungpo UIM Files Vol. 1.*
51 Sohn Eun-jeong, "Transcribed Interviews: Myeong Noh-seon" (2022).
52 Yeongdeungpo Labor Church, *Bulletins* (1979).
53 Yeongdeungpo Labor Church, *Bulletins* (1979–1980).
54 Han Myeong-hee, "The YDP-UIM And I," Yang Myeong-deuk, *Freedom for the Oppressed* (YDP-UIM & Dongyeon, 2020), 338.
55 Yeongdeungpo Labor Church, *Bulletins* (1980).
56 Kim and Yoo, *Cho Chi Song's Oral History* (Vol. 4, 2011).
57 In, "The Minjung Church As A New Strategy."

6

LEARNING FROM EACH OTHER

ACTIVISTS AND THE workers affiliated with the YDP-UIM often called Cho Chi Song the "Father of Workers" to recognize the role he played in nurturing the growth of the workers. This was, indeed, a fitting title. Yet Cho always believed himself to be the one who was indebted to the workers. He said, "The workers are my true teachers," and maintained an attitude of learning from the workers till the very last day of his life.

Learning from the Workers

Cho got into the UIM because of his formative experience working the coal mines in the summer of 1961 as part of the first labor immersion program organized by the IIE of the PCK. His exposure to the lives of the miners left him with a strong sense of calling that he ought to share the good news with those who were his coworkers that summer. This led him to participate in student labor studies program organized by the PCK IEC.

Later on, Cho became the intern at the PCK DOE who was responsible for taking his juniors to the coal mines, casting factories, cement factories, textile factories, construction sites, and many other places of intense industrial labor to gain the same kind of hands-on education. Repeatedly subjecting himself to the experience of hard labor and guiding other students to do the same, Cho learned that labor was, indeed, the best teacher.

Labor was and still is the most important element of training for the UIM. You have to focus while you are working. You

*can't think about doing another research or coming up with
ideas about how to do ministry. [. . .] All you have to do is
just keep toiling with your body. The job best be the hardest
one you can find. [. . .] I still make the UIM students look
for another job if I think the ones they found are too easy.
Or if they don't work very many hours. Or if they get to sit
down all day. They have to work as hard as they can short of
falling ill or collapsing in the middle of it. There can be no
compromise. If they have something that is any easier, they
have to switch (the workplace).* [1]

The programs offered by the PCK IEC while Cho was an intern
gained a reputation for providing the right kind of exposure to the
working society that a member of the clergy needed for carrying out
an effective ministry. Bishop John Daly believed this to be the case
and instructed all Anglican seminarians to participate in the PCK's
training before their ordination. Kim Seong-su, who later became the
first archbishop of an independent Anglican Church of Korea (SKH),
went through the same training under Cho Chi Song's supervision in
the coal mines of Dogye.

The pain of working long hours of hard labor utterly struck Cho
with the realization of how academic and abstract his understanding
of scripture had been.

*I don't think I truly understood what was meant by "blessed
are those who are persecuted for the sake of righteousness"
until, say, I was a decade into the UIM. [. . .] By then it
became clear what it meant for the workers and for me to
suffer persecution for the sake of righteousness. I don't think
people who've never experienced persecution for trying to
do the right thing will ever understand what that passage
means. I'm certain of it. You could have ten doctorates in
theology, and you still won't understand that passage unless
you experience persecution in your body. [. . .] I learned the*

*true gospel not from the professors of theology but from the
workers.*

*You get an answer to the question, "who is Jesus,"
whenever there is a solemn moment in which somebody really
shows you the meaning of the gospel and of justice. I've had
countless such moments with the (workers) who are treated
with contempt.*

*I think the greatest blasphemy against God is to pray,
"our father in heaven, hallowed be your name, give us this
day our daily bread," when you've just robbed people of
their daily bread despite your stores of food to last you for a
lifetime. [. . .] I couldn't pray like that in front of the workers
anymore. [. . .] Because the obvious question is, why would
you ask God for those things? Why wouldn't you give the daily
bread to the others yourselves (when you've already stored
enough food and clothes to last you an entire lifetime)? You've
even already robbed the others of everything they have. That's
no church. That's nothing sensible. It's certainly not a group
of people who really believe in Jesus. [. . .] Through the course
of my experience in the UIM, I've come to believe the church
(which lost its touch with the mind of Christ) itself needed
to be brought to salvation. The UIM would flourish once the
church had been reformed and renewed.*[2]

Cho believed it made absolutely no sense that a missioner could
serve the workers without first having become one, let alone without
ever having a genuine encounter with one. He believed true learning
was only possible once a person had set aside the pretense of somehow
helping the workers and instead chose to identify with the workers,
immersing into the reality and problems of their everyday lives.

*You have to feel it for yourself in your body—the back pain,
the drowsiness, the insult, the humiliation, everything. Then
you have to take a good look at the workers until you can see*

the depth of their perseverance, the weight that they bear, the
dignity of their character that borders on religion, even that
of Jesus Christ. [. . .] You need to become a worker to know
what it means to be human. To know what it means to be an
authentic Christian. To have a chance at salvation. To have a
chance at repentance. You have to labor until you reach such
experience in your very own body.

The true meaning of the gospel as understood by Cho Chi
Song was the proclamation of human dignity by the workers
who shed their blood as they patiently waited for justice. It
was also the process by which a Christian, upon hearing that
proclamation, identified one's self with the worker. Christ was
born a human so that he may bring salvation to humanity.
Likewise, Christians must become workers so they may bring
salvation to workers. This was also the way the Christians
would ultimately find their own deliverance.

There was nobody who could speak the truth as workers
did in my conversations with them. Their words naturally
inspired me. They could move both the heart and the mind,
bringing you to a certain understanding and a resolve. The
look on their face and the words that they used. [. . .] The
Bible says in the beginning there was the Word.[3]

Cho inclined his ears toward the truth contained in the raw stories
of the workers. It broke his heart to see them resign themselves to their
mistreatment for the lack of having acquired a critical consciousness
about the systems surrounding them. They were rightly angry, but they
did not think there could be a solution to the problems. Cho often felt
a greater degree of vicarious indignation than the workers themselves.
As such, he was overjoyed to see a worker have an awakening through
the small-group activities, determining for herself that she would break
the cycle of oppression.

Salvation and the ministry of the UIM was none other than the
process by which a worker regained her agency, awakened herself to

the labor laws, and rose to fight not only for herself but for the rights of other workers and the justice of society. Cho remarked, "I've seen many workers who have never heard the name of Jesus and yet thought and acted more like Christ than I ever did as an ordained minister." He considered such workers 100 times better than himself, saying "The gathering of such workers was the true church." This was the gist of what he meant when he said he learned the UIM not from seminary but from the workers.

The theology and scriptural interpretation he originally had did not help Cho find a way he could in good conscience say would lead the workers to their salvation. He found the breakthrough when he identified the suffering of the workers to the passion of the Christ. The mere process of reading the Bible through the eyes of the workers, grappling with issues with the workers, and fighting to improve the labor conditions facing the workers was a proper part of expanding the kingdom and doing God's ministry.

The community of workers was the church. There was no need for a separate ecclesiastical building. The stories they told were the sermons, their cries the prayers. Cho emphatically said, "There could be no better preaching, no better praying, no better repentance" than what he has seen in the communion of workers. He also stated that the church needed to find salvation before it could offer it to the workers. This seems to have been a criticism of the church and its slowness to repentance and understanding compared to the increasing measure of grace and the character of Christ that he could see in the workers who matured through the UIM activities.

Cho Chi Song discovered Christ in the workers. He loved them the way he would have Christ. Finally, he discovered that identifying with the workers was the true way to carry out the industrial mission. The two ideas that he ought to learn from the workers and that Christ was none other than the workers fighting for justice became a part of his lifelong profession of faith and philosophy of ministry.

In Organizing Lies Our Strength

Cho spent most of his time in ministry meeting with workers. The encounters used to lack depth in the early days of industrial evangelism, limited to the formal sessions of the factory worship and Bible studies. Once Cho realized such factory worships were not truly welcomed by the workers, he changed course and started to focus on building personal levels of trust and relationships with the workers. Cho needed the workers' trust before he could help them transform their lives, and the workers needed to be able to cry and laugh with Cho before they could trust him.

So began the informal factory visits. Cho would go to a factory with or without a formal event scheduled for that day and eat lunch with the workers in the cafeteria. When they went back to their stations, Cho stayed behind with the security guards to continue the conversations. When the workers started leaving at the end of their shift, Cho accompanied them. At times, he even waited in front of the factory at midnight to meet the workers who worked the late shift.[4] He had a considerable amount of freedom to visit the factories while he was still invited by the employers to lead the factory worships. The company employees must have thought he had a free pass to visit their premises.

Over the course of meeting many workers, Cho gained a thorough understanding of their work and living environments, including the stories of their backgrounds, the details of the jobs, how much they were paid, how many days they had off, the general mood of the workplace, the presence and character of the labor unions, and the workers' friendship networks. After a while, Cho came to know a few workers in each of the major Yeongdeungpo factories. He began to keep track of the factories he visited and the workers he met onto a large map of Yeongdeungpo, which later covered around 300 factories.

*I didn't meet the people with a predetermined goal of
what I wanted to accomplish. Rather, I indicated that I*

*was interested in learning what issues they had and how I
could be of help. I indicated that I wanted to have a deep
conversation about whatever they were concerned with. Then,
they would respond very naturally. People will naturally
organize when you have a focused discussion about their
underlying issues. [. . .] They respond to their most pressing
needs. Because a light goes on in their minds when they talk
about what they're interested in, or what they hoped could be
better.*[5]

Cho treated every worker he met with great respect, trying to respond sincerely and sympathetically to each of their stories.

*I didn't always know the pain, the wrongs, the anger the
workers had to live with. But they became all too obvious
once I went where they were. I could see them, touch them,
and feel them in my heart. I could identify with the workers,
and their anger became my anger. [. . .] Sometimes, I got
so angry at how the workers were wronged, I could hardly
contain it. Even if they were calm, even if they weren't angry,
I was angry.*[6]

The object of such visceral anger was labor exploitation. Cho was outraged at the employers who enriched themselves at the expense of the dignity of the workers. He was, furthermore, indignant at the complicity of the police and public authorities. Even the labor administration, the ostensible advocate for workers, shamelessly displayed its favoritism for the employers. Cho felt that he had to do something about the inequity. At the very least, the church and the UIM had to take a stand in support of the workers.

Justice required balance, but power was concentrated in the hands of the employers. They had the power of capital and control over the workforce that was willing to do their bidding with great efficiency. Should anyone dare to say no, they could turn to the ready support of the police, labor administration, and the rest of state power. This led Cho to believe that the church should at least become an ally for the workers to help restore balance and create a chance for justice.

> *Management had more power than the workers. I was certain, therefore, that the church should not try to stay neutral on the issue of labor-management relations. [. . .] Yet, the Korean church always insisted on maintaining neutrality. But standing in the middle does not mean neutrality when the scales have been skewed. You could be doing something in the name of serving the poor and still be serving the rich in reality.*[7]

Cho justified his preferential love for the workers in the fight for their rights by pointing out that the pretense of neutrality might end up enabling or abetting the wrongdoing of the combined force of the employers and the state. He also often said that one could never fully understand the Scripture, let alone become a true Christian, through intellectual study. Only by understanding the downtrodden and identifying with the anger of the impoverished workers could one become a true Christian capable of serving in an urban industrial ministry.

Cho believed that for the young working women to be able to correct the injustice they suffered, they needed a certain amount of power. This power could only be found through organizing. Hence, Cho began organizing the workers, initially in the form of the labor unions.

> *We believed organizing was necessary for the workers to be able to receive a just and humane treatment. They could only exercise power through organizing. Then the question was, how should they organize?*[8]

He had already experienced how dismal the workplace could be without organizing. This, fortunately, also taught him how a resigned worker could be shaken out of hopelessness. The key was to give the workers a taste of their own ability to create change by working together, starting with the smallest of improvements to their day-to-day lives. Cho recognized early on that the workers needed more than the occasional strikes to make fragmentary improvements to their wages or conditions. They needed to steadily build up their organization base.

> *There's no secret to organizing other than that you always have to get them to lay a claim to something (in their interest) and make it happen. A group of people are only organized if they can continually look and fight for new improvements, whether it be getting new heaters or getting better tables for their workstations. [. . .] Sitting down to read and theorize all day is a seminar, not organizing. A labor union that talked about matters of theory and principles all day could not become a true organization.*[9]

Once organized, the workers needed a variety of tactics they could use to struggle and win. This was an idea Cho picked up during his stay in Chicago where he was exposed to Saul Alinsky's concept of community organizing. The gist of it was that no legitimate demand would ever be met without substantial organization and sound strategy.

Another way Cho described the Alinskian organization was that it was a group of people who rose up in fierce, powerful opposition to injustice.

> *Their activism was inspired. You would have pastors, priests, and nuns come out, not to teach the Bible, but to carry around these pamphlets. Thousands of them. And there was no other reason for doing so other than that they were convinced that was as holy an activity as preaching or holding mass. I remember them going around, handing the pamphlets out, explaining to people what it was all about. For them, that was mass. And I say, what better mass could you have?*[10]

The workers, farmers, and residential activists of Chicago who organized themselves according to Alinksy's theory taught Cho Chi Song a number of important lessons. First, people needed to organize if they wanted to live in a humane and just society. As such, the workers and missioners in Yeongdeungpo also needed to find a method of activism that made sense in their local context. Returning from Chicago, Cho defined the UIM's ministry as a social movement that was driven by indignation against injustice in the workplace and aimed at correcting such injustice using the collective means to apply organized pressure.

Worker leadership was going to be an important element in all of this, which was why the YDP-UIM invested heavily into the various leadership development trainings. One of them was the Pioneer, a course for workers who had been a part of a small group for three to five years so they could become leaders among their coworkers. The course consisted of lectures and discussions that were great in both breadth and depth, addressing topics like why the workers needed organized activism, the methods and principles of such activism, the key issues in economics and industrial relations, the history of labor movements overseas, the labor rights afforded by the constitution, precedents in labor disputes, how to run a labor union, and organizational management. University professors like Park Hyeon-chae, Yoo In-woo, and Shin In-ryeong were invited as speakers. The workers who completed the Pioneer could claim at least an undergraduate level of knowledge about the topics.

> *A lot of the people who received the training went on to become officers in their unions. You know, the stewards, women's representatives, accountants, and so forth. In some unions, 80 to 90 percent of the officers were members of the Yeongdeungpo UIM. [. . .] Towards the end of a course, the workers would even have a candlelight service to make their leadership resolutions.*[11]

Cho held the worker leaders in very high regard, saying they had accomplished several times more than he had as a full-time missioner in the UIM. He believed they were the true drivers of the UIM's ministry.

There were hundreds of workers who were two or three times more committed to the UIM than I was. I'm sure that whenever I worried about 100 things, they worried about 200 things. So having a few hundred of those leaders could produce results that would have taken a thousand missioners like me.

Of course, such grassroots organization and leadership required a great amount of initial investment in the forms of time, money, and building of personal trust. The returns were great, nevertheless, as was demonstrated when the graduates of Pioneer took center stage during the late Yushin period from 1976 to 1979. A partial list of the struggles they led includes workplaces like Daeil Chemicals, Hanheung Moolsan, Haitai Confectionery, Lotte Confectionery, Namyoung Nylon, Pangrim Textiles, Daehan Weaving Company, Daehan Textiles, Wonpoong Textiles, Daehyup, Dong-gwang Trading Company, Dongyang Nylon, Hanyoung Textiles, Mando Mannequin, Samgong Machinery, Seoul Miwon, Seoul Trading Company, Signetics Korea, Crown Electronics, and Control Data.

Learning from Each Other

One of the big initiatives of the YDP-UIM was providing general education for the workers. From 1964 to 1967, this was done by inviting university professors or their equivalents as speakers for the lay industrial evangelism programs. Then the YDP-UIM shifted focus to providing union officer training in 1969. When this was put to a stop by the emergency decrees in 1972, the YDP-UIM shifted focus once again to grassroots organizing through the small groups, and Cho Chi

Song accordingly redesigned an educational program that matched the workers' needs to what the YDP-UIM was able to provide.

Both the lay evangelism and union officer programs shared in the fact that their educational goal was to cultivate an elite group of workers in each workplace who could evangelize or unionize the other workers. There certainly was value in this. The education for the LAIE resulted in an increase of Christians throughout the factories. It also helped the recipients of the education receive promotions to middle management, which resulted in a wider access to the workforce for the purposes of evangelism. The union officer training also contributed significantly to building the capacity of the labor unions and their democratization.

There was a limit, however, in the extent to which the education of a select group of workers could contribute to broader growth and transformation. The lay evangelists were talented members of a church. They were rarely advocates for the rights of their coworkers. The union officers, as educated as they were, proved to be highly susceptible to repression and placation. They often became ineffective advocates for workers at best and effective advocates of the employers at worst.

This taught the YDP-UIM that it needed to reorient its educational programs toward those who were lowest on the organizational ladder. Training the top was not going to create lasting justice. Adding to the impetus for change were the emergency presidential decrees that effectively banned all forms of overt public assembly.

The new goal of YDP-UIM's educational program was to raise the level of consciousness among the workers on the bottom rung so they could become the agents of change in the workplace. Informing this transition, again, were the eight months Cho spent in Chicago learning about the urban and rural activism that applied Alinsky's concept of community organizing. He also drew from what he learned in the union leadership training in Roosevelt University. Cho realized that the success of a movement depended on strong organization, voluntary mass participation, and dedicated leadership. Wealth and state power were powerfully united adversaries. The workers needed to be no less united in their common interests and moral high ground if they were to stand a chance. They also needed the sense of urgency that winning in their fight was the only way to be fully accorded their dignity.

Cho went right to task upon returning from Chicago to organize the women workers in Yeongdeungpo, recognizing that they were the bottom rung of its social order.

If one worker out of a hundred were to tell management all of her grievances, saying that she refused to work, the company wouldn't bat an eye. It would simply shrug it off. [. . .] But if ninety out of the hundred were to do the same, it would strike fear in their (the company's) heart. [. . .] If you wanted humane treatment, you needed to organize. Organizing was the only way the workers could exercise strength.[12]

The personal relationships Cho built during the years of industrial evangelism proved instrumental to building the grassroots network. The contacts he had built years ago across 300- something factories became the core members around whom the YDP-UIM organized the first of the small groups with seven to eight members each. Members were supposed to have a natural affinity, being from the same sections in the same factory and belonging to the same gender and age groups. Each group also had to elect its leader and democratically decide upon its activities. The missioners of the YDP-UIM were there to provide the assistance the workers asked for but otherwise stayed out of the groups' decision-making.

As such, each group lasted only as long as the members partici- pated. The groups were run with an adapted version of Paulo Freire's principle of conscientization. Learning took place as the workers presented their own questions, looked for their own answers in discus- sion, and applied them in their own lives. The only activity that was preset for every small group was to spend the first session talking about each of the members' stories. By sharing both the joys and sorrows they had experienced so far in their lives, the members, in the presence of one UIM missioner, articulated their sense of identity.[13] This led to a reflection about the kind of life the workers wanted to live thereafter.

The activities that followed were left wholly to the workers. Often, they would start by meeting to share a hobby or learn about a light topic of general interest. Examples of these included arranging flowers, embroidery, handicrafts, and topics in the humanities. Once the workers decided what they wanted to learn together, a YDP-UIM missioner was assigned to prepare the necessary materials, space, and lesson plans. The workers only had to focus on engaging with the principal activity.

Some of the popular topics were marriage, childbirth, personal finance, time management, women's rights, cultural activities, interpersonal relationships, the LSA and other labor laws, the UIM, and current social issues. Every topic was discussed at the request of the workers. As an exception, the missioners made sure by design that every small group would eventually discuss the LSA. Every lesson took the form of a participatory discussion led by the designated member who had previewed the lesson. This did not differ much from the method of "see, judge, act" that was used in the JOC. Park Song-ah (previously Park Jeom-soon), who was a worker in Namyoung Nylon, recounted her time in the small groups.

> *We could learn and share anything that we wanted. What I found the most helpful was the fact that we could be very comfortable with each other since we were all employed in the same context. There was an air of warmth, love, and life that started to rise among us in the small group. The room where we met may have been cramped, but it wasn't lacking in any way as a place of refuge and learning for us working women.*

Indeed, the workers transformed themselves through the small-group activities. Cho placed great priority in their ability to identify and solve problems for themselves as the method of bringing change to their lives. He said, "Workers can only grow if they act, and they can only act if their lives are changed."[14] He assessed the previous education of industrial evangelists and union officers who had only achieved partial success—it was because they were not followed by concrete action and changes in life.

One can picture the extent of the workers' transformation through an anecdote from Kim Yeon-ja, who used to work in Namyoung Nylon, about the days of the great repression. Rumors were going around at the time that the missioners might get their ordinations canceled or otherwise removed from the UIM ministry. Apparently, this created a discussion among the workers who wondered why the UIM needed ordained ministers. Surely, the workers could continue the ministry on their own. There had been a remarkable growth in the workers' sense of agency and confidence. When the YDP-UIM needed additional members on the staff to keep pace with the growing number of the small groups in the late 1970s, the workers rose to the occasion to raise the funds necessary to hire additional missioners. In 1976, they were paying the salaries of three of them. They showed a similar initiative during the building project of a new YDP-UIM center, fundraising among themselves to help make up for the shortage in the budget for the land purchase. One has to remember that these were some of society's most underpaid workers.

With the small groups, every struggle had to emerge from the problems identified by the workers who belonged to the workplace in question. No action could start until they had ample discussions about the problems and their proper solutions. Once the dialogue had taken place in most of the small groups of a given factory, the YDP-UIM organized a retreat for all the small groups to decide whether or not to initiate action. The three major factors considered in addition to whether there was consensus among the small-group workers were the following.

1. Were there at least 100 small groups outside the factory in question? (Could they muster sufficient small-group support?)
2. How were the social and political conditions? (Would public opinion or government try to suppress the workers?)
3. Could the workers count on external allies? (Were students, youth groups, churches, and others able to provide their support?)

If the answer to any of these questions was no, the workers postponed their action until all the conditions were met. In Myeong-jin, who took primary responsibility for nurturing the small groups, said the following:

> *We ate with them. Lived with them. Shouted with them. We shared both anger and laughter and did everything we could to help them reach a certain understanding. We weren't trying to teach. We were sharing our lives. [. . .] To our amazement, we soon discovered that the workers had been transformed during the time they spent with us. They understood they were dignified human beings created in the image of God and started to demand their rights as humans and as workers. They started to challenge the structural evil that oppressed them. They shed blood in the fights through which they accomplished some level of success in transforming the evil structures that had been the source of their suffering.*[15]

The relational foundations for the first small groups had been laid through the missioners' contact with the workers in 1969. Then they received their organizational form after Cho returned from Chicago in 1972, which lasted until the small-group workers were dispersed in 1979. As such, one could say the small-group activities and the associated education through action took place for a full decade in substance. In form, 105 small groups gathered 1,722 times in their first year in 1972, with a total of 22,545 persons who showed up for meetings (counting repeat visits). The groups continued to become more active until they were shut down, reaching their peak in 1979 with 150 groups meeting 5,200 times for a cumulative total of 62,400 visits. This was also the year when the YDP-UIM carried out its most significant campaigns.[16]

While the small groups were a setting in which the workers could learn about their dignity through practical activities, the night classes were a setting in which they could learn about the rest of the world. Many of the workers were young women who had gone to work in the factories after completing middle school. There was a thirst for the learning that they otherwise should have received. To fill this need, the university students of Saemoonan Church put together a night school in 1975. They borrowed two locations for the classes. Twelve workers met in Siheung Church and 22 others met in Mullae-dong Church, five times a week for 10 weeks.

The instructional objectives were "to enable the workers to know, discuss, and participate in political, social, economic, and cultural life." Part of this meant teaching the workers how to read and write in classical Chinese script. Despite the fact that schools no longer taught the classical Chinese script, newspapers and public documents still used it alongside the Korean script. Full literacy therefore required additional instruction. One class was dedicated to teaching classical Chinese characters required to read the news, while the other was dedicated to other practical topics.

In 1978, the university students of Yeomcheom Church joined the faculty, thus enabling the night school to offer another class for basic Korean and world history. By this time, each of the other two courses had about 100 workers who had completed them. The separate courses were integrated into a single "Labor School" curriculum in the fall of 1979. The topics it primarily covered were humanities, basic philosophy, economics, history, labor movement history, and labor laws.

The YDP-UIM also arranged several one-time speaker events on topics that Cho thought were helpful in promoting the health, education, and cultural life of the workers. These lectures spanned topics like oral hygiene, women's health, fashion, music, and interpersonal relationships. They were also open to members of the public who were not affiliated with the YDP-UIM, serving as an opportunity to form connections with entirely new workers. Many, in fact, joined either the YDP-UIM's consumer cooperative or Labor Church after attending one of the lectures.

The workers also engaged volunteers from the universities in dialogue sessions over topics of common interest. For instance, in 1972, a small group named Honeybees had a discussion with a group of students for several hours over the topic of careers for the modern working woman. They shared what they saw as the problem of women having to work very long hours for very little pay, and potential solutions. Cho was very mindful about not allowing the university students to patronize the workers simply because they had achieved a higher level of formal education. He stressed to the workers that they ought to speak as equals when addressing those who were from the universities, coaching them to be the leaders in the conversation.

Letting the workers make their own choices regarding their education allowed the kind of character growth that would never have happened in the more prevalent form of one-way transmission of information. The YDP-UIM often stressed that the workers should not settle at performing a little better on their jobs to make a little more money, saying that they ought to possess a well-rounded character.

> *Character is like the threads you use to weave a piece of fabric. The finer the threads, the finer the silk. [. . .] It's also like a ripe yellow melon. Unripe melons are very hard to get off from their vines. Ripe melons fall off at the slightest touch and is a sweet fruit for others to eat. That is what it's like to have a fine character.*[17]

The point of the analogy was that nothing could be done without character.

The missioners witnessed a wondrous transformation of the workers after the humanizing, egalitarian minjung education. They said they could taste the joy of Christ's resurrection after his death on the cross when they saw the workers come out of their lengthy struggles even more beautiful than before. Their stories were authentic, their prayers grounded, and their actions consistent with the depths of their hearts. The missioners thought this was what it meant to be a Christian and to be a part of industrial missions. While the workers learned their sense of identity by sharing life with the missioners, the missioners learned the true character of someone who lived by faith in the imitation of Christ. The community was one that learned from each other. Dr. Moon Dong-hwan, a theologian and minjung educator who had created the intentional learning community of *Saebyeogeh Jip* (House of the Dawn), marveled at how the small-group workers of the YDP-UIM faithfully realized the ideals of minjung education as a community whose members learned from each other so that they could change the world.[18]

YDP-UIM Staff: Servants of Workers

Cho was a seasoned instructor who trained many of the missioners who joined the UIM. His journey started all the way back in August 1957 when he joined the Christian Students for Labor Studies, shortly after which he was hired as an intern by the PCK DOE to train seminarians in the work projects. Cho gained a wide reputation as an effective trainer to the point that in March 1972, the National UIM Staff Conference appointed him as the head of the newly created and ecumenical UIM Training Center. Even the Catholics sent their seminarians and priests. Those who learned under the tutelage of Cho Chi Song until the KCAO took over the process in the mid-1970s included two Anglicans (Kim Seong-soo, Ahn Joo-yong), two

PCK Presbyterians (Kim Jeong-gook, Hwang Tae-joon), two PROKs (Koh Jae-shik, Jeong Tae-gi), and two from the Salvation Army (names unknown).

Cho believed a UIM missioner had to be a spiritual leader who could do more than what was on their job description. He considered personal character very important in judging a UIM candidate's quality. Accordingly, he chose to train ministers and students in whom he saw a genuine and charitable attitude over those who were highly competent and intelligent in the early to mid-1960s.

Cho had a reputation for producing leaders who were grounded in reality and were capable of dealing with practical labor issues. Knowing this full well, the PCK DOE hoped to appoint Cho as the chair of the Central UIM Committee. Cho declined, insisting he could not leave Yeongdeungpo behind. So, they reached a compromise in which Cho was to be appointed an instructor at the PCK UIM Training Center starting in July 1972 without taking any additional role in the PCK Central UIM Committee. Thus, Cho was spared the fate of working three jobs, serving only in the two roles of training prospective UIM missioners until they settled into their assignment and serving in the YDP-UIM.

Cho's training method was rigorous, and it was based on a number of foundational principles. Chief among them was that the missioners must learn to face the same problems confronting the workers, ultimately reaching a point where they could identify with the workers, speak the workers' language, and feel the workers' pain.

> *The best training was to simply go meet the workers, learning*
> *how to read their expressions, and letting their speech,*
> *attitude, action, courage, and everything to get through to you*
> *and become your teacher.*
>
> *You had to go to where the workers are and learn about*
> *their lives and issues as they were on the ground. You had*
> *to go down to their place. You could not become a missioner*

> *without making the effort to be where they were. [. . .] The*
> *notion that you could serve the workers without having been*
> *in their shoes was, in fact, delusional. [. . .] You needed to*
> *have the singular mindset that you will become one of the*
> *workers.*[19]

He explained the same principle in the UIM Staff Training Manual as well:

1. Speak the language of the workers, not the language of religion.
2. Do not talk about Jesus. Talk only about the workers.
3. Do not sit at your desks. Get out onto the streets.
4. Do not work with your mind. Work with your body.
5. Do not demand what the church wants. Incline yourself to what the workers want.
6. Do not try to analyze the workers' pain in your head. Feel it in your heart.
7. Social justice is not accomplished by theory or religious ideas. It is accomplished by a collective force that opposes injustice.
8. Labor is worship. There is true prayer and praise in labor. Labor is a precious offering to God. It is also the practice of neighborly love.
9. Fiercely commit yourselves to the mission. Do not spend a minute on anything that is not part of the UIM. Commit yourselves 100%.
10. Experiencing industrial labor is the basic training required of all missioners who will serve in the UIM.[20]

The level of importance that Cho placed on the tenth point can be seen in the fact that he elaborated on it through the nine others. The candidates for UIM assignment were directed to get the most difficult jobs they could find. In today's terms, they were to look for the "difficult, dirty, and dangerous" ones.

Every candidate had to go through the process of finding a job and getting hired alone. This proved to be difficult for the ones who were older in age. Jeong Jin-dong, for instance, was in his early 40s when he received the missioner training. His age was an obstacle in getting a job with most employers. When he thought he finally got a place with one, he found himself showing up to an empty workplace of a fraudulent ghost company. It took a month before he finally got employed as a money counter with a city bus company. Cho Soon-hyeong similarly struggled to find a job given her age. She finally managed to get employed by using the name of her sister-in-law, who was six years younger than herself.

Through the duration of the training, the candidate missioners were to live just as if they were one of the workers. For instance, they were to only live off of the wages they received. The exception was with a number of candidates who received a stipend from their sending organizations. In their case, the wages they received were turned into the training center.

The candidates were not even allowed to go to church on Sunday. The only people they could meet when they were not at work were coworkers and family. They were only permitted to attend the funerals and weddings of either their coworkers or family. Trainees had to keep their identities as seminarians or ministers strictly hidden. They were not to talk about Christ or religion. They were to only use the language and blend into the culture of the workers. The purpose of all these measures was to isolate the missioners from their original echelons of society so they could focus entirely on identifying with the workers.

All trainees had to spend between six and 12 months in this phase of the training. They were to keep a journal in which they wrote down their observations from work. This helped cultivate their ability to survey and analyze an industrial workplace. The regular reflections also helped keep the trainees accountable for how much they immersed themselves into the lives of the workers. Trainees were evaluated for how well they observed and recorded their tasks, thoughts, feelings, relationships, and other aspects of their daily lives. Cho also met the trainees once a week on Saturday evenings to provide verbal feedback.

> *Cho Chi Song: How was this week?*
> *Koh Ae-shin: It was infuriating. The section chief, who was obviously many years younger than myself, addressed me by saying, "hey you," or "hey kid."*
> *Cho Chi Song: I told you so. It applies to everyone who works in a factory. What you suffered is actually rather mild.*
> *Koh Ae-shin: I'm a respected deacon in the church.*
> *Cho Chi Song: But you're a mere* gongsooni *in the factory.*[21]

In Cho's mind, the candidates could only earn their right to serve the workers as UIM missioners if they also experienced the crushing labor and humiliation the workers had to endure on a regular basis. He intentionally withheld the words of affirmation that the candidates might have received if they were still in their original contexts. For instance, he said nothing about the blisters that formed on the tender hands of the candidates who were trying physical labor for the first time in their lives. An unremarkable part of a worker's life was to be treated as an unremarkable part of the training. Every passing day at work chipped away at the savior complex that may have been carried by the missioners. The beating to their body formed the idea in their minds that they were one of the workers more than they were one of their rescuers.

The academic part of training only started once the working phase had been completed. This was when the candidates learned the labor laws. They also received practical training with organizing the small groups, whether in the factories or another place. The first task was to begin a regular conversation group with the workers there, but this proved to be the most difficult part of the training. In most cases, the groups started and ended as experiments. Some of the groups, however, managed to develop a fully fledged labor dispute, serving as the candidate's introduction to the full gamut of organizing. This was the case for Jeong Jin-dong and his small group of cleaning workers in Cheongju City Hall.

The academic phase lasted for about three months, considerably shorter than the working phase. Cho usually sent the candidates to research organizations affiliated with the universities so they could learn from the best experts. Frequent partners in training were Yonsei University Institute for Urban Studies, Korea University Institute for Research on Labor and Employment, and Sogang University Institute for Labor Studies. With these organizations, candidates could learn about the domestic and international trends in labor, the history and policies of the UIM, labor laws, and more at the level of graduate study.

As the final stop before receiving their assignment, candidates learned how to perform the administrative tasks required in a UIM. Cho had the trainees try their hands at writing the account books, logs, reports, petitions, complaints, press statements, and a variety of other documents produced in the UIM. He also had them sit in during a counseling session. Trainees were sent to join current negotiations between workers and management to gain a sense for how a dispute could be carried out. Cho made sure he did not waste any effort training people who would not end up in the UIM. He only accepted candidates who had a good idea of where they were going to be assigned. Then he made sure he provided a very practical training that equipped the candidates with everything they needed to independently run a UIM.

Even after they were sent to their assignments, Cho's rule for the missioners was that they renew their experience with physical labor once every three years. This was so they could refresh their sense of what life is like in the workplace and continue to identify with the workers. The exception was Jeong Jin-dong and In Myeong-jin, who were too old and well known to be able to get work among the employers. They instead spent their time as rag-pickers in Cheongju. Cho advised the UIMs with multiple missioners to always have someone on the staff spending time away in a physical job. If that was not feasible, he advised everyone to spend concentrated periods of time doing physical labor. The idea was that physical labor was to the UIM missioners what the Vassa retreats were for Buddhist monks.

The efforts in training paid off, as missioners demonstrated they were more than capable of handling the UIM ministries to which they were assigned. The first cohort of PCK missioners that Cho Chi Song trained from 1971 to 1972 were Jeong Jin-dong and In Myeong-jin. Jeong was a latecomer to the UIM as a classmate of Cho Chi Song from seminary. He was faithful till the end, however, protecting the Cheongju UIM at the cost of even leaving the Chungbuk Presbytery when it caved to the government's pressure and attempted to close down the UIM. Thanks to his persistence, the Cheongju UIM became a nexus of the labor and minjung movement of Cheongju. In Myeong-jin was originally sent by the Gyeongbuk Presbytery to be trained as a missioner for the Daegu UIM, but when the presbytery gave up on launching the ministry, Cho recruited him to join the ministry in Yeongdeungpo. He had already formed a relationship with the YDP-UIM as a student who got involved in the aftermath of Kim Jin-soo's death. If Cho was the quiet thinker and strategist, In Myeong-jin was the engine of action that constantly drove the YDP-UIM into motion.

The second cohort trained from 1976 to 1977. They were all female: Myeong Noh-seon, Koh Ae-shin, and Cho Soon-hyeong. Myeong was already working in the YDP-UIM as the successor of Kang Haeng-nim before she received the missioner training. Koh Ae-shin was also already part of an urban mercy ministry in Mangwon-dong when Cho Chi Song recommended her for the Gumi UIM, at which point she received the missioner training. She was subjected to intense repression and a smear campaign in the late Yushin period by the police and corporations who claimed that the UIM should never be allowed to gain a foothold in an area where Park Chung Hee's ancestors were buried. When her own church barred her from entry, she had no choice but to leave the Gumi area.[22] Cho Soon-hyeong was Jeong Jin-dong's sister-in-law. She, too, received the missioner training in the middle of helping Jeong's ministry in the Cheongju UIM. After her training, she was formally assigned to Cheongju, where she took over after Jeong's death. She is still in the Cheongju UIM to this day.

Even after Cho left the YDP-UIM in 1982, the other denominations wanted him to continue training their UIM missioners. This led to the creation of an ecumenical training center under the KCAO, where Cho was appointed the head. The KCAO training center lasted from 1983 to 1984, taking two cohorts for a year each from the PCK, PROK Church, KMC, and Catholic Farmers' Movement. Those trained in this period included PCK's Lee Geun-bok, Sohn Eun-ha, Kim Youngnak, Park Jin-seok, Kim Gyu-bok, Yoo Jae-moo, and Ahn Gi-seong; PROK's Rim Heung-gi and Gih Gil-dong; and KMC's Yoon In-seong and Park Il-seong. Some of the PCK trainees went on to join the YDP-UIM staff. Some others planted workers' churches. Rim Heung-gi became the general secretary of the PROK UIM. Yoon In-seong planted a minjung church in Bucheon.

Staffed by the missioners whom Cho trained, the UIMs of Yeongdeungpo and Cheongju are still continuing their ministry at the time of this writing in 2022. The third generation of missioners planted workers' churches throughout the country's major industrial areas, carrying on elements of the YDP-UIM's ministry. In 1988, they formed the PCK Workers' Ministries Association, joined by churches that ministered to the urban poor. In 1991, the association was renamed the PCK Urban Minjung Ministries Association. The same group is still active today as the PCK-URM, or translated more directly, "Working Society of Jesus." This younger generation of minjung ministers were left with an indelible mark by the education they received under Cho Chi Song. They went on to apply many of the same principles in training their students, seeking to ground them in the lived experience of labor and equip them for action.

The Garden of Minjung Theology and Ministry

There were largely two faces of Korean Christianity in the 1970s. The first was the gigantic assemblies like the ones that gathered for Billy Graham's Crusade or Expo 1974. The other was the UIMs and other progressive Christians who led the activism for human rights and democracy.

The conservative churches that wanted to grow in numbers and receive material blessings often cooperated with the juntas in exchange for tax exemptions and accommodations for their massive religious assemblies.[23]

The progressive Christians opposed the state and its development policies that trampled on the lives of workers, farmers, and the urban poor. Theologians who joined the democracy movement after being dismissed from their university posts came to articulate the theological notion that God was with the ordinary people or minjung and worked to deliver them from their suffering. Jeon Tae-il's self-immolation in November 1970 especially led them to the belief that the goal of Christian ministry was to bring human and social liberation.

Seo Nam-dong believed that God was actively working to bring deliverance in the various minjung events like the oppression of the farmer Oh Won-choon, and the death of the YH worker Kim Gyeong-sook. He called the gathering of people who prayed and showed solidarity for such incidents the church of the *hyeonjang* (or spatio-temporal present). "The church does not reside within an ecclesiastical structure or institution," he explained. "Rather, under the guidance of the Holy Spirit, it rises and falls with the rise and fall of an event. [. . .] It performs God's mission through the voluntary formation and dissolution."[24]

Ahn Byeong-moo believed God acted upon history through the struggles of the farmers, workers, and urban poor. He believed such minjung activism was the Christian movement. There was a minjung event whenever and wherever the workers, farmers, poor, and otherwise downtrodden people exposed the contradictions of a society that marginalized the very people sustaining it and resisted their exclusion by the state and privileged class. Ahn described the Christian faith as being in solidarity with such resistance.[25]

Kim Yong-Bock spoke of the minjung as the people of God in a paper titled "The Biblical Background and Justification for the UIM." He wrote

> *One cannot discuss Jesus as the Messiah who ushered in the reign of God in history without talking about the minjung, for the Messiah came from the minjung, belonged to the minjung, and served the minjung. The minjung waited in anticipation of the Messiah. The politics of the Messiah was one in which the minjung became the agents. It was, in other words, the minjung and liberation movement. The politics of the Messiah is identified with the humanization of workers, which is identified with peace. Such is the faith behind the UIM, upon which it acts. Thus the UIM partakes in the kingdom of the Messiah.*[26]

Kim explained that the workers were the people of God whose struggles God used to accomplish his divine purposes in history.

The YDP-UIM was already practicing the participatory church in the late 1960s before academics started talking about minjung theology. It had discovered Christ's presence among the downtrodden and recognized that their gathering—the minjung's gathering—in the labor unions and small groups was the church.

Theologians were greatly inspired by the community life and witness borne by the dispossessed and powerless workers of the YDP-UIM, far surpassing the enthusiasm of any institutional church. They saw in the workers' fight to reclaim their rights and dignity as a minjung event that was comparable to the arrival of Jesus in Galilee 2,000 years earlier. The UIM was the venue of God's contemporary work of deliverance.

Gwon Jin-gwan, a professor in the Sungkonghoe (Anglican) University, remarked that "there were a handful of Christians who shared their lives with the minjung long before we had minjung theology, which was simply the by-product of academic and devotional reflection upon the lived experience that was already being accumulated throughout the UIMs. The principal agents in these stories were the ordained missioners, lay members, and workers of the UIMs, who were joined later by the Christian students."[27] In other words, he identified the root of minjung theology in the UIM.

Indeed, the UIMs had a special place in the hearts of many. They were dependable allies for the democracy activists, given their uncompromising struggle for justice in the workplace against the repression of the dictatorship. To the progressive theologians, they were the garden that sprouted the seeds of minjung theology. The minjung theologians considered it a great honor to be a part of the UIM and eagerly showed support for their various campaigns. The YDP-UIM often invited these scholars and ministers for a variety of worship and speaking events in the Labor Church throughout the 1970s and early 1980s. These included the minjung theologians Seo Nam-dong, Ahn Byeong-moo, Kim Jeong-joon, Moon Ik-hwan, Moon Dong-hwan, Kim Yong-Bock, Seo Gwang-seon, and Hyeon Yeong-hak, as well as progressive academics and ministers like Kim Chan-gook, Min Gyeong-bae, Han Wan-sang, Lee Woo-jeong, Lee Sam-yeol, Lee Jae-jeong, Kim Dong-gil, Lee Moon-yeong, Koh Yeong-geun, Park Hyeong-gyu, Kwon Ho-gyeong, Cho Seong-gi, and Cho Hwa-soon.

No less than what it did for theologians, the UIM nourished the growth of the minjung church. After all, the archetype that the minjung ministries adopted was the prayer and worship of the workers. Christians in Korea had almost no experience resisting the power of the state except when a number of ministers were imprisoned by the colonial authorities for refusing to participate in Shinto shrine worships. This changed with the rise of the UIM, whose members demonstrated a martyr's spirituality that was willing to risk material persecution in its rebuke of state power and capital. They left a powerful impression on the bystander Christians. This soon led to the recognition that following Christ required resistance to the oppression of not only the workers, but also of the farmers, urban poor, and anyone else whose rights were violated. The UIMs were joined by a broad range of ecumenical and Catholic allies who formed the KCAO on September 23, 1971, which became a forum for collective social action and training of minjung ministers and activists.[28] Thus trained, a generation of students, seminarians, and young members of the clergy became a generation of progressive Christians who knew how to act. They formed a network among their churches and with the UIM, forming an advanced front in the struggle for democracy and human rights.

When the Shingunbu regime banned third-party labor interventions through a new piece of legislation in 1980, the PCK ministers who had been trained by Cho planned individual minjung churches to continue industrial missions despite the severe limitations on centralized, networked activities. The workers' churches formed from 1983 to 1985 when a large number of PCK missioners finished receiving their UIM training included those in Seongsu (Samil Church, Yoo Jae-moo), Anyang (Hanmuri Church, Park Jin-seok), Daejeon (Bindeul Church, Kim Gyu-bok), Daegu (Dalgubeol Church, Ahn Gi-seong), and Guro (Didimdol Church, Kang Woo-kyeong).

These churches followed the model of YDP-UIM's Labor Church, adjusting their worships and programs so they could speak more to the workers. Most of the ministers offered labor counseling, night classes, and childcare services as part of benchmarking the YDP-UIM's ministry.[29]

This led to a natural exchange between the comparable ministries of the PCK, PROK, and KMC. Their worker-oriented programs began to lose comparative importance when the broader labor movement finally gained substantial maturity and autonomy following what was called the Great Workers' Struggle in 1987. As such, the labor churches renamed themselves in broader terms as the minjung church. A meeting of representatives in July 1988 led to the creation of the National Minjung Church Alliance. The YDP-UIM provided the venue for the meetings. Similarly, the PCK Workers' Ministries Association also combined itself with the churches that ministered to the urban poor, renaming itself as the PCK Urban Minjung Ministries Association.[30]

Nevertheless, their roots being the industrial ministries, the minjung churches tried to keep their ministries worker friendly. For instance, they kept the annual Labor Sundays, took collective action for the workers' issues, and formed organic relationships with the local labor movements. The minjung churches of the PCK also acted as the YDP-UIM's partners in formulating the mission's policy and discussing the state of worker missions within the UIM seminar that was held under the auspices of the DOE. Together, they recommended the creation of a Central Counseling Center for Workers to the General Assembly and installed 11 Call Centers of Hope under the local presbyteries in major industrial complexes throughout the country.

Such initiatives were the product of the training and baptism of the minjung ministers in the UIM. Having spent formative months in intense physical labor, they still had the spirituality of workers. Although the only UIM organizations that have formally survived are the YDP-UIM and the Cheongju UIM, the spirit of their ministry had in fact spread throughout the country in the various minjung churches, which formed the basis for a new chapter in missions for an industrialized society.

NOTES

1 Kim and Yoo, "Workers' Culture," *Cho Chi Song's Oral History* (Vol. 1, 2011).
2 Kim and Yoo hee, *Cho Chi Song's Oral History* (Vol. 12, 2011).

3 Kim and Yoo hee, *Cho Chi Song's Oral History* (Vol. 12, 2011).

4 Kim and Yoo, "Workers' Culture."

5 Kim and Yoo, *Cho Chi Song's Oral History* (Vol. 8, 2011), 93.

6 Kim and Yoo, *Cho Chi Song's Oral History* (Vol. 12, 2011), 19.

7 Kim and Yoo, *Cho Chi Song's Oral History* (Vol. 8, 2011).

8 Kim and Yoo, *Cho Chi Song's Oral History* (Vol. 8, 2011).

9 Kim and Yoo, *Cho Chi Song's Oral History* (Vol. 8, 2011).

10 Kim and Yoo, *Cho Chi Song's Oral History* (Vol. 8, 2011).

11 Kim and Yoo, *Cho Chi Song's Oral History* (Vol. 8, 2011).

12 Kim and Yoo, *Cho Chi Song's Oral History* (Vol. 8, 2011).

13 Cho Chi Song, "The Story of the Yeongdeungpo UIM," *My Life, My Story 2* (Yeonee Books, 1997), 287.

14 Yeongdeungpo UIM 40th Anniversary Committee, *Yeongdeungpo UIM: A 40-Year History* (YDP-UIM, 1998), 134.

15 In Myeong-jin, "The Strategy of the Yeongdeungpo UIM in the 1970s," *Yeongdeungpo UIM: A 40-Year History*, 143.

16 Kim Myeong-bae, *Yeongdeungpo UIM Files Vol. 1* (YDP-UIM & Soongsil University Center for Culture and Mission Studies, 2020).

17 Seo and Sohn, "Interviews of the Older Members of the UIM."

18 The Christian educator, Moon Dong-hwan, wrote in *Arirang Hill Education* that in the midst of suffering the *minjung* can resist oppressive powers and envision and create new life through mutual encouragement and resilience.

19 Kim and Yoo, *Cho Chi Song's Oral History* (Vol. 10, 2011).

20 Cho Chi Song, "UIM Staff Training Manual" (unpublished document, YDP-UIM).

21 Kim and Yoo, *Cho Chi Song's Oral History* (Vol. 10, 2011).

22 Seo Deok-Seok and Sohn Eun-jeong, "Koh Ae-shin's Interview," *Interviews of Related Individuals for the Biography*, transcribed by Hong Yoon-gyung (2011).

23 Chang Sook-kyeong, *The UIM and Labor Movement in the 1970s* (Seonin, 2013).

24 Seo Nam-dong, "The Figuration of the Han and Its Theological Reflections," *Exploring Minjung Theology* (Hangilsa, 1983), 83–87.

25 Ahn Byeong-moo, "Jesus and the Minjung," *Jesus of Galilee, Korea Theological Study Institute* (2019).

26 Kim Yong-Bock, "The Biblical Background and Justification for the UIM," *Yeongdeungpo UIM: A 40-Year History* (YDP-UIM, 1998).

27 Gwon Jin-gwan, *Jesus, the Figure of Minjung and Minjung, the Figure of Jesus* (Dongyeon, 2009), 575.

28 PCK Department of Evangelism UIM Committee, *The Church and UIM* (PCK Education & Resourcing Ministry, 1981), 59–70.

In 1971, Christians began participating in the democracy and minjung movements in earnest after creating the KCAO, creating a powerful core of resistance. This was later renamed in 1976 as the Council of Churches for Social Missions, if the name is translated directly from Korean. Nonetheless, the English name of the organization remained KCAO. Cho Chi Song served as the first general secretary after the renaming.

29 Hwang Hong-ryeol, *The History of Korea's Minjung Ministries and Minjung Missiology* (Handl, 2004).

30 Hwang, *The History of Korea's Minjung Ministries and Minjung Missiology*.

7

THE FOOLS KEEP MARCHING ON

IT IS HARD to say when exactly Cho retired from the YDP-UIM. For reasons unknown, he started to suffer severe migraines between 1978 and 1979 during the intense repression of the late Yushin regime.

> *I got severe migraines and felt very dizzy. [. . .] I went to the Yonsei Severance Hospital, Hangang Seongshim Hospital, St. Mary's Hospital, and a traditional Korean clinic to get acupuncture. I even got hospitalized for a month in Japan. [. . .] The doctors kept saying I was fine, but the migraines didn't go away. [. . .] I later even suffered partial paralysis around my mouth.*[1]

Many people assumed Cho's health had deteriorated because of the torture he suffered while he was in detention. The truth, however, was that Cho was only ever detained temporarily for interrogations and was never subjected to torture. A UIM researcher, Jeong Young-cheol, thought this fact a little curious. Many of the other UIM missioners were often imprisoned under the rule of Park Chung Hee. How was it that Cho Chi Song, the head supervisor of arguably the most active UIM, was never given a prison sentence?

> *I was never sentenced. Never spent time in prison. At most I'd be detained where they took me for the interrogations, where I'd stay for maybe three days or a week or two at most. Most of the questioning was really over by the second day, and there wasn't much that happened after that. [. . .] This was because the issues were pretty straightforward. I'd say, for example,*

the workers had worked 10 hours a day but were only paid
for eight hours. Then I said we calculated how much they
should receive according to the Labor Standards Act, which
amounted to 1.6 billion won total for all workers over the
span of three years. So, I'd tell the investigators, all I did was
say the workers should get another 1.6 billion won. When
I asked what's so wrong about that, they really didn't have
much else they could ask me.

Of course, they captured and tortured all sorts of
people who opposed the regime, whether they were university
professors or members of the national assembly. But they
didn't go quite as far with the clergy. If they did, I would
have left the UIM a lot sooner. [. . .] I'm rather fragile, you
see (chuckles).[2]

Whatever the cause may have been, Cho continued to suffer from poor health. The frequent visits to the hospitals did not help to improve it. Cho felt it was about time he stepped away from the UIM.

One House

In 1983, the tenacious attacks by the anti-UIM forces led to the 68th General Assembly's review of the six highly regressive recommendations of the Committee on Church and Social Issues concerning the UIM. These included changing the name of the UIM back to Industrial Evangelism, cutting it off from all foreign assistance, dissolving the YDP-UIM Committee, and replacing all active UIM missioners among other measures that would have effectively rolled the UIM back by 20 years.

The reformist and progressive forces within the PCK vigorously opposed all recommendations, saying their adoption would be tantamount to the forfeiture of the UIM. The protests of young ministers and seminarians during the 69th General Assembly that met in Young-nak Church the following year in September fortunately succeeded in blocking all but the first recommendation of changing the name back to Industrial Evangelism.[3]

Even so, this incident greatly discouraged Cho Chi Song and the other YDP-UIM missioners. "I thought to myself, well what [was just discussed in the General Assembly] was no way to carry on the UIM. Now that I'm sick, there's nothing more that I can contribute. My role was over. I was sick in two ways. I was sick in my body. And I was sick in my spirit with what you could call disappointment or despair."

The fact that the General Assembly even entertained the thought of kicking out all the current UIM missioners was the straw that broke Cho's back, along with the bodily exhaustion that had been accumulated through the years of repression. He submitted the first letter of resignation on July 17, 1982, to the YDP-UIM Committee, which declined the request and instead put Cho on a paid leave, during which Cho did nothing but recover his health and attend the Labor Church services. This decision to keep Cho Chi Song around the UIM seems to have been motivated by the committee's concern that Cho's sudden disappearance would have resulted in a leadership gap.

The following spring, the KCAO requested that Cho took over the training of UIM missioners. Cho initially declined, citing his sick leave, but Rev. Kwon Ho-kyung, the president of the KCAO, pleaded with him saying that there was nobody else in the Korean church who could lead the training. Cho relented. With the YDP-UIM Committee's permission, he was formally sent to the KCAO as the UIM training director on March 18, 1983.

After two years in the KCAO from 1983 to 1984, Cho began looking for a place in the country where he could retire to and look after his health. He invited a handful of people to join him in creating a community of UIM colleagues, calling on Koh Ae-shin and Park Young-hye from Yeongdeungpo and Jeong Jin-dong and Cho Soon-hyeong in Cheongju. After some discussion, the five decided they wanted their fellowship to also contribute to the spiritual formation, education, and training for others in Christian social missions. For this, they needed the involvement of academics. As such, the five invited professors Kim Yong-Bock, Lee Sam-yeol, and Sohn Deok-soo. Per Lee's recommendation, Han Wan-sang also joined.

The group agreed to build a home to serve as a retreat and training center. None of the individuals had the necessary capital, but they did have experience with efficacy cooperatives. Five UIM missioners, four professors, and their spouses thus formed the 13-member cooperative, appointing Cho Chi Song as the director and groundskeeper of the retreat center they would name the Okhwa-dae Retreat Center.[4]

Cho asked Jeong to recommend a few locations in Chungcheong Province where they could build the center. He took other members when they were free to survey the sites to slowly build up plans. One of the locations was Okhwa-ri, a village near Cheongju that was the home to Okhwa-dae, one of the nine sites of stunning sceneries known as the "Okhwa Gugok." Back in the Joseon Dynasty, the Chuwoljeong, Magyeongjeong, and Seshimjeong pavilions used to face each other here with the Dalcheon River flowing in between while scholars taught their disciples in Okhwa Seowon. The plot belonged to someone who was about to leave to live in the city, leaving behind a decrepit farmhouse and a patch of rice paddy. Cho and the company loved it and signed the purchase contract as soon as they saw it.

Construction started in March and lasted till June 1985. Cho stayed on site, drawing the blueprint and overseeing construction. One of the unique features of the house was that the entrance faced the hillside, away from the village. This was a purposeful design to make the visitors' traffic less conspicuous, which Cho did not want to be a source of disruption to the rest of the village life. The exterior of the building was also kept simple, sticking to the basic bricks and roof tiles one could easily find in the countryside. Cho's previous experience with building the YDP-UIM center came into service. He personally managed the purchase of materials and hiring of workers, keeping costs to a minimum and getting the structure ready to be licensed in just three months.

The Okhwadae Retreat Center opened in December 1985. As defined in the constitution, it was to be a nonprofit retreat center for those involved in missions or other social projects. It also promoted fraternity among the members.[5] A sign at the front read, "One House," written in the calligraphy of Rev. Kang Heenam. When I visited Okhwa-ri in December 2020 with YDP-UIM missioners a little before the second anniversary, after Cho Chi Song's passing, the sign was still up.

The One House was an open space for old friends in the UIM to reconnect and for those in social missions to rest and replenish their energies. Those involved in Christian activism and the minjung church movement often visited to learn from Cho the spirit of the 1970s or discuss the future of social movements. This helped them determine the next steps that the Christian movement had to take. For instance, the PCK-URM, comprising second-generation UIM missioners whom Cho had trained, listened carefully as their old teacher spoke his thoughts on what the minjung ministry had to do in order to continue the legacy of UIMs.

The center was also supposed to serve as a think tank that fostered study and discussion of the Christian labor movement and social missions, training the next generation of highly capable labor activists. This initiative, unfortunately, never panned out, partly because of Cho's poor health, largely because of the social and geographic barriers to training labor activists as a third party in a rural location. Sporadic education and training for some of the labor activists of North Chungcheong Province did take place. Examples include the Daejeon Hanwoo Union, Cheongju Dyeing Company Union, Shinshin Taxi Union, and Jungwon Taxi Union, all of which were supported by the Cheongju UIM.[6]

Meanwhile, academic work of a different nature took place. Funded by the WCC URM, Kim Yong-Bock recorded Cho Chi Song's oral history of the Yeongdeungpo UIM in the 1960s and 1970s. This project lasted for many years after its start in 1986.[7] Under his guidance, Yoo Seung-hee, a graduate student of Christian studies in Ewha

University, recorded 36 tapes that were transcribed into 12 volumes by the staff of the YDP-UIM. These were precious resources for the study of UIM in Korea, especially since very few other sources survived the multiple searches and seizures by the government. Cho Chi Song himself was very hesitant about leaving his thoughts behind in writing. The tapes and their transcriptions will continue to be valuable additions to the handful of official meeting minutes and reports for the continued study of the UIM. The transcribed tapes were the most important sources for writing this book as well.

Cho was often visited by the younger missioners of the YDP-UIM who wanted to talk to their revered predecessor and pioneer about the past, present, and future of the UIM. They wanted wisdom, in particular, for how they could revitalize the ministry. Their elder listened carefully, providing words of encouragement and affirmation. He took care not to give any specific advice, however. Times had changed. Cho recognized the younger missioners had to face different problems than he did in the 1970s.

The women of the small groups from the 1970s also visited Okhwa-ri, now with their own families. They looked back on the most intense moments of their lives and belatedly marveled at what they had accomplished together. They were also permanently impressed with the taste of the hand-pulled dough stew Cho served with the freshwater snails he caught in the Dalcheon River.

In 1992, eight years after its construction and 10 years after its inception, the cooperative reached the first of its two crossroads. Cho sent a letter out to the members to call for a meeting. The only original goal the home had seemed to fulfill was serving as a retreat center, but its maintenance was becoming costly. The operating costs were paid with the monthly dues of 10,000 won from each of the 13 members plus however much visitors gave on a pay-what-you-can basis. This often resulted in a deficit even after counting just the cost of the food. Either the cooperative needed to recruit more members, increase the dues, or find external sources of funding.

Cho himself was happy to continue his role for no pay. He found it replenishing to simply live in the clean and quiet rural environment. The upkeep for the retreat center, however, was another matter. The cooperative also had to face the reality that its members were aging. One could only expect a decrease in the amount of time and energy the members could commit to maintaining the retreat center. The issue was further accentuated by the fact that a number of its members had taken on public duties. Han Wan-sang became a cabinet minister, Kim Yong-Bock became the President of Hanshin University, and Lee Sam-yeol became the chair of the Korean National Commission for the UNESCO.

Despite Cho's letter, fewer members showed up than was required for quorum. A full decision had to be tabled, but those present nevertheless acknowledged that they could not proceed with the previous ambition of letting the center provide research and education. The home would continue to serve only as a retreat and fellowship center. The One House met its second crossroads in January 2005, when Jeong Jin-dong, who had been one of its key helpers, suffered a stroke. With Cho's health also deteriorating, the cooperative had to make the choice to dissolve itself. In 2007, the cooperative sold the land and distributed the proceeds in proportion to the shares of initial investment. Cho Chi Song moved to live with his daughter in Pangyo, Seongnam on July 17, 2009.

Memories of Okhwa-ri

In terms of personal happiness, the years Cho spent in Okhwa-ri were the best years of his life. He was still subject to government surveillance in his initial days of retirement, for the authorities were concerned that he might spread his troublesome organizing in the rural environment. Intelligence detectives camped out in the corner store or somewhere in the mountain to watch him. Over time, it became apparent Cho was simply enjoying his bucolic life. Apart from getting occasional visits, there was not much going on. The surveillance began to loosen.

The villagers of Okhwa-ri remember Cho Chi Song as "the quiet pastor from Seoul who came to live in retirement." It was easy to become the topic of gossip in a small rural community. Cho made a point of running the One House in a way that would not disturb the rhythm of the village life. He placed the guesthouse and kitchen between the center and the mountain to create an isolated space for visiting groups to go about their business without making the villagers feel restless.

Cho offered a different version of retreat depending on who was visiting. To the workers, he only offered rest. To the missioners, he assigned jobs around the house and created one if there was not any. The logic, Cho Soon-hyeong explained, was that the workers needed to get away from their usual labor, while the missioners and reverends would benefit from getting away from their sedentary states.[8]

There was only one time Cho organized the villagers of Okhwa-ri in collective action, and that was to get their roads paved. The dirt path leading into Okhwa-ri got very muddy and uneven every time it rained. This was a source of great inconvenience for the community, but none of the local authorities seemed to do anything about it. Cho thus wrote a petition to the county office asking for paved roads with the villagers' signatures. It was an eye-opening experience for the villagers who have only ever resigned themselves to the government's control. Now they knew that they could, in fact, make certain demands.

The last road to be paved was the one that led to the One House. This demonstrated for the villagers that Cho was willing to put his interests behind that of the others. Moved by the sincerity of his character, they later gave him a plaque of appreciation. This created relationships that led to some of the villagers visiting the YDP-UIM and other places in Seoul. Upon hearing of Cho Chi Song's passing, one of the deacons of Okhwa-ri church shared his memory fondly. "He was so quiet. I had no idea he was so well known and used to do such great things. I am sad to hear of his passing. I am certain God has rewarded him greatly."[9]

Cho's health seemed to improve for a while during his stay in Okhwa-ri. About two years into the stay, he was able to function without taking medication. He also very much enjoyed farming, using the plot attached to the house to grow vegetables and grains. Eating the fresh produce and breathing the clean air cooled by the streams of water, Cho recovered his physical and psychological health. The visitors were also treated to barbecues in the back hut featuring fresh greens, maize, potatoes, and sweet potatoes that Cho raised. It was delightful for all parties involved to converse with the pioneer of industrial ministry, now turned farmer.

The sound of classical music could still be heard around Cho Chi Song. He put up a speaker on the hut and played the tapes while tending to his garden or cleaning the lawn. He also made a belated discovery of his enthusiasm for art, taking pictures of nature in Okhwa-ri or carving the blocks of wood he found around the nearby hills. He also took up painting and calligraphy. The gourds, woodwork, paintings, and photos produced in his new hobby made excellent gifts that he enjoyed giving to his friends and successors in the UIM. The product of his handiwork served as a warm reminder of the earlier days of the YDP-UIM, reminding their recipients that the spirit of the ministry was still alive.

Cho also occasionally created pieces as he looked back on the most intense moments of the 1970s. These took the form of poetry or computer graphics, which he taught himself, or Christmas and New Year's cards that he sent to his old colleagues and supporters. They were often full of satire and wit, at times reaching more complex intellectual reflection.

One of the most memorable pieces that Cho created was a photograph titled "Hot Potatoes" (see Figure 7.1). It was a brilliant recreation of Christ's last supper for which he used potatoes as the figures for the characters in the scene.[10] The photo was hung up on

Figure 7.1. Hot Potatoes.
(image provided by author)

the living room wall. Cho often asked if the visitors could spot which one of the potatoes was Judas, to which many responded by looking for a fault in the potatoes. "It's the one looking the other way." Or, "It's the fat one who had too much to eat."

Cho would redirect their attention away from the imperfection of the potato to the cups in front of them, which he made with acorn shells. Only then did they realize that one of the potatoes had its cup flipped upside down. The message was that the Christians who refused to take the cup of suffering and sought only comfort (or material blessings) were no different than Judas.

Cho said, now and then, that if he had not escaped North Korea or become a UIM missioner, he would have become a musician or painter. There was good reason to believe this, given the amount of his creative expression and the level of concentration he displayed in whatever he did. He certainly seemed to have the character of an artist.

Although he welcomed visitors who were still active in the church or UIM, Cho tried not to discuss the details of their present work while in Okhwa-ri. Times had changed since the 1970s, and Cho strongly believed it was not his place to comment on the current affairs as someone who has already retired and left the scene. This was an extension of his conviction that the urban industrial ministry could not properly exist divorced from the context of the workers.

The one exception was Jeong Jin-dong, who was Cho's classmate in seminary and still served in the Cheongju UIM. With Jeong, Cho often talked about the trends in the labor and minjung movements. Cho spend his Sundays in the Cheongju Labor Church in the Cheongju UIM, occasionally preaching for special occasions. Jeong was the foremost leader in the minjung and democracy activism of Cheongju, serving in the UIM until the day he collapsed from a stroke. He always had a very special place in Cho's heart.

One of the greatest joys for the retired missioner was being visited by the old workers who had since built their own families. Having met the workers when they were as young as his daughters, getting to see their children filled Cho with the joy of a grandfather.[11] Old and new friends in the YDP-UIM came down to Okhwa-ri to modestly celebrate his 60th birthday in 1991, then his 70th in 2001. Cho's old colleague, Park Hyeong-gyu, preached for the latter. Many of the women who were a part of the small groups in the 1970s were also there, sharing many memories.

Looking Back and Ahead

Cho was proud of what the YDP-UIM accomplished in the 20 years he spent there. He believed his final task in the remainder of his life was to take stock of its history as it pertains to Korean Christianity and democracy. Of course, authoritarianism was still alive and well. It would still take a number of years before one could evaluate the 1970s with detached eyes. Nevertheless, Cho believed he had to pass on the stories he knew before they faded from memory.

Yet, he refused to pen a book in his own name. He believed himself to be the hands of action. The hands to write history must belong to someone else. People had asked him for his authorship, which he politely declined. At most, he agreed to give a spoken presentation or an interview. Among them were the interviews he gave to the young researchers who were writing a paper on the UIM of the 1970s and to the KDF for its project to archive the broader democracy movement.

Then finally in 1986, he began giving an ongoing series of oral history for the next 20 years. This was at the initiative of Kim Yong-Bock, who was collecting primary materials for his broader, long-term theological study of the UIM not only in Yeongdeungpo but also in the rest of Asia and the world.

Kim believed Cho Chi Song's years in the YDP-UIM marked the climax of the history he studied. Such was his high regard for the YDP-UIM in the 1970s. Kim regarded the Korean UIM and its perseverance against the Yushin regime one of the most powerful moments in the "social biography of the minjung" since Jesus Christ in Galilee.

UIM in Korea was lauded not only among Christians, but also among most theologians and historians who have heard of it. For instance, Bruce Cummings, a renowned scholar of Korean history in the University of Chicago, wrote in *Korea's Place in the Sun* that the UIM had an explosive power that accelerated the downfall of the Yushin order, writing, "For many years the Urban Industrial Mission (UIM), an organization run by Christians, sought to make workers aware of their rights."[12]

Han Hong-goo, who taught modern Korean history at Sungkonghoe (Anglican) University, also wrote in a column for *Hankyoreh* (January 18, 2013) that the women's labor movement in the 1970s that caused the downfall of the Yushin regime was closely connected to the UIM and JOC. Han also added, "If there was a moment in which the Korean public felt it could trust the Christians despite their recent ignominy, it was likely thanks to the UIM that actually followed Christ into the low places."

Kim Jin-ho, Ahn Byeong-moo's student and fellow at the Third Era Christianity Institute, commented that the UIM was "one of the very few successful protestant movements."

As the first real protestant social movement since the war,
the UIM stood defiant in the face of neglect and attack from
the mainstream church. Its influence was in no way lacking
compared to that of the mega-churches. This was likely thanks
to the worldwide network of resistance that had been formed
across Protestants and non-Protestants alike by the UIM [. . .]
which often formed meaningful pressures on the Korean
government and corporations.[13]

Chang Soo-kyeong, who wrote multiple papers on the UIM from the Center for Korean History in Korea University, wrote that the UIM differed greatly from the rest of the Protestant church that often strove for growth in close alliance with the Yushin regime.

The UIM and labor movement of the 1970s were often
thought of as being one body. Predictably, they were
persecuted by the public authorities, which, because of their
persistence, only made them into a broader antiestablishment
movement. Thus, the UIM left a noteworthy legacy in the
labor and democracy movements of the 1970s, traversing
across the various spheres of religion, politics, and society
in the particular historical circumstances of the Yushin
regime.[14]

Of course, the UIM did not always receive praise and support. In fact, it had to deal with far more criticism and repression. The authoritarian military regime consistently slandered the UIM, calling them Communist agitators using the disguise of religion to incite the workers to political action. Nevertheless, Cho remained unwavering in his commitment to the workers. "They knew that we weren't

Communists. It was better to spend the time talking to another worker than worrying about all that nonsense."

He was also confident in the UIM's moral high ground. "Would the UIM have failed because of persecution? No way. If it was the sort of thing that a little persecution could snuff out, Christianity would have disappeared long ago. [. . .] The persecution by the powerful and wealthy was, in fact, a benefit to us. It was glory on our part to be subject to the slander."[15]

The struggles were a sacred part of the ministry for Cho Chi Song. There was no room for politics. His singular focus was helping improve the lives of the workers and advancing their self-directed movement. The goal was organizing the workers for the sake of the workers, not for some other political party or cause.

> *After the introduction of direct [presidential] elections, even*
> *they (the activists) pitted themselves against each other,*
> *divided into supporters of Kim Young-sam versus Kim*
> *Daejung. [. . .] These were supposed to be the people who*
> *struggled in common for labor and human rights movement.*
> *Now they were pulling each other by the collars of their*
> *shirts. That is senseless. I never took part in that kind of*
> *fight. I wasn't a part of political demonstrations. I didn't go*
> *out and shout* Down with the dictator! *All I ever did was*
> *demand that the workers be paid and treated fairly. That they*
> *shouldn't be paid for eight hours when they worked 10. That*
> *they shouldn't be physically and verbally abused. That's what*
> *I stuck to. The kind demands I made was that the abusive*
> *supervisor be fired, or the workers should refuse to work.*[16]

There were clear parameters to Cho's activities: geographically, they only took place in Yeongdeungpo; in terms of audience, they only addressed the workers (whether employed or laid off); in terms of content, they only treated labor issues. Cho was very guarded about doing anything outside of these, no matter how righteous the cause may have been. For the most part, he maintained a disciplined distance from everything that was not directly a part of the UIM.

The one reluctant exception he had to make was signing a public statement regarding the US government's actions following the fire in the US Cultural Center in Busan in April 1982. The statement was issued by the KCAO, which included elements overtly critical of the US government. Cho believed the statement should focus on the persecution of workers, believing the political elements of the criticism superfluous. He was in the minority, and yet, as the general secretary of the KCAO, he had to sign the document others had drafted. Cho believed the political content of the statement was what provided the authorities the pretext with which to intensify the repression. Indeed, things may have unfolded very differently if the content of the statement was kept narrowly focused as Cho recommended.

Within the YDP-UIM, nonetheless, Cho actively shut down even partial attempts to politically mobilize the workers. He also tried to resolve the labor disputes without making them broader issues if he could help it. For this reason, he opposed the YH Trading Company's occupation of the headquarters of NDP, a political party. He thought a better strategy would have been for the union to occupy the offices of the labor administration.

This also meant reprimanding the workers if they got involved in what seemed to be a politically charged issue that was not necessary. Such an incident happened in 1978 during the combined Easter service in Yeouido. Six members of the YDP-UIM (Chang Namsoo, Kim Hyeon-sook, Jeong Myeong-ja, Kim Bokja, Kim Jeongja, and Jin Hae-ja) took over the podium and cried out a certain slogan associated with another labor group that the missioners believed to be politically charged. Public displays of defiance were fine, but they had to be for the agreed-upon reasons. Cho also once decided he will have to dismiss Shin Chul-young from the YDP-UIM after Shin's arrest for his involvement in creating the National Confederation of Democratic Workers during the 1980 Seoul Spring. The organization's aim included mobilizing the workers as a political force, which Cho thought was unacceptable for someone in the YDP-UIM. He softened his mind, however, and decided not to act on the decision by the time Shin was released from prison.

The YDP-UIM made contacts with politicians only when there was a very specific issue for which they formed a temporary alliance. For instance, politicians could still help the enactment of a particular labor law or policy. They could also display solidarity for well-defined problems confronted by the workers. As a general and unbreakable rule, however, the workers and missioners of the ministry had to refrain from all public speech or action that showed support for a certain political faction or its message. They were also to refrain from making contact with politicians. This was partly because of the general PCK culture of treating missions as a matter that transcended politics. In much larger part, it was simply a part of YDP-UIM's distinct tradition of keeping a certain distance from politics.

Cho was wary of politics because he believed true participation was only possible for those who already had some power in substance (whether through organizing or ownership of capital). Unless the workers had first organized themselves into a force with some level of genuine power to advocate for their own interest, they were susceptible to political mobilization. In other words, Cho was neither indifferent nor opposed to politics. He simply believed the workers needed to possess some amount of tangible power before they could set their own agenda that was not forced upon them by someone else coveting their votes. The power of the workers lay in organizing, and the organizing needed to start without political slogans.

> *How would it help the workers (and their political development) to make them chant for the resignation of a cabinet minister or president when they haven't even had the experience of organizing themselves to sack a bad supervisor in the workplace?*[17]

> *I didn't start with the UIM to bring democracy to the nation or an end to the dictatorship. That's why I told In Myeong-jin he shouldn't sign the statement of opposition to the emergency decrees when he did. My stance was always consistent. Do not get involved in politics. You can go to prison, but it better be from helping the workers, not from getting involved in politics. Maybe this means the student activists will call us cowards. I say, let them.*[18]

Cho was not particularly impressed with those who got into politics, either. He recounted of a time he met Kim Young-sam when he was the president of the NDP. During the Seoul Spring in 1980, Kim Young-sam apparently promised Cho that he would take whatever the good reverend had to say for formulating his government's labor policy, should he win an election. Cho said he never heard from the man ever again after he actually became president. This confirmed Cho's belief that it was best not to place too much of one's hope in politics. The only outcome in politics will have to be made by the people who had organized themselves into a position of genuine strength.

This attitude toward politics was made evident again when a labor activist turned politician later visited Cho in Okhwa-ri. Bang Yong-seok, once a steward of the Wonpoong Textiles Union, later made his entry to politics with a proportional seat in the National Assembly. He was part of the NCNP, and as such was appointed a minister of labor when Kim Dae-jung won the presidency. When Minister Bang thereafter visited Cho Chi Song in Okhwa-ri, he was greeted by his old friend who said, "I'm not calling you minister, I'm still more comfortable with the union steward." The message as candid as it was deep. For Cho, being a union leader was a far more important job than being a lawmaker or cabinet minister.

As such, Cho had no regrets investing all of the productive energy that he had into the UIM. That was, except for the areas where he felt he could have done even more. One of those that he told Kim Yong-Bock was something that came to his mind once he had the benefit of hindsight after moving to Okhwa-ri.

Despite the intense repression toward the end of its formal existence, Cho found that there was a genuine but missed opportunity in the Wonpoong Textiles Union. Its members had reached a remarkable level of maturity and self-organization. Each of the 900 was fit to be the steward.[19] Indeed, when the repression began reaching new heights, some key members suggested that they disperse and organize the workers of other workplaces that were not yet unionized. Cho especially remembers Park Soon-hee, who was Bang Yong-seok's deputy steward, and her colleagues who said they "felt a sense of duty to create a second, third, and fourth Wonpoong Textiles Union." The idea was "to replant themselves to the other factories, just as seedlings are replanted from their seedbeds into the paddy fields."[20]

The workers acted on the idea, actually moving into various other industrial areas like Iri (now Iksan) and Daejeon. As seasoned veterans of labor organizing, they helped set up the new workers' movement wherever they went. Cho regarded this attempt very highly and even wrote an article titled "May the Winds of Wonpoong Blow" in the Wonpoong Union's newsletter to commend those that went. However, that time in 1983 was bad for Cho in terms of his health. He had already taken a step back from ministry and never got to see the Wonpoong alumni elsewhere in action. His regret, therefore, was that more of the same initiative had not been taken with the rest of the members of the Wonpoong Textiles Union. They were, after all, the last of the truly worker-controlled unions that were only squashed out of existence after years of repression. Had they mustered just 400 among themselves to go out and start new movements elsewhere like the handful above, the impact could have been greatly multiplied. But alas, the opportunity had passed.

> *In the early days of the church, the authorities struck the*
> *disciples who were gathered in Jerusalem. What did that*

do? The believers were scattered, and they started to preach the good news in places outside of Jerusalem. Wonpoong was the seedbed where we sprouted the seedlings. We didn't have enough hands to replant them into the paddies. But the government thankfully came along and struck Wonpoong, doing the work for us. Now they were ready to go out and replant themselves throughout. Unfortunately, we at the YDP-UIM had lost our relationship with the Wonpoong Union, and we weren't in a position to make that kind of a thing happen.[21]

Indeed, even if Cho had come up with the idea before his retirement, given the fact that Wonpoong and the YDP-UIM had decided to part ways by then, he would not have been able to propose launching such an involved initiative. Losing that connection and thus opportunity was, therefore, Cho's regret. True to its grit, the Wonpoong Textiles Union continued to survive by adopting the new body of the Korean Council for Workers' Welfare, a labor organization existing outside of the institutional framework. Cho, however, believed Wonpoong had potential to do so much more. Perhaps when he told Bang Yong-seok that he still preferred the union steward in him, Cho Chi Song was implying Bang had missed his opportunity to tap into a truly explosive potential in the union he led as its final steward. Had he seized that chance, being a cabinet minister would have been the less impressive part of his pedigree.

Cho valued the relationships he had formed with the workers and made a point of sustaining them throughout his life. He also believed that those workers, especially the small-group women, would similarly sustain their relationship to the cause and the movement for the rest of their lives. They may get married, leave the country, move to another city, or move to a farm. Wherever they are, they could explain the true meaning of the UIM to their husbands, in-laws, nieces, nephews, aunts, uncles, and anyone else around them, creating thicker and thicker layers of support for the workers' movement. In fact, this was the only hope Cho had for raising more supporters for the cause.

The former members of the YDP-UIM could have created a tremendous social, nationwide force as long as they remained connected after leaving Yeongdeungpo. They could have transformed many aspects of society beyond the workplace. As such, another one of Cho's regrets was the fact that he did not succeed in facilitating the robust network of YDP-UIM alumni after they left Yeongdeungpo. What Cho often saw in the workers was that they became isolated upon leaving the workplace and began to live highly individualized, fragmented lives. The essence of the small-group movement was that there was first some kind of gathering that later matured into intentional action. Even if the workers had left the context of the factories, the same essence of the UIM could have been continued, fanning the spark into flames, and driving transformation action for the rest of the workers' lives. If only they could have continued.

A Memorial on "Holy Ground"

Around the time he turned 77, Cho began visiting the hospitals again frequently. His health was deteriorating, in no little part because of the simple fact of aging. Despite the good that it did for his recovery, the rural lifestyle in Okhwa-ri still required a certain level of physical exertion, which the elderly Cho found increasingly more challenging. The decision was therefore made that he would move back into the city with his daughter in her apartment in Pangyo, Seongnam, in the summer of 2009. Thanks to the proximity, he was able to more frequently meet his old friends like Oh Jae-sik, Cho Hwa-soon, Park Hyeong-gyu, Kim Yong-Bock, and Kim Gyeong-nak. This allowed the old missioner to look back on the days they spent together as well as catch up with the more recent events.

In 2010, about 25 years since Cho's resignation, the YDP-UIM was busily working to restore its name that was tarnished through years of propaganda. It was also working to heal its relationship with the higher organs of the PCK, which had been strained in 1984 surrounding the decision of the 69th General Assembly to revert the name and, therefore, the substance of the UIM back to industrial evangelism in an apparent submission to the wants of the government.

Although the 72th General Assembly restored the name "UIM" in 1987, there were still many more hurdles that had to be surmounted before the UIM could fully restore its reputation within the PCK. There were also financial difficulties caused by the previous assembly decision to block direct foreign financial support for the ministries, which were still called, within the country, "problematic, un-evangelical groups that incited workers to political agitation."

Rev. Sohn Eun-jeong, the 8th general secretary of the YDP-UIM, and the YDP-UIM Committee, decided that the next move in the healing process was to create a history archive in the mission center and to get the center designated by the PCK as a historic site in Korean Christianity. This would help set once distorted records straight. They also decided to push for the installation of a memorial stone (see Figure 7.2) at the center to celebrate its part in the democratization movement. There was also substance to go with the symbolism. The creation of a history archive would become a long-term project to find, research, publish, and exhibit valuable sources that will ultimately serve as reference for research and decision-making in future ministries.

Part of the work had already been done in proxy fashion when the YDP-UIM donated part of its archival materials to the KDF to be cataloged as part of its larger archives. The YDP-UIM also had access to tapes of the interview with Cho Chi Song and In Myeong-jin, the first and second general secretaries. Their oral history would provide much to be studied about the UIM and the democracy movement in the 1970s. In a fresh change of pace, this project worked out seamlessly. The memorial would be installed at the YDP-UIM, becoming a physical manifestation of the public vindication. The stone would celebrate the mission's role in the country's democratization and its solidarity with various activists for democracy, which it had accomplished even while remaining true to the essence of the church and its ministry for the workers.

Riding on the momentum, YDP-UIM Committee also requested that the PCK General Assembly's Committee on History designate the center as a historical site in Korean Christianity. The request was reviewed and passed by the 95th General Assembly on September 9, 2010. Thus, the YDP-UIM center became the PCK's eighth historic site. The history committee's rationale was that, despite the lack of historic significance in the physical features of the center, the intangible historic value of what had happened in and around it warranted the designation.

> *The center is only 30 years old, having been built in 1979. There is nothing unique about its architecture. Nevertheless, its intangible value is clearly evident, having been the home to those who were dedicated to God's justice and peace and acted in missions for the industrial society. The significance and value of the center and its missional history for our country's democratization has already been recognized by the rest of society. As such, this assembly recognizes the value of the center as the birthplace of the UIM and resolve to designate it as a "Historic Site in Korean Christianity."*[22]

The historic designation by the PCK and memorial installation by the KDF were the first steps toward healing the deep wounds left by the denomination abandoning it in the past amid the relentless propaganda by government and media. It was a first step for restoring lost honor. The decisions were also significant in that the YDP-UIM was being recognized as a carrier of authentic Christian faith and a symbol of the country's broader democracy and human rights movement. It was a big change after having been ostracized by both the church and secular society.

On November 25, 2010, the YDP-UIM Committee hosted a worship service in the third-floor auditorium of the YDP-UIM to give thanks for its designation as a historic Christian site. The service was followed by the unveiling ceremony for the memorial stone. Kim Jeong-seo, the moderator of the General Assembly, led the worship that day, preaching on Joshua 4:19–24 with a sermon titled "What do these Stones Mean?"

> *We designated this place as a historic site in Christianity.*
> *We are setting a stone here to memorialize our country's*
> *movement for democracy. This is so that we can remember the*
> *suffering that had to be endured for the sake of truth, justice,*
> *service to the helpless for the sake of the love of Christ. The*
> *stone and signs we put up today will be a reminder for our*
> *descendants of how God has been present with the UIM. They*
> *will be a reminder of the shining part of the church's history*
> *when it chose to stand with the suffering workers.*[23]

Father Ham Seh-woong, president of the KDF, told the story of the remarkable perseverance and resilience of the workers, and the YDP-UIM, during the days of terror under the Yushin Regime. He asked that the ministry continue to serve the least among us in society who continue to suffer, including women and the precariously employed. Dan Byeong-ho, the first representative of the Korean Confederation of Trade Unions, sent a video message of congratulations, asking for the YDP-UIM's support for the precariously employed workers who were now being forced to work below a living wage.

Ahn Do-seon (Anthony David Francis Dawson) who had come to assist the YDP-UIM from the Uniting Church of Australia from the early to mid-1980s, also sent a video message, congratulating the YDP-UIM and recounting:

> *Serving in the YDP-UIM to restore and build up the dignity*
> *and self-respect of the poor and the oppressed so they may*

> *come to the realization of their creation in the image of God*
> *was a priceless opportunity for me to learn to work "with"*
> *rather than "for" the people whom I serve.*[24]

Cho Chi Song was not able to attend the ceremony, still recovering from a recent surgery. Nevertheless, he sent a video message with a weaker voice but strong spirit that the viewers ought to remember the crucial meaning of the memorial.

> *Everyone who sees the stone ought to remember how*
> *much suffering the workers had to endure. [. . .] They*
> *ought to see how the missioners of the UIM had also*
> *to suffer and overcome various kinds of trial despite a*
> *tremendously challenging environment. That's how the*
> *mission has been sustained. [. . .] I hope people will see*
> *more than just a stone. I hope they will see the sweat and*
> *blood shed by the workers and the missioners when they*
> *see it.*[25]

In Myeong-jin and Shin Cheol-young were present to bear tearful witness to the days of the persecution. Having been Cho Chi Song's colleague in the 1970s, they had been with him through some of the most challenging years. The event concluded with a benediction from Rev. Bang Ji-il, now 102 years old. He had been a constant source of advocacy and protection for the UIM throughout his days as the YDP-UIM Committee chair, Moderator of the Gyeonggi Presbytery, Director of the Evangelism Department, and Moderator of the PCK General Assembly. His blessing was to "keep marching on, carrying the good news of the cross." Guests and friends of the YDP-UIM helped unveil the plaque attached next to the first-floor entrance, whose words designated the center as a historic Christian site. The party then moved out to the spot to remove a tall, white veil. Underneath, a large, gray boulder stood (see Figure 7.2).

Figure 7.2. A Memorial on Holy Ground. Text on the rock reads: *The Home of Labor Missions, a Historic Site for Democracy*

Beneath the title on the rock was a paraphrased summary of Luke 4:18–19: "Good news for the poor, freedom to the oppressed." Those were the words that had become a symbol for the UIM since 1968. The final line on the stone noted that this memorial was a joint recognition given by the YDP-UIM Committee and the KDF.

The following year on January 17, CBS Radio invited Cho Chi Song to the show *CBS Invitational* to interview him about the recent recognition as the pioneer of UIM. The show host asked what activities there were in the UIM from the 1960s to 1970s and how Cho felt about the mission getting a historic designation and memorial stone after 52 years since he started ministry. Finally, the show host asked what it all meant for the church in Korea. Cho's answer was:

> *The church has to take a stand, and it has to take the stand*
> *of those who are suffering. When I go among those who suffer,*
> *there I can see the living and moving Christ. But when I go to*
> *a lavishly ornamented church, I find myself doubting if Christ*
> *is really there. In my mind, a church can only work out the*
> *true salvation of Christ if it has experienced suffering as a*
> *result of trying to share the pain of the minjung, as a result of*
> *trying to solve the problems experienced by the workers.*[26]

Cho had not visited the YDP-UIM in a while when he came up to Seoul for the radio show. Given the opportunity, the current missioners of the YDP-UIM arranged a meeting between Cho Chi Song and the current generation of labor church ministers for a friendly dialogue. There, on the second floor of the YDP-UIM center, Cho shared his stories from the 1970s. Then he went down to the first floor, examining the plaque of historic designation and the memorial stone. His eyes turned red for a minute, perhaps because he was overwhelmed by the memory of the cry and struggle of the women he used to serve with. He gently stroked the stone. Perhaps the weight of the tears and bloodshed on that holy ground was still a little too much to console with the stone that stood over it.

The Fools Keep Marching On

Two years after the historic designation ceremony, the YDP-UIM invited Cho Chi Song to celebrate his 80th birthday on October 6, 2012.[27] Cho had always maintained a strict separation of his public and private life, even withholding the news of his father-in-law's passing or his eldest daughter's wedding. As such, he initially also refused the birthday celebration. His former students, however, respected and loved him and insisted that he accepts the invitation. They took care to keep the celebration modest, even giving it an air of formality so as to avoid making it sound too personal. The cover was to give Cho

Chi Song and those who present a mid-progress review on the writing
of this book in a presentation titled, "The Fools Keep Marching On."
The event was co-hosted by the YDP-UIM, its alumni, Seongmunbak Church, and the PCK-URM. Everyone present had learned
from Cho Chi Song, whether directly or indirectly. They were also his
successors to carry on the legacy of the UIM within the PCK. At their
insistence, Cho eventually relented and attended the ceremony. His old
friends and colleagues also joined to celebrate. The once young workers
were now a part of the more senior members who were in attendance.

In Myeong-jin preached that day on Psalm 9:10–17 with a
sermon titled "Make Strong the Work of our Hands." He recounted
the life story of Cho Chi Song, pointing out that he had consistently
focused on serving the workers and advancing the UIM.

*Some people dismiss Rev. Cho Chi Song as an opponent of
the church. This is because they only take a cursory look at his
criticisms against it. But I say to you, the Rev. Cho I know
had entered seminary and industrial missions because of Jesus
Christ. He lived a life of service to the workers, which was
his way of following Jesus. Scripture teaches us to love our
neighbor. So Rev. Cho did through his lifetime. He consistently
served the workers as if he was serving the Lord. So I ask
you. Is this not the true essence and character of the church?
It certainly is the character of Rev. Cho. His criticism of the
church was a paradoxical statement that you become the true
church when you abandon the distorted image of faith and
Christ and begin to place your faith in the real Jesus Christ.*

*Rev. Cho eschewed using formal titles like "president" or
"general secretary." At most, he wanted to be called someone
who was on the YDP-UIM "staffer" [translated literally]. He
rejected money, honor, and everything else as being vain by
faith. Tell me, can you find another minister in the Korean
church today who is like Rev. Cho?*

The essence of the UIM as we learned it from Rev. Cho was that we are to "serve the workers as you would serve the Lord." The title of his interview published in TIMES *Magazine also said, "When They are Angry, I am Angry." The pain of the workers was the pain of Cho Chi Song. Their anger was his anger. Such was the way in which he served the workers as if he served the Lord. I am certain that God desires those of you who will take up our mantle will continue to firmly uphold the legacy of Rev. Cho in the UIM as he modeled it.*

The attendees had a conversation about the progress of the book following the service, which I had started to write in 2011. Dr. Lee Jae-seong of the Sungkonghoe University expressed the following hope:

Asking a '"good question" can be greater than giving a clever answer. [. . .] In an age where "good questions" have all but disappeared, I hope the biography of Rev. Cho and the "good questions" it asks to the churches and society will serve as a mirror we can use to examine our souls.

Rev. Lee Geun-bok, the third general secretary of the YDP-UIM, spoke of the life of Cho Chi Song as he saw it.

Rev. Cho's life is a mirror and compass for churches and Christians who are falling prey to the temptations of wealth and success. [. . .] He despaired of the church in the distortions it allowed itself before power and wealth. Rev. Cho always said, "the workers are better than the church." Yet, at the same time, Rev. Cho practiced the essence of the church with his whole being.

Shin Chul-young, who worked as a lay missioner in the YDP-UIM from the late 1970s to early 1980s, said the following:

More than in anything else, Rev. Cho played a great role in
transforming industrial evangelism into industrial missions.
[. . .] This transition was a departure from that which was
familiar and comfortable. It was a turn toward thorny road.

Kim Gap-jun, who had helped Cho Chi Song in the days of the
Lay Association for Industrial Evangelism as a worker in Hanguk (later
Wonpoong) Textiles, recounted she and her coworkers spent with the
old missioner:

I used to think I'll go to heaven when I die. But Rev. Cho
said Jesus was present with us here today. So I became very
committed. There was no room to be lazy, since I figured Jesus
was right here (next to me). At some point, I realized I was
becoming more like Rev. Cho the more I was around him.
[. . .] I started carrying around industrial evangelism tracts
that explained the labor laws inside my bag and started to
distribute them to each of the factory sections regularly.

Oh Jae-sik, a former president of World Vision, was the man
who went out of his way to connect the YDP-UIM to sources of
foreign financial support when the domestic persecution strained its
relationship with the PCK. His role was integral in the mission finding
the strength necessary to persevere through the trials. Looking back on
the days he stood with the YDP-UIM together, he said:

God used Rev. Cho and the Yeongdeungpo UIM to make
the church a bastion of democracy and workers' rights just
when our society fell into its darkest moments. They became
the salt and light of this world. Getting to be a part of their
wonderful story was a true honor that will last me a lifetime.

The celebration ended with the current YDP-UIM staff reading
the poem, "March of the Fools," written by Cho Chi Song. Everyone

in attendance responded by singing the song, also written by him, titled "The Road to Freedom."

After his 84th birthday, Cho Chi Song's health suffered from the combined effects of aging, his chronic migraines, and more advanced symptoms of Parkinson's disease. He had to mostly stay home, relying on a wheelchair. His tongue had stiffened, making him slower to speak. He also had some trouble keeping his hands steady. Nevertheless, Cho was always well kempt, ready to greet visitors and former students with dignity. He listened to the news they had to share with interest about the current developments around the nation, especially the massive candlelight vigils whose chant was, "The truth shall never sink."[28]

Despite his illness, Cho happily welcomed missioners like Koh Ae-shin, Cho Soon-hyeong, and Sohn Eun-jeong when they visited. He was even in good enough spirits to share a joke. Cho and Park Gil-soon, his wife, were very intentional about respecting the working time and conditions of the caretaker who assisted with Cho's needs. This was a testament to his students of his enduring love for all people who work.

Cho Chi Song died on January 22, 2019. He closed his eyes in peace inside his daughter's apartment in Pangyo where his wife and daughter held his hands until the passing. He was 86. There was a modest funeral service at the YDP-UIM, where he had served for 20 years. His remains were buried in Donghwa Park in Paju, where one could see his lost hometown to the north.

About 100 days after the funeral, Park Song-ah, a former worker of Namyoung Nylon and now president of the Squirrel Fellowship, received a phone call from Park Gil-soon with instructions to come take 50 million won that her late husband wanted to donate to the fellowship. As it was, the informal credit union had been struggling in the books because of a number of long-term payment delays. The money was meant to help stabilize its operation as well as for providing relief to a worker who may have been in need. Park Song-ah left for Pangyo with Sohn Eun-jeong, trying to convince Park Gil-soon that she should use the money to support herself. Park Gil-soon would not be moved, reminding them exactly why she and Cho had married. "He wanted you to have it. I want to give him a reason to be glad when we meet again in heaven."

NOTES

1 Kim and Yoo, *Cho Chi Song's Oral History* (Vol. 2, 2011).
2 Jeong and Sohn, "Cho Chi Song's Interview."
3 In Myeong-jin, "A Challenge for the UIM," *The Story of Seong-munbak's People* (Christian Literature Society of Korea, 2013).
4 Seo Deok-Seok and Sohn Eun-jeong, "Koh Ae-shin's Interview," *Interviews of Related Individuals for the Biography* (transcribed by Hong Yoon-gyung, 2011).
5 Cho Chi Song, et al., "Community Constitution for the One House" (1985).
6 Seo Deok-Seok and Sohn Eun-jeong, "Cho Soon-hyeong's Interview," *Interviews of Related Individuals for the Biography* (transcribed by Hong Yoon-gyung, 2020).
7 When Kim Yong-Bock was the head of the Sandol Labor Culture Center, he carried out an oral history study of the YDP-UIM per the suggestion of George Todd. The original goal was to publish the tapes into a book, but Cho Chi Song would not agree to it. The tapes were therefore transcribed and kept in collection.
8 Seo Deok-Seok and Sohn Eun-jeong, "Cho Soon-hyeong's Interview," *Interviews of Related Individuals for the Biography* (transcribed by Hong Yoon-gyung, 2020).
9 Verbal account of an anonymous deacon of Okhwa Church, 2020.
10 Cho Chi Song's photograph "Hot Potatoes."
11 Seo and Sohn, "Interviews of the Older Members of the UIM."
12 Bruce Cummings, *Korea's Place in the Sun* (Changbi, 2001), 372.
13 Kim Jinho, "Society of Gods," *Hankyoreh* 21, Issue 857.
14 Chang Sook-kyeong, *The UIM and Labor Movement in the 1970s* (Seonin, 2013), 381.
15 Kim and Yoo, *Cho Chi Song's Oral History* (Vol. 2, 2011).

16 Jeong and Sohn, "Cho Chi Song's Interview."

17 Kim and Yoo, *Cho Chi Song's Oral History* (Vol. 2, 2011), 50.

18 Jeong and Sohn, "Cho Chi Song's Interview."

19 Kim and Yoo, *Cho Chi Song's Oral History* (Vols. 8–9, 2011).

20 Kim Nam-il, *History of the Wonpoong Textiles Union* (Samchang, 2010).

21 Kim and Yoo, *Cho Chi Song's Oral History* (Vol. 8–9, 2011).

22 Yang Myeong-deuk, "Ministry Documents from the Yeongdeungpo UIM," *Freedom for the Oppressed* (YDP-UIM & Dongyeon, 2020), 547.

23 Yeongdeungpo UIM Committee, "Bulletin for the Thanksgiving Service for the Historic Site Designation and Democracy Memorial Unveiling Ceremony" (2010).

24 Anthony David Francis Dawson (Ahn Do-seon), emails (November 2010).

25 YDP-UIM, "Video Footage of Cho Chi Song" (2010).

26 CBS Invitational, "Cho Chi Song: Pioneer of the UIM" (January 17, 2011).

27 YDP-UIM, "And We Fools Keep Marching On," *Cho Chi Song's 80th Birthday Celebration* (October 2012).

28 *PCK News*, "Cho Chi Song, Pioneer of the UIM, Passes Away" (January 22, 2019).

BIBLIOGRAPHY

Ahn, Byeong-moo. "Jesus and the Minjung." In *Jesus of Galilee*. Seoul: Korea Theological Study Institute, 2019.

"A Song for the Workers of Seoul." New York: *TIME Magazine*, January 3, 1977.

"And We Fools Keep Marching on." In *Cho Chi Song's 80th Birthday Celebration*. Event program notes. Seoul: YDP-UIM, October 2012.

"Bulletin for the Thanksgiving Service for the Historic Site Designation and Democracy Memorial Unveiling Ceremony." Seoul: YDP-UIM, 2010.

Chang, Sook-kyeong. *The UIM and Labor Movement in the 1970s*. Seoul: Seonin, 2013.

Chi Song Cho, Myeong-hee Han & Myeong-deuk Han. *Freedom for the Oppressed*. Seoul: Dongyeon, 2020.

"Cho Chi Song, Pioneer of the UIM, Passes Away." *PCK News*. Seoul: PCK News, January 22, 2019.

"Cho Chi Song: Pioneer of the UIM." *CBS Invitational*. Seoul: CBS, January 17, 2011.

Cho Chi Song. "UIM Staff Training Manual." Seoul: YDP-UIM. Unpublished document.

Cho, Chi Song, *et al*. "Community Constitution for the One House." Seoul: YDP-UIM, 1985.

Cho, Chi Song. "A Half-Piece Story the UIM." Seoul: YDP-UIM. Unpublished lecture notes.

Cho, Chi Song. "An English Letter Requesting Prayer." Seoul: YDP-UIM.

Cho, Chi Song. "Hot Potatoes." Seoul: YDP-UIM. Photography.

Cho, Chi Song. "The Story of the Yeongdeungpo UIM." In *My Life, My Story 2*. Seoul: Yeonee, 1997.

Cho, Chi Song. "Why Cooperatives & How." Seoul: YDP-UIM. Unpublished document.

Cho, Chi Song. *Cho Chi Song's Oral History* Vol. 1–12. (Interviews). Seoul: YDP-UIM, 2011.

Cho, Chi Song. Interview by Yeong-cheol Jeong & Eun-jeong Sohn. Seoul: Korea Democracy Foundation, 2002.

Cummings, Bruce. *Korea's Place in the Sun.* Translated by Kim Dongno & Lee Gyoseon. Paju: Changbi, 2001.

Dawson, Anthony D. F. (Ahn Do-seon). Emails. November 2010.

Gwon, Jin-gwan. *Jesus, the Figure of Minjung and Minjung, the Figure of Jesus.* Seoul: Dongyeon, 2009.

Hwang, Hong-ryeol. *The History of Korea's Minjung Ministries and Minjung Missiology.* Seoul: Handl, 2004.

In, Myeong-jin. *The Story of Seongmunbak's People.* Seoul: Christian Literature Society of Korea, 2013.

Interviews of Related Individuals for the Biography. Interviews by Seo Deok-Seok and Sohn Eun-jeong. Seoul: YDP-UIM, 2011.

Jeong, Byeong-joon. "50 Years of UIM." In *I Am Working As My Father Is Working.* Seoul: PCK National Mission Ministry, 2007.

Kim, Jinho. "Society of Gods." Seoul: Hankyoreh 21, April 25, 2011.

Kim, Myeong-bae, et. al. *Yeongdeungpo UIM Files.* Seoul: YDP-UIM & Soongsil University Center for Culture and Mission Studies, 2020.

Kim, Nam-il. *History of the Wonpoong Textiles Union.* Seoul: Samchang, 2010.

Kwon, Jin-gwan. "Social Movement As A Collective Learning Process." In *Class Culture and Identity Among Korean Workers in the 1960–1970s.* Seoul: Hanul Academy, 2006.

Labor Church Bulletins. Seoul: YDP-UIM, 1979–1980.

Myeong Noh-seon. "Transcribed interviews." Interview by Sohn Eun-jeong. Seoul: YDP-UIM, 2022.

Myeong-jin In, Chul-yeong Shin, Stephen Lavender, et al. *Yeongdeungpo UIM: A 40-Year History.* Seoul: YDP-UIM, 1998.

Oh, Cheol-ho. *Industrial Evangelism Handbook.* Seoul: PCK Education and Resourcing Ministry, 1965.

"Order of Kim Jin-soo's Funeral Service." Unpublished program notes. Seoul: Council of Churches for Urban Industrial Issues (CCUI), 1971.

Park, Jeom-soon. "Beautiful Memories." In *30th Anniversary of the Squirrel Fellowship,* Program notes. YDP-UIM, 1999.

Seo, Nam-dong. "The Figuration of the Han and Its Theological Reflections." In *Exploring Minjung Theology.* Seoul: Hangilsa, 1983.

Song, Hyo-soon. *The Road to Seoul.* Seoul: Hyeongseongsa, 1982.

Soon, Jeom-soon. *For the Eight-Hour Workday.* Seoul: Pulbit, 1984.

"Statement On Current Affairs." Seoul: PCK General Assembly, 1978.

The 30th Anniversary of the Squirrel Fellowship. Unpublished reports. Seoul: YDP-UIM, 1999.

The Church and UIM. Seoul: PCK Education & Resourcing Ministry, 1981.

The Fire of the Age 3: Kim Jin-soo. Seoul: Korea Democracy Foundation, 2003.

"The May 16 Coup and Labor Movement of the 1960s." In *Testimonies from the Ground: Labor in the 1970s*. Seoul: NCCK & Pulbit, 1984.

Yang, Myeong-deuk. *Freedom for the Oppressed*. Seoul: YDP-UIM & Dongyeon, 2020.

Yoo, Ok-soon. "Building a Democratic Labor Union in Control Data." In *I, A Working Woman 1*. Seoul: Greenbee, 2011.

INDEX OF NAMES

Kim Dong-hyeok, 36, 180, 181
Kim Dong-wan, 191
Kim Gap-jun, 36, 50, 54, 113, 281
Kim Geum-soon, 102, 184
Kim Go-man, 102
Kim Gwan-seok, 191
Kim Gye-won, 188
Kim Gyeong-nak, 48, 56, 58, 62,
   64, 122, 123, 124, 132, 148,
   185, 191, 203, 272
Kim Gyeong-sook, 103, 115, 128,
   245
Kim Gyu-bok, 244, 248
Kim Hye-ran, 126
Kim Hyeon-sook, 267
Kim Il-sung, 4, 86
Kim Jae-gook, 125
Kim Jae-joon, 191
Kim Jae-shik, 87
Kim Jeong-gook, 238
Kim Jeong-ja, 93
Kim Jeong-joon, 207, 247
Kim Jeong-ran, 186, 196
Kim Jeong-seo, 275
Kim Jeongja, 267
Kim Jin-ho, 265
Kim Jin-soo, 56–64, 69, 121, 150,
   243
Kim Jong-ryeol, 194
Kim Mi-soon, 184
Kim Rok-ho, 196
Kim Ryeo-seong, 36
Kim Sang-geun, 191
Kim Seong-hye, 186
Kim Seong-seob, 81, 122
Kim Seong-soo, 237
Kim Seong-su, 220
Kim Soon-hee, 184
Kim Soon-rye, 102, 103
Kim Sou-hwan, 191

Kim Yeon-ja, 74, 184, 233
Kim Yong-Bock, v, xv, 192, 194,
   246, 247, 256, 257, 259, 264,
   270, 272
Kim Yoon-gi, 57
Kim Young-hee, 186
Kim Young-sam, 266, 269
Kim Youngnak, 244
Ko Seong-shim, 79, 80, 82
Ko Un, 128, 193
Koh Ae-shin, 241, 243, 255, 282
Koh Hwan-gyu, 190
Koh Hwang-kyung, 190, 206
Koh Jae-shik, 186, 238
Koh Yeong-geun, 247
Kom Yong-baek, 36
Koo Haeng-mo, 162
Kwon Ho-gyeong, 191, 247
Kwon Ho-kyung, 255

Lavender, Steven (Na Byeong-do),
   86, 128, 143, 144, 150, 187
Lee Bong-soo, 122
Lee Byeong-cheol, 49
Lee Chang-bok, 191
Lee Don-myeong, 193
Lee Eui-ho, 159
Lee Geun-bok, 154, 164, 186, 194,
   244, 280
Lee Geun-sil, 1, 2
Lee Geung-ha, 159
Lee Gi-yeon, 207
Lee Guk-seon, 33, 191
Lee Gwan-young, 195
Lee Gwon-chan, 23, 188
Lee Gyu-sang, 191
Lee Hae-hak, 191
Lee Jae-jeong, 247
Lee Jae-seong, 280
Lee Jeong-gil, 26
Lee Jeong-gyu, 190